Adam Versényi explores the history of Latin American theatre from pre-Columbian days to contemporary drama. Theatre in Latin America has historically been a powerful force for social change and has frequently combined religious and political concerns with performance practice to create a style of drama unique to the region. Versényi investigates this special inter-connection of religion, politics, and theatre, and finds this relationship present from the earliest contacts between Cortés and the Aztecs through Spanish-influenced theatre to the politically charged contemporary drama of Cuba, Argentina, Chile, and elsewhere. Versényi concludes his study with an analysis of liberation theology and its secularly derived theatrical counterpart, liberation theatre. Yet this study does not simply provide a theatrical history of Latin America. Rather, the volume offers a detailed understanding of how theatrical, political, and theological elements have consistently intertwined in Latin American history and why that has been the case.

All quotations are translated into English and the book contains an appendix of playwrights. It will be of interest to scholars and students of theatre history, Latin American and Spanish studies, and theology.

THEATRE IN LATIN AMERICA

THEATRE IN LATIN AMERICA

Religion, politics, and culture from Cortés to the 1980s

ADAM VERSÉNYI

*Assistant Professor of Dramaturgy, University of North Carolina at Chapel Hill
and Dramaturg, Playmakers Repertory Company*

CAMBRIDGE
UNIVERSITY PRESS

Published by the Press Syndicate of the University of Cambridge
The Pitt Building, Trumpington Street, Cambridge CB2 1RP
40 West 20th Street, New York, NY 10011–4211, USA
10 Stamford Road, Oakleigh, Melbourne 3166, Australia

First published 1993

Printed in Great Britain at the University Press, Cambridge

A catalogue record for this book is available from the British Library

Library of Congress cataloguing in publication data
Versényi, Adam.
Theatre in Latin America: religion, politics, and culture from
Cortés to the 1980s / Adam Versényi.
p.   cm.
Includes bibliographical references and index.
ISBN 0 521 41938 7
1. Theater – Latin America – History.   2. Theater and society – Latin
America.   3. Theater – Religious aspects.   1. Title.
PN2309.V46   1993
792′.098 – dc20   92-33869 CIP

ISBN 0 521 41938 7 hardback

*For Laszlo G. Versényi, who should have seen it, and for
Sue L. Versényi, without whom it would not have been possible.*

Contents

ix

Preface

One of the most exciting areas of theatrical activity in the world today is Latin America. Whatever its form: collective creation, formal dramaturgy, or cultural celebration, theatre in Latin America is presently a powerful force for social change. The emergence of Christian base communities that have used Bible study as a means of confronting and converting social reality into something more akin to what is promised in scripture, has been paralleled by the emergence throughout the region of theatre groups that use performance as a means of objectifying a community's problems. Such performances are often the result of an extensive, in-depth investigation by the community's inhabitants themselves. These performances, as well as those that are the result of the more traditionally accepted form of a play written by an individual, frequently combine political and religious concerns. Such a combination is secularly derived but it mirrors the concerns of the region's liberation theology movement. The result of this creation is a form of artistic activity I choose to call liberation theatre.

This book addresses the roots of liberation theatre by investigating the interconnections of religion, politics, and theatre in selected regions and time-frames from pre-Columbian days to the twentieth century. Although a great deal has been done recently to rectify the situation, North Americans, especially the inhabitants of the United States, remain woefully ignorant of the history of our neighbors to the south. With the possible exception of Mesoamerican architecture, such ignorance is apparent in our dearth of knowledge concerning Latin American arts. Consequently, a certain amount of historical background (which Latin Americanists may find superfluous) is inevitable. It is not my intention, however, to supply simply a theatrical history of the region, as fascinating as that in itself can be. Rather, I hope to present the reader with a detailed understanding of *how* religion, politics, and theatre have been consistently intertwined in Latin American history, and *why* that has been the case.

To that end I have eschewed attempting to provide the reader with a global rendition of these trends in Latin America. Such a rendition founders under the sheer weight of detail it would be necessary to include, and would become an encyclopedic rather than a critical investigation of the specific aspects of Latin American theatre identified. What I have attempted, then, is to focus upon certain countries that at given times have exhibited the interconnection of religion, politics, and theatre more forcefully than others. For this reason the reader will encounter a certain amount of geographical hopscotching. As I think the following pages will make clear, however, what is described as occurring within a specific locality can also be extended to a statement about Latin American theatre in general. Even recognizing the cultural distinctions that exist between the countries in the region, it is possible to speak of a Latin American sensibility in the theatre. There is one final point to be made about the countries I deal with here, namely the absence of Brazil. While the convergence of religion, politics, and theatre certainly exists in contemporary Brazilian theatre and society, as well as in Brazilian theatre history, Brazil presents certain factors unique to the region that deserve to be treated separately. This work covers only the Spanish-speaking countries in Latin America.

Acknowledgments

Numerous people assisted me at various times while I was writing this book. Without their generous willingness to share their expertise, completion of this work would have been impossible. For help in formulating my ideas at an early stage thanks are due to George Woodyard, Emir Rodriguez-Monegal, Ramón Layera, and Elsa Gambarini. The book began as a doctoral dissertation at the Yale School of Drama and its final form owes a great deal to the preliminary groundwork laid there with the assistance of my doctoral committee: Leon Katz and Joel Schechter of the Yale School of Drama, and Marion P. Holt of CUNY. A number of people were kind enough to read portions of the book at various stages and for their invaluable advice thanks are due: Sharon Magnarelli, Karen Sánchez-Eppler, Benigno Sánchez-Eppler, and Clive Barker. For their comments on the completed manuscript I am indebted to Lars Schoultz and David Perry. For their unflagging efforts in tracking down my often arcane requests my gratitude is due to the Inter-Library Loan Departments of Yale University, the University of North Carolina at Chapel Hill, and Duke University. Two Fulbright Lecturing Grants to Colombia afforded me the opportunity to observe Enrique Buenaventura and Santiago Garcia's work at first hand. Such observation would not have been possible without the invaluable assistance of Consuelo Valdivieso at the Fulbright Commission. A debt must also be acknowledged to that small, but ever-growing, band of scholars who have gone before me in the investigation of Latin American theatre: José Juan Arrom, Willis K. Knapp, George Woodyard, Leon F. Lyday, Frank Dauster, Carlos Solórzano, Kirsten Nigro, Pedro Bravo-Elizondo, Claudia Kaiser-Lenoir, and Beatriz Rizk, among others. Their work served as inspiration, and whatever contribution I make to the field finds its roots in what they have done before me. To all the Latin American

xiii

theatre artists who have given freely of their precious time over the years to talk with me or reply to my letters, *les dan mis gracias*. Portions of Chapter 1 appeared previously in different form in *New Theatre Quarterly*. Without the patience and assistance of my editors, Victoria L. Cooper and Sarah Stanton, the book would not have arrived at its present form.

Finally my unflagging gratitude goes to my parents, Laszlo G. and Diana A. Versényi, for giving me the opportunity to explore other cultures and languages from an early age, and to my wife, Sue L. Versényi, always and forever my first reader.

CHAPTER I

Religion, politics, and theatre: Cortés greets the twelve Franciscans

In 1519 Hernán Cortés landed on the Mexican mainland. By 1522 he had conquered the Aztec capital and converted it into the captaincy general of Nueva España, the headquarters from which he was to launch his conquest of the rest of Central America. In the spring of 1524 the twelve Franciscan friars requested by Cortés to take charge of the Indians' religious instruction arrived in Mexico City – Tenochtitlán. When Cortés was told of their approach he went to greet them on the outskirts of the city. Accompanied by most of his Spanish soldiers and a long procession of Indian leaders, Cortés knelt and kissed each friar's hands. His soldiers did the same and the Indians followed suit. Bound together in this one historical incident are three interwoven threads that have characterized Latin American history both prior to the Conquest and until the present day. In the simplicity and power of Cortés' action can be seen the interconnected strands of religion, politics, and theatre. While there is no one incident that reflects this triad in the European contact with the Maya and Inca cultures, the history of their conquest contains the same clear combination of forces.

That the same man who included theatrical entertainment for his troops, in the form of a puppeteer, on his expedition to conquer Hibueras in Guatemala, left history with such a brilliantly dramatic display should come as no surprise.[1] But Cortés was much more than a military leader with a theatrical flair; he was also an astute politician. He had expressly requested that Franciscan friars be the first to undertake Christianization of the New World, and his reasons for such a request were manifold. On a practical level, the Franciscans were the best prepared to undertake such a mission. The followers of the Franciscan rule established by Juan de Guadalupe, from the ranks of which the twelve sent to Cortés were chosen, already had the experience of evangelical work amongst the rural peasants and

I

neglected townspeople of the province of Granada, a region which had been newly conquered from Moors. A bull issued by Pope Alexander VI in 1496 had given the Franciscans the status of *predicadores apostólicos*, in order to enable them "throughout the world among the faithful and the infidel, [to] preach the word of God and the Holy Gospel." Juan de Guadalupe's disciples carried out the evangelical mission of Christianizing the Moslem farmers and townspeople that none of their colleagues would attempt. Such work amidst an alien people, language, and culture within Spain itself perfectly prepared the Franciscans for the role Cortés had chosen for them.[2]

Politically, the mendicants were the logical choice for Cortés. Their conversion of the Indians' souls would be the necessary complement to his conquest of their bodies. In addition, Franciscan mysticism and vows of poverty ensured that they would not attempt to usurp his secular power and authority. The Franciscans, in fact, were the perfect allies, for they could be counted upon not only to hold the Indians in sway, but also to help Cortés check the worldly aspirations of the Spanish colonists, the royal officials, and the Court of Spain, by giving him a spiritual and theological basis for his authority. He thus lost no time in securing such an alliance. By kneeling and kissing their hands (the friars prevented him from kissing their garments), Cortés "conquered" the astonished Franciscans, "converting" them into his allies. The far-reaching nature of this act can be seen in the pages of the *Historia ecclesiástica indiana* by the Franciscan, Gustavo de Mendieta. In his treatment of Cortés, Mendieta "kneels and kisses" his hand applauding him for his spiritual self-conquest.[3]

For the Franciscan friars, Cortés' carefully staged reception had tremendous mystical and theological implications. With Columbus' discovery of the "West Indies" in 1492 and Vasco da Gama's trip round the Cape of Good Hope to India in 1499, Franciscan mysticism discovered the possibility of a Christianity which would be not only conceptually universal but territorially global in scope. Columbus and da Gama's discoveries meant that the gospel could be brought to all parts of the world and to all men, it was no longer limited to the geographical constraints of the Old World. The realization that every person on earth could now be converted was a "vision...so blinding and so radiant that its fulfillment must inevitably fore-shadow the rapidly approaching end of the world. It seemed to these mystics that after all the races of mankind had been converted nothing further could happen in this world; for anything else would be an anticlimax."[4] The Franciscan missionaries employed biblical exegesis to support their mystical temperament and to further their terrestrial aims. Thus the parable concerning the eleventh hour in Matthew 20, confirmed the idea that man was living in the last age of the world; and the parable concerning the three invitations to supper in Luke 14 became the theological underpinning for the Conquest. Mendieta approved of secular humanist Juan Ginés de Sepúlveda's exegesis of Luke 14 in converting the heathen.

Sepúlveda suggested that the servant's first invitation corresponded to the Christian Church prior to Emperor Constantine's reign (311–337), when coercion was not employed to bring converts into the fold. The third invitation, however, corresponded to the Church during and after Constantine, when there was, for the first time, a unified Christian Empire. Such unification meant that the Church now had a secular arm which, when authorized to do so by the spiritual power, could employ force to convert the heathen.[5] While such an exegesis afforded the Franciscans the luxury of utilizing secular power to achieve their own ends, the use of a nonecclesiastical exegesis foreshadows the mendicant orders' inability to establish themselves in the New World without the backing of the secular authority. Such dependence was to prove the downfall of the mendicants' enormous influence in colonial America. This was not yet the case, however, when Cortés placed himself at the feet of the twelve Franciscan friars. Their number was no accident. They had set sail quite consciously considering themselves the successors to Christ's twelve apostles and, while Cortés had probably calmly calculated the political consequences of his actions, he displayed the religious fervor of a man of his position, time, and temperament in carrying them out.

If the Franciscan friars were surprised by Cortés' behavior, the Aztec leaders who accompanied him must have been amazed. They saw for the first time European men dressed in coarse clothing similar to that of their own priesthood. These same men, they were soon to discover, professed to be uninterested in gold, the one constant craving of all the Europeans they had previously encountered. It was to these men that their conqueror Cortés, the man whom they had taken to be a god or a representative of the gods himself, bowed in homage. His gesture of taking the friars' hands to his mouth and, even more so, his attempt to kiss the hems of their robes, must have astonished the Aztecs in its near repetition of the dirt-eating gesture of humility and honor with which they themselves greeted those they wished to honor. Such a gesture is continually mentioned in the chronicles when the Spaniards first encounter the Indians and can be seen represented on sculpture and other artwork of the period throughout Mesoamerica. In addition, the similarity between Cortés' welcome to the friars and Moctezoma II's welcome to Cortés a few years before must have made a deep impression upon the Aztec leaders.

SPANISH AND AZTEC THEATRICAL DISPLAY DURING THE CONQUEST

Although Cortés did not reach the Yucatán until 1519, Moctezoma II may have known of the existence of strange ships in the Caribbean as early as 1507. He certainly received reports of their presence long before the Spaniards' approach to Tenochtitlán, and every report seemed to follow a series of evil omens the most frightening of which was a comet.[6] The Aztecs perceived these omens as predicting doom for their empire. This heightened climate was added to the coincidence that Cortés' arrival in 1519 corresponded with the year I Reed in the Aztec calendar. This was the date when the god Quetzalcoátl had promised to return. Cortés' appearance during I Reed led the Aztecs to suspect that the Spaniards might actually be gods, possibly including Quetzalcoátl himself. As a consequence, Moctezoma had elaborate costumes of feathers and gold made and sent them via messenger to Cortés aboard his ship, where he was clothed as a god. The costumes were for Quetzalcoátl, Tlaloc, the rain god, and Tezcatlipoca, a patron of royalty. Moctezoma hoped in this way to propitiate the strange gods, causing them to reveal their identities or go away. Cortés, however, quickly realized he had been taken for a deity and took full advantage of the situation. Chaining the messengers, he fired his cannon, which caused them to faint. He then revived them with wine, which made them drunk. The messengers confused reports of Cortés' theatrical actions (costumed as a god, he assumed the role) could not have eased Moctezoma's heavy heart.[7]

After a few decisive battles, Cortés' approach upon the Aztec capital was made virtually without bloodshed. His superiority in battle was certainly not the result of numerical strength but of firepower and, more importantly, vastly different traditions of warfare. For the Aztecs warfare was a ritual activity that had been performed along certain guidelines laid down by Tlacael around 1427. At a moment of near complete defeat for the Aztecs, this singular leader, who never desired to be chief himself, transformed the Aztec nation from victims into vanquishers. He did this by reorganizing the army along strict lines of discipline, and instilling Aztec society with the sense of being a predestined people. They became a warrior–mystic race whose divine mission was to take sacrificial victims in battle.[8]

Such battle was highly ritualistic, in a format largely composed of elaborate announcements of hostilities prior to any actual fighting. When they did fight, they fought with obsidian blades, wore splendid costumes, and carried brilliant standards. Since the point was to capture prisoners for subsequent sacrifice, they avoided killing their opponents, and if their leader was slain or their standard taken, they surrendered, with both sides deciding between them the amount of tribute to be paid by the losers. So necessary to the continuance of Aztec society was human sacrifice, in fact, that in times of peace an artificial form of warfare, called "Flowery Wars," was devised to provide the necessary victims. Under the terms of a prearranged compact, the Aztecs and their neighbors to the east agreed to meet in equal number and do battle in a specially designated area. The sole purpose of this type of warfare was to obtain victims for sacrifice. Moriarty has pointed out the similarities involved in both the ritual nature of this kind of combat and the conception of honor that accompanied it, and the medieval "Mêlée."[9] It is also an incipient theatrical form in which a battle is consciously staged. The difference being that this type of "performance" lacks spectators. Against this highly structured style of warfare Cortés launched a war of total conquest. It was so antithetical to the system that they had developed that the Aztecs did not know how to respond.[10] After a failed attempt to ambush the Spanish in Cholula, the remaining Aztec cities quietly surrendered.

Moctezoma II and his nobles prepared an elaborate welcoming ceremony for Cortés. Meeting him at the southern entrance on the outskirts of Tenochtitlán, Moctezoma is said to have addressed Cortés as a descendant of Quetzalcoátl, saying to him: "O our lord, thou hast suffered fatigue; thou hast spent thyself. Thou has arrived on earth; thou hast come to thy noble city of Mexico. Thou hast come to occupy thy noble mat and seat, which for a little time I have guarded and watched for thee."[11] Although it is questionable whether or not Moctezoma believed Cortés was Quetzalcoátl returned, his adoption of the story explained his own actions, and inactions, towards the Spaniards. The similarity between his welcome of Cortés and Cortés' welcome to the friars is striking, and it is to be assumed that Cortés consciously reinforced the similarities to impress the Aztec leaders with the Franciscans' position. By humbling himself before the friars Cortés increased the power of the mendicant presence. At the same time, he utilized the ecclesiastical power they represented, and which he confirmed, to consolidate his secular authority over the recently conquered Aztecs.

In order to understand the Aztec response to Cortés' carefully staged greeting to the friars, it is necessary to return to pre-Columbian times and examine the relationships between religion, politics, and theatre in indigenous society. How would the Aztecs have responded to Cortés' piece of theatre? Would they have seen it as a staged event? Besides the easily perceived significance of their conqueror kneeling before a different authority in their presence, would the Aztecs have understood the broader religious and political implications of Cortés' act?

RELIGION, POLITICS, AND THEATRE IN INDIGENOUS SOCIETY

To the Aztecs daily existence was a metaphysical drama based upon the interplay of space and time. In a certain limited sense, that of ritual representation such as that present in the "Flowery Wars," a theatrical element pervaded their lives. In their language, Nahuatl, the words "movement," "heart," and "soul" all share a common root. The structure of the language reflected the structure of a society for which life (the heart) was impossible without movement. Such a fundamental belief led to the Aztec obsession with, and creation of, a highly evolved calendrical system.

The Nahuas... believed that movement and life resulted from the harmony achieved by the spatial orientation of the years and the days, in other words, by the spatialization of time. So long as this harmony continued, so long as the four directions of the universe were each allotted thirteen years in every century and their supremacy unquestioned during the specified time, the Fifth Sun [the era current at the time of the Conquest] would continue to exist – it would continue to move. Should this balance some day be disturbed, another cosmic struggle for supremacy would be initiated. There would be one final earthquake – one so powerful that "with this we shall perish."[12]

This understanding of the interrelationship of space and time, combined with the Aztec narratives of genesis, produced a specific orientation underlying all actions in everyday life. The narratives told of how the gods created the world out of their own blood. In so doing they themselves became dependent upon the world for their own survival. Periodic infusions of offerings of the human heart and blood were essential if the gods, and the god's creations, were to continue to exist. This combination of forces provided a basis for Tlacael's creation of a trained corps of warrior–mystics devoted to their god, Huitzilopochtli.

Huitzilopochtli, a god associated with the day, was born of Coatlicue, an earth-mother goddess. Coatlicue, a priestess, was sweeping out her temple one day when she discovered a ball of down which she placed in the bosom of her dress for safekeeping. By the time she had finished sweeping the down was gone and she was miraculously pregnant. Believing themselves to be disgraced, Coatlicue's 400 sons and her daughter Coyolxauhqui all joined together to kill their mother. As she died Huitzilopochtli swore vengeance. He appeared fully armed, chased off the 400 sons and cut off Coyolxauhqui's head.

Modern scholarship has held that the Aztecs saw the 400 sons as representations of the 400 stars and Coyolxauhqui as a representation of the moon. Their defeat by Huitzilopochtli signified day's victory over night. For the Aztecs this battle was reenacted every night as the sun died in the west and then, after a night of strenuous combat, was reborn in the east. Subsequent investigation has shown that Aztec symbolic representations of the sun, the moon, and the stars are attached to other situations and deities as well, and that such a neat progression from night to day is more probably a Western construct imposed upon Aztec conception. In any case, this concept of a battle between night and day was one recorded by the friars.[13] According to such a concept sacrificial offerings of human heart and blood renewed Huitzilopochtli's strength in his nightly war with the forces of darkness. Like their god, the Aztecs themselves became great warriors skilled at ceremonial warfare and human sacrifice. Their mission was no less than the prevention of the final catastrophe, the death of the Fifth Sun.

AZTEC RITUAL–DRAMA

Ritual warfare and sacrificial offerings are not, in and of themselves, full-blown theatre. The latter distinguishes between the audience and the performers, the former do not. Victor Turner has defined ritual as "prescribed formal behavior for occasions not given over to technological routine, having reference to belief in invisible beings or powers regarded as the first and final causes of all effects."[14] He goes on to say that "I like to think of ritual essentially as *performance, enactment*, not primarily as rules or rubrics. The rules 'frame' the ritual process, but the ritual process transcends its frame." This distinction is especially valid in regards to Latin America, where indigenous ritual forms were incorporated into the mendicant evangelical theatre. The spectacle inherent in Aztec ritual warfare and sacrifice contained within it many elements of an incipient theatre the mendicant orders skillfully used to their advantage as they undertook the task of Christianizing the New World. The rules framed the ritual process and the ritual process transcended its frame, but the context had changed.

Dominican and Augustinian mendicant forces followed the Franciscan shock troops into the battle for the indigenous populations' souls and it is to a Dominican, Fray Diego Durán (*c.* 1537–1588) that we owe our gratitude for his descriptions of Aztec ritual representations in his *Historia de las Indias*. Durán was brought to Mexico at the age of five or six, and his upbringing in the New World gave him a particularly astute understanding of the meaning of sacrifice. Two ritual representations of special interest to this study that were observed by Durán are those done for Huitzilopochtli and Quetzalcoátl:

The dance they liked best was that done with adornments of flowers with which they crowned and surrounded each other. For this dance they built a house of roses in the principal *momoztli* of their great god Huitzilopochtli's temple, and constructed a few handmade trees, filled with sweet-smelling flowers, where the goddess Xochiquétzal was made to sit. While they danced, a few boys dressed like birds, and others dressed like butterflies, heavily adorned with rich plumes of green, blue, red, and yellow descended.

They climbed the trees, running from branch to branch, sucking the dew from the roses.

Then the gods, each one dressed in all their adornments as if they had stepped off the altar, appeared. They dressed the Indians in the same fashion and then, their blow-guns in hand, began to shoot at the make believe little birds in the trees. From there the goddess of the roses, who was Xochiquétzal, came out to receive them, taking them by the hand and making them sit down next to her, treating them with great honor and respect as such gods deserved. There she gave them roses and incense, calling her representatives and making them comfort them. This was the solemnest dance this nation had, and thus there are very few times now that I see another danced without wonder.[15]

As Fernando Horcasitas has noted, it is difficult to imagine this scene as a hieratic dumbshow. It seems logical to assume that the dance was accompanied by song, music, and dialog, especially between Xochi-quétzal and the other gods.[16] In any case, the description presents us with a ritual dance of a theatrical nature in which boys play the roles of birds and butterflies and adults represent the individual gods complete with their identifying clothing and insignia, and sets are elaborately constructed. It is only a short historical step from here to the type of schematic, allegorical representation present in the medieval cycle plays, and from there to a more developed form of characterization. Even more striking in its elaborate preparation and religious content was the annual festival for Quetzalcoátl (Cortés' first indigenous costume) described by Durán.

Forty days prior to the most important day of the festival, the merchants bought a slave who would represent Quetzalcoátl during those forty days. He had to be "healthy of hands and feet, without any blemish or brand, neither one-eyed, nor cloudy eyed, neither one-legged nor one-handed, nor deformed; not bleary-eyed, drool-ing, or toothless, without any sign of boils, pustules, or scrofula. In all, that he should be clean of any stain."[17] He had to be, in other words, a perfect example of the ancient Mexican man. Once he was purchased, the slave was bathed and:

[They] dressed him exactly like the idol was dressed, placing the crown and the bird's beak upon his head, giving him the mantle, the jewel, the stockings and gold earrings, the loincloth, buckler, and scythe that pertained to the idol.

This man was the living representation of the idol for those forty days. He was served and worshipped like the idol, and his own guard and many other people accompanied him every day.

They also kept him caged at night so that he wouldn't flee, as has already been noted about the slave who represented Tezcatlipoca. Then, each morning, he was taken from the cage, placed in a prominent spot and served an excellent meal. After he had eaten, they put roses in his hands and garlands of roses around his neck and went with him to the city. He sang and danced throughout the city so as to be recognized as the likeness of the god...

And hearing him approach singing, the women and children emerged from their houses to greet him and offer him many things fit for a god...

Nine days before the appointed day of the festival, there came before him two of the oldest and most venerated temple dignitaries who, humbling themselves before him, with great reverences said to him in a respectful, hushed voice, "Lord, your majesty should know that nine days from now your labor of singing and dancing will be at an end and you must die." To which he had to respond that the time was right. If the priests noticed that the slave was upset or saddened by his impending death, he was drugged with *itzpacalatl*, a potion that made him forget his destiny and he was soon dancing and singing again.

When the day arrived which, as we have said, was midnight on the third of February, after having done homage to him with music and incense, the slave was taken and sacrificed. At the appointed hour his heart was offered to the moon and he was then thrown in front of the idol, in whose presence they killed him, letting the body fall down the steps.[18]

These two rituals were described by Durán two generations after the Conquest, when the indigenous ruling class had been quite thoroughly supressed. As related to him by the Indians with whom he came into contact, such spectacles as those of Huitzilopochtli and Quetzalcoátl are remarkable for the theatrical display involved. All the elements that we normally associated with a more fully developed theatre were present in this indigenous ritual–drama: representational actors, spectators, a defined stage, and a thematic content developed and carried to conclusion, dialog, music, and dance. Such drama, moreover, was an important part of the culture's social, religious, and political life. When the slave-as-Quetzalcoátl's heart was offered in sacrifice and his blood shed, not only was the god's sacrifice for his Aztec brethren reenacted, but the human slave's blood served to propitiate and strengthen the god himself, thereby maintaining equilibrium in the universe and the stability of the Fifth Sun. Such duality, as we have seen, was essential to the successful completion of the festival.

The festival of Quetzalcoátl presents us with a type of experience, the sacred rite, that the modern theatre has explored from Artaud to

Growtoski. It is the seed of, though by no means the same as, one of the recurring fascinations of twentieth-century theatrical technique: the continuing explorations of the duality inherent in acting itself, where the person portraying a role can either ask us to enter into the fiction of the actor's character with him, or can present that character to us as a fabrication, commenting upon it as he or she does so. Since the Aztec actor's performance ended in his actual death, the duality present in theatrical characterization was, on one level, extinguished. However, since he was frequently drugged, believing himself to be in a state of grace, the death was not feared but welcomed as a step towards deification. In addition, the sacrificial victim's body was rapidly skinned, the flayed skin coming off in one complete piece which was then donned by others who took the name of the divinity the victim had represented. As Turner has written: "The experience of subjective and intersubjective flow in ritual performance, whatever its sociobiological or personalogical concomitants may be, often convinces performers that the ritual situation *is* indeed informed with powers both transcendental and immanent."[19] In technical terms, then, there was a conflation of the entire matrix of actor/character/audience, with the actor being seen as actor, and as god (character); while the audience member, through his donning of the dead victim's skin, became both the god represented, and by "getting into his skin," the dead actor as well. This being a ritual performance, its ultimate end was transformational, the convergence of the community in worshiping the god. The theatre's division between spectator and actor was nonexistent in pre-Columbian indigenous display. What the subsequent evangelical theatre retained and developed were the spectacular and transformational aspects of ritual performance, wedding them to Christian theological and political concerns.

The duality inherent in the type of sacrificial characterization described by Durán was merely a part of a larger sense of duality that imbued Aztec life. While the mystico-militaristic conception of sacrifice as necessary to the maintenance and movement of the Sun had been Tlacael's organizing principle for Aztec ascendancy, the notion of an ever-present, constantly impending cataclysm that would destroy their entire universe led the *tlamatinime*, or Aztec wise men, to search for the philosophical and metaphysical meaning behind such a world. Returning to the Toltec myths upon which Tlacael's new society had been based, and discovering that man's existence had always been mysteriously necessary to the gods, the wise men searched for the motive for man's creation. The answer they arrived at was quite different from the mystico-militaristic one of divine/human reciprocal sacrifice, and is reflected in the following from the *Códice Florentino*:

> Our Master, the Lord of the Close Vicinity,
> thinks and does what He wishes; He determines, He amuses himself.
> As He wishes, so it will be.
> In the palm of His hand He has us;
> at His will He shifts us around.
> We shift around, like marbles we roll;
> He rolls us around endlessly.
> We are but toys to Him; He laughs at us.[20]

As León-Portilla comments, the *tlamatinime* were led by this sort of view of the divine to a completely different vision of religion in which Ometeótl (as "our mother, our father" and "invisible and intangible," a duality in himself), the "Lord of the Everywhere" created man for the pleasure of watching his momentary passage upon the earth. "Since it was impossible for man on *taltípac* to know the underlying motive for creation, the wise men attributed it to the Divine's wish for a spectacle, for entertainment, a play which human beings would perform in a world of dreams."[21] In both its mystico-militaristic and its metaphysical manifestations Aztec understanding of existence exhibited a profound sense of the theatrical, a sense that was inextricably linked to the religious and political life of the Aztec empire.

As a result of the presence in the Aztec region of the mendicant orders, who fervently believed in the practice of utilizing the indigenous languages and culture as a means of proselytization, incipient indigenous theatrical forms, primarily those of ritual and ceremony (the pageantry of state occasions), have been well documented. As we shall see, the mendicant's millenarianism and their subsequent battle for power with the secular church and colonial powers, as well as with the Crown, was also a strong factor in their interest in, and documentation of, indigenous activity. Their moral and theological right to exclusive control over their Indian converts would be strengthened by their ability to demonstrate the salutatory effects of conversion upon the heathen, and the pernicious practices to which they would return if left in the hands of secular masters.

RELIGIO-THEATRICAL ACTIVITY IN MESOAMERICA
AND SOUTH AMERICA

Further south, in Mesoamerica and South America, the documentation of religio-theatrical indigenous activity in pre-Columbian times is greatly impoverished by a lack of mendicant presence. Our understanding of such activity is also hampered by the zeal of people like Bishop Diego de Landa, who carefully destroyed any indigenous books or codices he discovered. This lack, coupled with the habit the various Incas had of destroying all records of past history and starting the world afresh when they came to power, accounts for the small quantity of detailed chronicle material. The information that does exist, however, shows indigenous forms in the south quite similar in character and content to those of the north.

As we have seen in Durán's descriptions of various Aztec religious spectacles, Nature played a large part in scenic, dramatic, and thematic elements of ritual practice. An emphasis upon Nature was also evident in the indigenous activity to the south. Both the Maya and the Inca cultures were pervaded by pantomimic dances that exhibited a fascination with the animal world around them, the wonders of cultivation, and humanity's place in this seemingly miraculous system. "From watching the animals, zoological festivals are born; from the practice of cultivation, agricultural festivals intermixed with phallic myths appear; the return to the past carries them to legend and history, and the desire to invoke superior beings leads them to myth, which takes the form of religion that is manifested in liturgy."[22]

Among the Quechua in Peru, religious rites were performed for fertilization of both the earth and of women, for exorcism of malignant spirits, and for purification of the earth and its inhabitants. The purification festival is particularly striking for its performative nature. In it a warrior, carrying a lance in his hand as the Sun's messenger, and adorned with many colored feathers, came running out of the Sacsahuamán fortress. He ran to the center of the principal plaza, where four other warriors awaited him. He touched their lances with his own and they then each ran towards one of the four roads which, leaving Cuzco, lead to the four corners of the empire.[23] Through a performance, the Inca empire was transformed into a purified state.

As there existed a highly stratified society with a very strong aristocracy, the majority of religious ritual activity seems to have been performed for that class. Such was the ritual in honor of the god of virility, Huari, in which the Inca approached the Sun's statue, did obeisance, and was followed by his lords, who drove their sons before them, whipping them and exhorting them to be as courageous as they themselves were.

As we have seen among the Aztecs, understanding and practice of religion was carried out differently by aristocracy and commoners. This was also the case in the Incan empire, where the popular religion consisted of worshiping the *huaca* (ancestral god) of one's clan. The Inca's ancestor was the Sun, and the entire population, aristocracy and commoners alike joined in the worship of their ruler's ancestor. Such worship was extraordinarily spectacular and magnificent; Cuzco possessed a magnificent temple to the Sun whose cornices, images, and utensils were all of pure gold. The High Priest's daily dress was a robe of coarse wool; he was a vegetarian and never indulged in any drink stronger than water. While performing the temple ceremonies, however, his dress was quite splendid. It consisted of a tiara that included a circular plate of gold representative of the sun, and a half-moon of silver underneath the chin. It was adorned with macaw feathers and covered with jewels and plates of gold. A long, sleeveless ceremonial tunic reached to the ground, covered by a retrimmed pelisse that was also studded with jewels and gold plates. He wore fine wool shoes and large gold bracelets on his arms.[24] Such garments were strictly for use in Sun worship and when the Inca and his entire court were present, costumed in full regalia, the sight must have been a lavish spectacle indeed.

The existence of a duality between the mystico-militaristic exercise of religion and that of the *tlamatinime* in Aztec society was matched by a division of religious thought and teaching among the Andean peoples. There was a pervasive belief shared by all levels of society that anything that had to do with one's daily well-being was imbued with the supernatural. This produced innumerable objects and gods to worship, with the Sun god taking precedence over them all. At the same time the Incas, and some of those around them, believed in the existence of a Supreme Being, called *Illa Tici Uira-cocha*, whom all the other deities obeyed. For them Uira-cocha was the vital organizing force behind the universe. They devoted long hours to the attempt to comprehend it. These two religious orientations, that of the pervasive supernatural and the worship of Uira-cocha, combined to form a highly organized society, socialistic in principle, but intensely hierarchical in practice.

Theatre and spectacle were an integral part of the maintenance of the empire. Rites of an historical–military nature and in honor of Nature abounded, with the specific pedagogical purpose of ethical education. These were rituals performed to discourage lying, robbery, homicide, and a number of other vices. Since religion was an arm of the state, these rituals bred obedience to both at the same time. The Incas skillfully maintained the status quo by encouraging their subjects to perform celebratory dances and songs to the great exploits of their kings. A permissive attitude towards intoxication frequently accompanied such dances, and the historical feat described was sometimes actually performed. This was the case when the Inca Tupac Yupanqui, in honor of his victorious son, staged a battle in which he directed the defense of Sacsahuamán fortress while 50,000 men attacked it.[25]

The explorer Pedro Sarmiento de Gamboa describes how, upon triumphing over enemies of his realm, the Inca Pachacuti Yupanqui "ordered made a great festival and performances concerning the life of each Inca. These celebrations, which they called *purucaya*, lasted more than four months. At the end of the performances of each Inca's life and deeds, large, sumptuous sacrifices were performed before each Inca's tomb."[26] Sarmiento de Gamboa also comments that, upon their victorious entry in Cuzco, "each squadron of warriors, as well as they were able…performed the battles in which they had triumphed."[27] Such performances were of a highly political nature, confirming the primacy of the emperor and exalting his warrior–actors.

The third great indigenous civilization of Latin America, the Maya, also performed rituals and ceremonies of a religio-theatrical kind. One, which finds its origin in the *Popul Vuh*, is *El baile de los gigantes* (Dance of the giants), which tells the story of the twins Junajup and Ixbalamqué in their battle against the giants Gukup Cakik, Xipacná, Caprakán, and the lords of Xibalbá. While the purpose of the story in the *Popul Vuh*, the Mayan Bible, was to teach theogony, cosmonogy, arithmetic, and astronomy, it was exploited by colonial powers after the Conquest for its similarity to the story of David and Goliath and its references to the beheading of St. John.

In this theatrical dance, two twelve-year-old boys who play the roles of the two *Gavites* (the young Sun and the young Moon) ally themselves with the *Gigante Blanco* (White Giant) against the *Gigante Negro* (Black Giant). There are five acts or movements to the piece describing the various battles between the two sides. The action is frequently suspended while the characters do homage to the Sun. In the final movement the Sun's son kills the Black Giant, cutting off his head. The piece ends with extensive worshiping of the Sun. *El baile de los gigantes* celebrates the triumph of skill and religious force over ignorance and brute force. The Maya strongly believed that the universe was organized in such a way that good would always defeat evil.[28]

THE *RABINAL ACHÍ*

In addition to the various political and religious theatrical spectacles described, Maya culture has left us the only known extant script from indigenous times, the *Rabinal Achí*. The story of this play is simple. The two main characters are the enemy warriors, the *Varón de Queché* and the *Varón de Rabinal*. The *Varón de Queché* is now the *Varón de Rabinal*'s prisoner after a long war in which he took the *Varón de Rabinal*'s king, *Cinco-Lluvias* (Five Rains), prisoner only to be defeated by the *Varón de Rabinal*. They now offer him a place in the Rabinal tribe, if he will humble himself before *Cinco-Lluvias*. He refuses to do so, and the play ends with *Cinco-Lluvias*' warriors killing the *Varón de Queché* in sacrifice.

This story is told by means of a long series of formal challenges interspersed with dance and music. Anthropologically, the play tells us a great deal about Mayan warfare, ritual, prisoner exchange, and other customs. It is also a veritable lode of Mayan theatrical technique. Each actor wore a heavy, highly detailed wooden mask and multicolored plumage that corresponded to his character. Since these masks were of considerable weight, the actors, especially those playing the roles of the *Varón de Rabinal* and the *Varón de Queché*, were often replaced two or three times during the course of the play. Another actor would don the mask and pick up from where his predecessor had left off.[29] This was especially necessary since the play was sung not recited, and the actors continued to sing during all of the dances that are interspersed throughout the story.[30] While the endless repetition of challenges and phrases can make reading the *Rabinal Achí* a rather tedious task, the musical quality of the language is easy to comprehend, and an almost operatic rendering of it is easy to envision. Pedro Henriquez Ureña has suggested that the formal qualities of the *Rabinal Achí* could be similar to those of the ancient Greek drama before the advent of the third actor, where only two actors engaged each other on the stage, interrupted at precise moments by a Chorus who pronounced a few necessary phrases.[31] This is exactly what occurs in at least half of the *Rabinal Achí*.

Henriquez Ureña's hypothesis seems to me to be further supported by a comparison of the play with Aeschylus' *The Persians*. Both are apparently static dramas consisting of long passages of descriptive narration. If one reads either script with an eye towards its performance, however, it becomes clear that the rich poetic imagery was mirrored by sumptuous costuming and lavish aural accompaniment, whether it took the form of the vocal manipulation of the Attic theatres or the musical accompaniment of the *Rabinal Achí*. In both plays choral dances are essential to the story's development and both end with a brilliant spectacle of political and religious significance when, in *The Persians*, Xerxes' rent garments are removed and replaced with new ones; and in the *Rabinal Achí* when the Chorus of Eagle and Jaguar Warriors kill the *Varón de Queché* on the altar, offering up his heart in sacrifice. Georges Raynaud, who first translated the *Rabinal Achí* into French, has emphasized its religious aspects even further:

When song was no longer of an absolute use for common conversation, it remained, possibly in melopea form at first, as a more or less poetic accessory to language and, above all, to the collective or individual's prayers, hymns dedicated to the gods.
Dance as well (including in it, if it at one time existed collectively, the simple unorganized agitation of various parts of the body), dance guided by musical sounds, consisted of a social–religious creation. Dance in itself was a prayer, a hymn, the mimed expression of symbolic ideas; a collective form of an act, so ancient and so universal that it could be traced to animalism itself: language spoken through gestures.[32]

"Language spoken through gestures" or, more precisely, language as equivalent to gesture, gesture being the initial movement that motivates the act, is the subject of Tzvetan Todorov's impressive semiotic study of the Conquest. In his book, *The Conquest of America*, Todorov presents Spaniards and indigenous peoples in dialog with one another – a dialog he joins in in an attempt to understand the mechanics of conquest, a machine that inexorably subdues the Other, the alien or, in this case, the culture. Todorov demonstrates that it is Cortés' pursuit of the knowledge necessary to interpret indigenous signs, coupled with his ability to utilize that information, that makes the incredibly swift Spanish domination of Mexico possible. While we have seen the importance of movement in space and time in Aztec thought, Todorov emphasizes another aspect, its cyclical nature.

The appearance of the Spaniards was not a part of the harmonious cycle that sprang from the movement of the Sun from east to west, which meant that night followed day, sacrifice imitated the Sun's progress across the sky, and warfare's highly codified system had as its end the propitiation and maintenance of the Sun. The Spaniards were completely alien to this design. They could not be encompassed by it. They were of a different language. Reading accounts of the Conquest, in fact, one is struck by their similarity to the stories of Westerners who have attempted to live within Japanese culture. Those Westerners quickly realize that much of what they have ever done, learned, or experienced is irrelevant and that they must start all over again. Such was the relationship of the Spaniards to the Aztecs and vice versa, and it makes one wonder whether Columbus did not reach Asia after all. In any event, as art historian Mary Miller has remarked, the Conquest was the only time in history that spacemen actually landed.[33]

Since their cosmogeny admitted no foreign element (it was complete in and of itself), the Aztecs desperately searched for a means of incorporating the Spanish presence into their own world view. The only place they could find it was in the mythology of the Toltec people they themselves had conquered, some of whose myths promised the return of their god Quetzalcoátl. If Cortés was Quetzalcoátl or his messenger, then a cycle could be conceived in which the Toltec god returned to announce the imminent end of the Aztec empire. Cortés' ability to grasp and speak this Aztec language of cyclical signs, what Todorov calls his ability to "adapt and improvise," made his achievement possible. By the same token, it was the Aztec failure to break free of their signs, their failure to "speak" the Spaniards' "language," that led inevitably to their subjugation. The Aztec empire fell, in one respect, from an inability to comprehend the linguistic codes with which they were presented.

THE MENDICANTS

The mendicant orders sent to New Spain had one central aim: converting the indigenous population to Christianity. In order to convert other people one needs to communicate with them. Where Cortés adapted and improvised theatrically in aid of conquest, the friars adapted and improvised theatrically in aid of conversion. Upon arrival in the New World they were faced with a terrible problem: they lacked any knowledge of the indigenous languages. While they went about the business of gathering enough information to comprehend the alien idiom, the task at hand was an urgent one both spiritually and temporally. If the discovery of the New World was, as we have seen, believed to be a prelude to the Apocalypse, then the need to Christianize these new peoples was immediate. The friars were also well aware that it was only a matter of time before the promise of wealth drew both the secular church and the laity to New Spain. The unwashed hordes were breathing down their necks and the mendicants needed to establish themselves firmly in the New World as quickly as possible. Able to grasp the forces at work on their battlefield as astutely as Cortés grasped those at work on his, the friars saw at once the importance of the theatrical possibilities inherent in the ritual of indigenous society. Lacking a common spoken language with the Other, they turned to a visual and aural one. They communicated in order to convert, and the method of communication was the theatre.

Cortés' greeting to the friars, as we have seen, was a consummate performance and his concern for staging throughout the time of the Conquest is truly remarkable. Upon being chosen to lead the expedition, his first concern was for a proper suit of clothes in which to play his new role. His noisy welcome to the first Indian messengers to board his ship was merely a precursor of the elaborately staged stratagems he was to use throughout his campaign. Cortés, a member of Spanish society in what Américo Castro has called *la edad conflictiva*, seems to have had an innate sense of the importance of appearance. In a certain sense, one's position in Spanish society after 1499 was strictly a matter of appearance. It mattered not whether you were a *converso*, a *cristiano viejo*, or a *cristiano nuevo*, but what you *seemed* to be to those around you. How you presented yourself, how successfully you played the role society demanded of you, was the key. The

societal tensions that were to create the elaborate intricacies of the
Spanish baroque had begun.

Looked at from a historical distance, the intersection of Christianity and indigenous religions is itself a matter of seeming. The image
of Paradise painted in Pierre d'Ailly's *Imago Mundi*, the idea of having
rediscovered the Garden of Eden, the persistent belief that certain
signs indicated the prior presence of St. Thomas in the New World,
and the tremendous burden of the imminence of the Apocalypse; all
these ideas or images imbued the Franciscan millenarianism the
friars brought with them to Nueva España. Each is a matter of
seeming, of the historical juncture of appearance. For the friars in
1524, however, these junctures were not matters of appearance but of
fact. The necessity of converting the indigenous populations made
them so.

INDIGENOUS RELIGION AND CHRISTIANITY

There were a number of points on which indigenous religion and
Christianity appeared to agree: the presence in the New World of the
cross, baptism, confession, and communion. The cross appeared in
numerous places in Mexico, most notably as it adorned depictions of
Quetzalcoátl's robe, or when it took the shape of a tree that in one
case seems to bleed. From another, an impaled body appears to
hang; before another, a figure, supposedly a child, is held aloft as if
in adoration. None of these crosses is a Latin one, the arms are all of
equal length.[34] Sahagún, Diego de Landa, and Durán all mention
ceremonies of baptism practiced by the Indians.[35] While these
ceremonies involved sprinkling with and immersion in water, and
seem to have been connected to the naming of children, they were not
performed by the priests and appear to have had none of the same
meaning as the Catholic ceremony. Mendieta and Sahagún both cite
instances of the use of confession. The practice had to do with the
expiation of drunkenness or infidelity and seems to have chiefly
resulted in a postponement to old age of certain actions since sin was
considered to be more a physiological malady, a kind of poison that
had invaded the system, than a spiritual weakness. By administering
confession and penance one purged oneself of the poison.[36] Acosta,
Motolinía, and Sahagún all describe variations of a ceremony similar
to the Christian communion in which cakes or actual replicas of idols
were baked out of amaranth seeds and then eaten in conjunction with

the consumption of the human flesh of the sacrificial victims. Even relatively recently in Mexico, peasants were discovered consuming amaranth seed cake replicas of the independence leader Benito Juarez at festivals.[37]

Sahagún's account of feast- and fast-days gives the most complete record we possess that the Spaniards clearly viewed the Indians' periods of abstinence as equivalent to the fasting practiced in Catholicism, even though they condemned at the same time the extreme instances of self-torture that accompanied the indigenous fast-days.[38] Such similarities in religious practice between Christianity and indigenous forms seem to us now, with our extensive knowledge of other religions, rather tenuous at best. For the friars, however, these similarities, especially as they presented themselves in performance, were a means of capturing an entire people's souls for Christ.

INDIGENOUS AND MENDICANT THEATRE

We have seen how lavish some of the indigenous rituals could be and the Aztec, Maya, and Quechua cultures all provided for the necessary artists in their system of education. The hierarchical structure of the indigenous culture gave the responsibility for education to the priesthood. Whether the ultimate goal was to produce great warriors, as among the Aztec, or not, the means used were similar. Composers, dancers, musicians, singers, and all sorts of artisans were trained in these schools. Sahagún describes the degree of specialization present in the Aztec schools called *cuicacalli*:

There were also then prizes… They gave presents to all the singers: singers of the dance; composers of songs; directors of the song. This was also true for the musicians: those who played the drum; to those who had the *huehuetls* and who played them; to those who spoke the words of the poet; to those who composed the melody; to those who whistled or clapped their hands (in imitation of battle noises); to those who directed the others; to those who danced representing some thing; to those who danced in groups; to those who enacted the farcical songs; to those who chanted the funeral dirges; and to those who did acrobatic dances.[39]

Durán speaks of "dramaturgos," who were the indigenous priests and monks that ran the schools where they composed "very pleasing dances, farces, interludes, and songs."[40] As the early Franciscan friars moved from province to province constructing churches and monasteries with the Indians' aid, they also invoked their prerogative of control over education, founding schools as they went along. In doing so they discovered the existence of the indigenous trained professionals and lost no time in incorporating their skills into the theatrical forms they were creating. By employing a theatre of pageantry and display similar to the native rituals and ceremonies they had observed, the friars sparked the enthusiasm of the professionals and awed the populace, both reactions that hastened the indigenous peoples down the path to conversion.

While Cortés' action in greeting the twelve Franciscans he had requested served his own immediate ends in terms of his postion in Mexico, it was also an acknowledgment of the Franciscans' legal postion, a position Cortés, the master of legal precedent, was quick to recognize. The Franciscans brought with them a very specific legal authority which they were to exercise virtually unrestrained for the greater part of the first century of colonization. That legal authority was the *patronato real* ceded to the Spanish Crown by the Pope in 1508. Under it, the Crown was granted the exclusive right to collect tithes and to present or nominate whomever it desired to receive benefices in their new colony. By special dispensation the regular clergy were allowed to be ordained as parish priests. The mendicants were confirmed in their nearly absolute position of authority by Cortés and, through him, the Aztecs, by the Pope, and by the Crown. This position was not to be eternal but for the moment it made their missionary status unusually secure. Such security, coupled with the demands of their new work, led to the creation of new architectural forms as the mendicant orders built their churches and monasteries throughout New Spain.

No longer threatened by hostile forces, the church was not required to double as a fortress and it took on a form nearly unknown in Spain, that of the *capilla abierta* or "open chapel" in order to meet the religious, political, social, and administrative demands placed upon it. The precipitous events of the Conquest together with the apostolic fervor generated by the impending Apocalypse, created a climate in which rapid conversion of the indigenous population was absolutely essential. To this end it was not at all uncommon for the friars to say Mass before thousands of Indians at a time. The open chapel, giving out, as it did, onto a large courtyard (*atrio*) modeled upon that of the Aztec temples, provided the necessary structure for the numbers the mendicants dealt with.[41] At the same time it was an ideal setting for an audience at the theatre. Fernando Horcasitas has commented upon this aspect of the *capillas abiertas*:

Almost all of the open chapels seem to be ideal stages for dramatic productions. This is due not only to their form but also because they so easily lend themselves to the introduction or addition of platforms and other provisional wooden constructions, curtains, machinery, rope, etc. The open chapel possesses, in addition, all the necessary qualities required for magnificent acoustics. It has a hard floor; the person speaking has his back against a stone wall which reflects his voice; the voice can be projected outward without fear of echo or resonance; there is a roof or "head" that ensures that anyone situated beneath it hears clearly (and in the courtyards all the faithful were beneath the open chapel, even if this only meant beneath one of its steps).[42]

Although the actual acoustic properties of the open chapels are debatable (it would take a systematic study of them to be sure upon the point), even photographs of the structures make plain their similarity to contemporary theatres, not to mention their resemblance to the proscenium frame.

PEDRO DE GANTE AND THE BEGINNINGS OF EVANGELICAL THEATRE

It was in a church of this type that Pedro de Gante, one of the three clerics in New Spain prior to the arrival of the Twelve, was to initiate the mixture of indigenous forms and Christian doctrine that would characterize the evangelical theatre to come. In a letter to Felipe II, written in 1558, Pedro de Gante gives a brief history of his work in New Spain, in order to bolster his request that the king stop the practice of giving towns and their inhabitants to the colonists. He maintained such a practice was endangering the Indians' chances for salvation. In his description of his own work Pedro de Gante relates how he began, shortly after Cortés' victory, to gather together the sons of the principal Aztec leaders and lords. These boys were placed under lock and key in the monastery of San Francisco in Mexico City. Free from the corrupting influence of their families, they were taught Christian doctrine, how to read and write, and how to preach. Those who demonstrated the greatest ability were sent out on Sundays and feast days to preach to the indigenous populations around Mexico City. They went in groups of two or three and traveled distances of anywhere from two to twenty leagues. When any of these novitiates discovered or heard of any return to idolatry, a group of the most skillful of them was sent to disrupt the ceremonies and smash the idols. We may look askance at such arrogance today but it was the arrogance of a religion absolutely convinced of its superiority. Pedro de Gante's actions were only a precursor of the type of imperial arrogance, whether that of a religious or political system, that has characterized Latin American history to the present day.

Given Pedro de Gante's tactics, it is no surprise that he complains to Felipe II that:

the common people were like unreasonable animals, indomitable, whom we could not bring into the fraternity and congregation of the Church, to the doctrine, or to a sermon, without them fleeing like the Devil before the Cross. We were about this endeavor for more than three years, without ever, as I have said, being able to attract them without them fleeing before the friars like savages, and even more so before the Spaniards.[43]

In order to remedy this situation Pedro de Gante, like all the early Franciscans, an acute observer of the indigenous customs, hit upon a brilliant strategem:

but by the grace of God I began to get to know them and to understand their conditions and values. I saw that they showed their adoration for their gods by singing and dancing before them. I saw that when someone had to be sacrificed for something, for instance, to bring about victory over enemies, or for temporal necessities, before killing them, they danced in front of the idol. Seeing this, knowing that I had to work among them, and realizing that all their songs were dedicated to their gods, I composed very solemn songs about God's law and the faith concerning how God became a man in order to save the human race, and how the Virgin Mary gave Him birth remaining pure and intact. This was all done two months, more or less, before Christmas. I also gave them marks of livery to paint on their mantas so that they could dance with them since such was their practice, dressing themselves for happiness, mourning, or victory depending upon the dances or songs done. Then, when Christmas approached I had everyone from the region and from ten leagues around Mexico City invited to the festival of the Birth of Christ our Redeemer. So many came that they could not fit in the patio, even though it is quite large. Each province built a hut for its principal figures. Some came from seven or eight leagues carried sick in hammocks, others six or seven leagues by water. All of them listened that very Christmas Eve to angels singing in the sky, who said, "on such a night was born the Redeemer of the world."[44]

Pedro de Gante's use of *cantares solemnes* in the Convento de San Francisco built, as tradition has it, on the site that had once housed

Moctezoma II's zoo, combines the aesthetic resources and theatrical skills already present in indigenous culture with the new Christian doctrine. It was apparently so effective a combination that Indians from all over the city and its outlying regions not only came to hear these "solemn songs" sung in their own language, but henceforth willingly sent their sons to the monastery school and flocked to Mass themselves. A means of communication had been found. While these initial steps by Pedro de Gante seem, at best, to have effected a superficial sort of conversion on the masses of people, the subsequent evangelical theatre was to develop his first endeavors into a strong force for conversion to Christianity.

Pedro de Gante's methods were the beginning of the mendicants' attempt to adapt and utilize portions of the native theatrical forms to carry out their missionary work. In sharp contrast to the way in which any vestiges of pre-Columbian familial, social, governmental, or ritual warfare structures were ruthlessly destroyed, the friars sought to maintain parallel forms of the religious structure substituting Christian content for the misguided paganism of indigenous religion. Where the Aztecs had seen their relationship to divinity as dependent, yet collaborative, Christianity now demanded complete subservience to God. Ritual warfare and human sacrifice were replaced by a system of tribute paid to the new society through its religious structure, and the didactic and ritualistic nature of Catholicism replaced the didactic nature of pre-Colombian tradition and ritual.[45] In addition, the Aztec system of domination over much of central Mexico meant that a kind of "lingua franca" existed and it appears that the friars quite consciously attempted to convert Nahuatl into a universal language which, since the secular authorities had not mastered it, would have been exclusively under their control. Even more germane to our discussion of the mendicants' use of theatre is the fact that the Church itself subsidized the arts, paying singers and dancers for their services in a manner virtually identical to the Aztec partial support of singers, dancers, actors, and artisans.[46]

MENDICANT EVANGELICAL THEATRE

We have seen the way in which theatrical spectacle and ritual was incorporated into daily life in indigenous culture. While the nature of incorporation was different after the mendicants' arrival, such indigenous beliefs were actively encouraged as a means of strengthen-

ing the bonds between the new religion and its charges. Thomas
Gage, an English priest who later renounced Roman Catholicism for
the Church of England, describes a dance-play dealing with the
death of St. Peter or the beheading of John the Baptist that he
witnessed during his missionary stint in Central America in the mid-
sixteenth century.

In these dances there is an Emperour, or a King Herod with their Queens
clothed, another clothed with a long loose cape who represents St. Peter, or
John the Baptist, who while the rest danceth walketh amongst them with a
book in his hands, as if he were saying his prayers, all the rest of the dancers
are apparelled like Captains and Soldiers with swords, Daggers, or Holbards
in their hands. They dance at the sound of a small drum and pipes,
sometimes round, sometimes in length forward, and have and use many
speaches to the Emperour or King, and amongst themselves concerning the
apprehending and execution of the Saint. The King and Queen sit down
sometimes to hear their pleading against the Saint, and his pleading for
himself, and sometimes they dance with the rest; and the end of their dance
is to crucify St. Peter downwards with his head upon a Cross, or behead John
the Baptist, having in readiness a painted head in a dish, which they present
unto the King and Queen, for joy whereof they all dance merrily and so
conclude, taking down him that acted Peter on the Cross. The Indians that
dance this dance most of them are superstitious for what they do, judging as
if it were indeed really acted and performed what is only by way of dance
represented. When I lived amongst them it was an ordinary thing for him
who in the dance was to act St. Peter or John the Baptist, to come first to
Confession, saying they must be holy and pure like the Saint whom they
represent, and must prepare themselves to die. So likewise he that acted
Herod or Herodias, and some of the Soldiers that in the dance were to speak
and accuse the Saints, would afterwards come to confesse of that sin, and
desire absolution from bloodguiltinesse.[47]

The similarity is evident between the Indians' beliefs in such a dance
and those held in a ritual such as that of Quetzalcoátl. This intimate
connection between religion, theatre, and daily life is repeated
numerous times in the reports of the mendicants' evangelical theatre.
Motolinía describes a performance of an *auto sacramental* called *La
natividad de San Juan Bautista* (The nativity of St. John the Baptist;
1538) which was preceded by a mass and ended with the baptism of
an eight-day-old child called John.[48]

The dividing lines between actor and role (not to mention the play
and the spectator) are blurred in this example. Whether to a greater
or a lesser degree, the actor and the role become one. This

convergence of actor and role is a direct descendant of pre-Columbian religious ritual and spectacle practice with a specific pedagogical end. The friars actively encouraged such practice as a means of effecting their own religious and political agenda of conversion. Even the Jesuit theatre in Mexico, which appeared later than the mendicant theatre and was addressed, in its didactic and rhetorical form, to a much smaller, specialized class of the population, indulged at times in similar connections between theatrical representation and the daily existence of their students. Guillermo Lohmann Villenna describes a production of a play called *Historia alegórica del Anticristo y el Juicio Final* (Allegorical history of the Antichrist and the Last Judgment) in Lima in 1559: "In order to represent more clearly the resurrection of the dead, the Jesuits had extracted from the gentile graves disseminated around the city, many indigenous skeletons and even cadavers preserved in their entirety. This caused great fright in those who found themselves present at that performance."[49]

As Fernando Horcasitas has pointed out, what this type of connection between actor and role creates is a *"drama vivido"* or *"drama que se vive."* The relationship of audience to actor is fundamentally different from that of the mainstream Western theatrical tradition. In these works the spectator, having assisted in the production in some way (made things for it, contributed a little money, made the food, or provided the costumes for the festival) buys no ticket, and arrives at the religious, social, and economic center of the town for the performance. The saint being depicted is the same saint seen on the altar, while the spectator attends Mass before the performance, and the performance itself surrounds and invades the audience's space, to the point where the spectators have to avoid being hit by the actors or becoming the butt of their jokes. The performance does not end with applause but with a communal meal or drinking party, and it is quite possible that an actor is a member of the spectator's family and accompanies him or her home.[50]

There was a further link to indigenous tradition in the style of production for some of these plays. Elevated stages, similar in concept to the European medieval drama's use of mansions, were employed. They frequently appeared as platforms along the route of a religious procession allowing a kind of multiple staging that was familiar to the Indians from their own forms of religious presentation.

While the highly developed spectacle that emerged out of confluence with indigenous forms was necessary in order to grab and hold the Indians' attention (especially at the beginning, when the friars lacked the linguistic competence to communicate), the content of the plays written or adapted by the friars, or by Indians under their supervision, was ultimately of greater importance. It was in the content of the plays that the friars perceived the real means of conversion. Once the indigenous population's attention had been captured, the stories they were told would (so the friars believed) induce them to reform their pagan ways.

An accurate chronology of the plays available to us from New Spain, with the exception of a few dates provided by Motolonía, is impossible to determine.[51] The evidence available leads most easily to the conclusion that these plays were performed under Franciscan auspices, primarily in the Tlaxcala region near Mexico City, in the early part of the sixteenth century from approximately 1530 on. One of the earliest of these plays, which Horcasitas tentatively dates 1531–1535, was *El juicio final* (The last judgment). It is a huge theatrical spectacle involving Christ, the Antichrist, and various devils and angels, that emphasizes the importance of marriage through the punishment of an adulterous woman named Lucia on the Day of Judgment. Here is Las Casas' description of the performance:

Nothing so admirable has ever been done by men as a performance, one among many others, done by the Mexicans in the city of Mexico of the final judgment, of which all those who saw it will carry the memory of it with them for many years to come. There were so many things to notice and admire about it, that neither great expense of paper nor of words will suffice to praise it too highly. What I remember at the moment was only one of the remarkable things about it, which was that eight hundred Indians joined together to perform it. Each one of them had his role and acted, and said the words it was incumbent upon him to do and say without a single one of them impeding another's performance. In the end, they say that it was such a thing [to behold] that if it had been done in Rome, it would have rung throughout the world.[52]

As Horcasitas has pointed out, even making allowances for Las Casas' well-known tendency towards exaggeration, half the number of Indian actors willingly performing in Nahuatl only ten years after the Twelve's arrival, and on a scale to match a Wagnerian opera, is astounding.

As Arróniz has so aptly observed, the purpose of such a spectacle was, like baptism by aspersion, in which as many as 5,000 Indians could be baptized at once, to convert at one time a mass of Indians (actors and spectators) by penetrating their idolatrous consciousness.[53] The content of the play was directed to the Aztec nobility, who, although severely diminished, still retained authority, in an effort to get them to depart from their tradition of concubinage. The Antichrist's presence was a reminder that any men outside the Church who pretended to exercise religious authority (such as indigenous priests) were to be avoided.[54] The form of the play, however, must have rested solidly upon indigenous theatrical practice utilizing, as it did, scenic display, pantomime, song, and dance.

Another play from this period, and an especially interesting one in light of the Aztec ritual of human sacrifice, is *El sacrificio de Isaac* (The sacrifice of Isaac; *c*. 1536–1539).[55] This short *auto* includes a devil's attempt to get Hagar and her son Ishmael to corrupt Isaac by tempting him to disobey his parents, and Abraham's willingness to sacrifice his beloved son. Both actions are frustrated, the first by Isaac's innate goodness, the second by an Angel who appears and stays Abraham's hand.

The play urges complete obedience to authority whether it be God, one's elders, or (presumably) others in positions of authority such as the friars themselves. In this way an important aspect of indigenous education, subservience to authority and a recognition of one's own social status and place, was utilized in the service of Christianization. The play also emphasizes that the Christian God is a God of grace not of sacrifice, who rejects the human sacrifice offered by Abraham, and the play leaves out the substitution of a lamb for Isaac in order to avoid giving the Aztecs any heretical ideas.[56]

La adoración de los Reyes (The adoration of the Magi; *c*. 1540–1550) is a play with a marked resemblance to the medieval *The Service for Representing Herod* in the Fleury Manuscript. It is basically the biblical story of the Magi's arrival, Herod's rage upon consulting his priests, his attempt to deceive the Magi, their visit to the manger, and their subsequent escape. The play contains Nahuatlisms in both the language employed and in the means of production. The parallels between this story and that of the actual events of the Conquest when Moctezoma II was terrified by a comet and other omens prior to the Spaniard's arrival, could well have influenced (at least subconsciously) the Indian audience, making them more susceptible to the Christian message inherent in the play.[57]

Invención de la Santa Cruz por Santa Elena (How St. Helen found the

Holy Cross; 1714) is the Spanish title of a copy of a lost Nahuatl manuscript. The play's ostensible focus is the conversion of the Emperor Constantine but it again offers a marvelous opportunity for spectacle in its depiction of wars, St. Helen's sea voyage, the digging up of the crosses, and numerous other incidents. The emphasis seems to be upon the power of sacred relics themselves, an odd thing for the mendicants, who were still trying to extirpate idol worship, to focus upon. A possible explanation is provided by Horcasitas, who accepts the copied manuscript's date of 1714 as closer to the date of the original, and suggests that certain elements of the play, the *graciosos*, the mention of the god of Hell (Mictlantecuhtli), sacrifice by flaying (Tlacaxipehualiztli), and necromancers, could be an incipient nationalism of the kind which appears in certain religious paintings of the same period from New Spain where the Holy Family eats in a Mexican peasant tavern.[58]

Souls and Testamentary Executors is the title of an English translation by Byron McAfee of a Nahuatl manuscript called *In Animastin Ihuan Alvaceasme*. The play seems to come from the mid-sixteenth century and is clearly a didactic drama designed to stress the importance of saying Mass for the dead in Purgatory, the importance of the ten commandments and of the five sacraments. A widow and the executors of her dead husband's estate squander the money he left to the Church to see him through Purgatory. Along the way they break every commandment and flagrantly violate the sacraments, but in the end they are justly punished. The action of the play provides a great deal of opportunity for spectacle (not the least of which is a fireworks display), dance, and music.

LA CONQUISTA DE RODAS AND *LA CONQUISTA DE JERUSALÉN*

We have seen how both the indigenous ritual spectacle and the evangelical theatre that was built upon its foundations sought to eliminate the line dividing actor from spectator in order to achieve certain religious and political ends. But there was another aspect to theatrical representation, its magical possibilities, its ability to entrance and appeal in a way that dry dogma could not, that attracted the friars to theatrical forms. Durán tells us that a type of theatre was used for specifically magical purposes by Moctezoma II. He describes how, when Moctezoma wished to have a huge piece of rock dislodged in order to send it to his workshops, he called for what seem to have been actors (*representantes*) to use their words to break the stone into pieces and assure success: "[He ordered] comics and actors to come and perform interludes, ribaldry, and buffoonery before the rock... the singers began to sing pleasing and joyful songs, and the clowns and actors performed their interludes and farces with much clowning which moved everyone to laughter and happiness."[59] This conception of theatre as a magical medium, one with the ability to transform objects in an almost alchemical manner, seems to have been on the minds of the Franciscans who wrote and directed two of the most spectacular pieces of evangelical theatre we possess: *La conquista de Rodas* (The conquest of Rhodes; 1543) and *La conquista de Jerusalén* (The conquest of Jerusalem; 1543). The alchemical transformation they were after, through the medium of theatrical representation, was the transformation of a multitude of Indian souls into Christian ones.

The story of these two performances returns us once again to events of the Conquest, for *La conquista de Rodas* was performed in Mexico City, Moctezoma II's Aztec seat, and *La conquista de Jerusalén* in Tlaxcala, the land of the Aztecs' traditional enemies, the people they had opposed in the Flowery Wars, and who had been Cortés' allies during the war with the Aztecs. This old rivalry was present in the conception and production of *La conquista de Jerusalén* in response to that of *La conquista de Rodas*. Fray Antonio de Ciudad Rodrigo tells us that: "The Tlaxcalans wanted first to see what the Spaniards and the Mexicans were doing, and having seen how they performed *La conquista de Rodas*, the Tlaxcalans determined to perform *La conquista de Jerusalén*... and in order to make it a more solemn occasion they agreed to leave the performance until Corpus Christi."[60] *La conquista de Rodas* was performed in 1543 in celebration of the peace treaty achieved between Charles V and Francis I the previous year. Las Casas describes it as follows:

In the Plaza de México there were large buildings like artificial theatres, tall as towers, with many elegantly appointed mansions, one over the other. Each one had its performance and function with singers and minstrels bulging with shawms, sackbuts, flageolets, trumpets, timbrels, and other musical instruments, so that I believe they gathered together from throughout the province more than a thousand musicians and singers of measured music for that day alone. There were castles and a wooden city fought over by Indians who attacked from without and who defended from within, there were large vessels with sails that navigated across the plaza as if they were upon water, although they were going across the ground. When they built the city and the aforementioned buildings, somewhere around fifty thousand men officially worked on them, and it was a wondrous thing to see the silence with which they worked, resembling nothing so much as a monastery of friars at choir or chapter, which was how those of us who, from time to time, went out to see how they were doing described them. The buildings, mountains, crags, fields or meadows, and forests they made, and the live animals they placed in them in the royal houses where the Viceroys and the royal Audiencia usually lived; all on top of the corridors, dining rooms and false gates constructed for only that day, and the decorations and escutcheons of flowers, those and a thousand other delightful things they made were such that nobody could elucidate and much less praise them too highly.[61]

The sumptuousness of the scenographic display, in which actors moved from one *apartamiento* or a type of medieval mansion stage to another, seems to have been the most impressive thing about the performance, although the sight of so many Indians engaged in a gigantic pantomime clearly made its mark on Las Casas. Even taking into account Las Casas' tendency towards exaggeration, the final performance must have been quite a sight indeed.

The Tlaxcaltecas rushed home and began work in an attempt to surpass their rivals in Tenochtitlán. They were momentarily stopped by the fact that the center of the city was at the time under construction, but they quickly improvised: "they leveled everything off and stuffed it with earth, and built five towers: the principal one in the middle, larger than the others, and four others in the four corners."[62] This stage seems to have been meant to convey the impression of a small castle, for the five towers "were surrounded by a wall with many battlements, many windows and elegant arches, all full of roses and flowers."[63] Across the plaza from these towers of Jerusalem was the Emperor's lodging, to the right of Jerusalem were the quarters of the Spanish army; and facing that, the area representing the provinces of New Spain. The center of this immense stage was Santa Fe, "where the Emperor and his army had to be lodged; all these places were enclosed and painted on the outside to simulate brick walls, with their front walls, embrasures, and battlements represented naturally."[64]

The ostensible content of the play is the 1099 Conquest of Jerusalem by Godfried, but it seems from Fray Antonio de Cuidad Rodrigo's description that the work's author was up to something considerably more complicated: a correspondence between the Ottomans and Crusaders of the Middle Ages and the opposing forces in the Conquest of the New World. Following this principle, all of the actors were Indians but the Turkish Sultan and his aide-de-camp were costumed as no less than Cortés and his aide Pedro de Alvarado. The leader of the Spanish troops in charge of the siege of Jerusalem was portrayed as Antonio Pimental, Conde de Benavente, and the leader of the fictitious Indian troops (inserted into history by the friars) who would have helped conquer Jerusalem, was none other than Antonio de Mendoza, the current viceroy. The Turkish troops were played by Indians prepared for baptism and, after they were defeated, they were actually baptized onstage in the same way as the child was baptized at the end of *La natividad de San Juan Bautista*.

We have, then, in this magical/theatrical work that sought to transform (convert) alchemically the indigenous population through the medium of performance, Indians portraying, with all the fervor they can muster, the Crusaders; and an Indian army inserted into history in order to transform them magically into complicit forces in the Conquest of Jerusalem. These two armies are opposed by another Indian army portraying the Turkish forces whose participants, when defeated, are baptized *en masse* in both their roles as Turks and, in actuality, their true roles as Indians. At the same time we have an Indian army defeating an army led by Cortés and Pedro de Alvarado, thus reversing the history of the Conquest. This same army that defeats Cortés, however, is led by the Viceroy Antonio de Mendoza reaffirming the contemporary authority of the Spaniards.

What can have been the Franciscan motive for presenting the seemingly insulting image of Cortés as an infidel? On the one hand, there is the conjecture made above that it may have raised the motivation and fervor of the Indians playing the Crusaders to think that they were (at least theatrically, although we have already seen how blurred the line between theatre and reality was for the indigenous population) conquering their conqueror. On the other is the Franciscan political position at the time of this performance. Cortés, their protector and advocate, was no longer governor nor captain general. Burdened by many problems of his own, he was in the midst of preparing to return to Spain. Although it was a risky proposition, the Franciscans probably believed that they could afford to treat Cortés in such a manner, especially since the current viceroy was presented as leading the conquering troops. Their political survival demanded that they disassociate themselves from Cortés and find a means of coexistence with the current secular authority.

The Franciscans had only recently won a critical battle on another front, the internal politics of the Church. Fiercely attacked by the Dominicans and others in 1539 for their practice of mass baptism by aspersion the Franciscans had only won confirmation of their methods by the Ecclesiastical Junta two months before. *La conquista de Jerusalén* is, in the end, a gigantic demonstration of Franciscan baptismal methods, a demonstration that took place, moreover, on Corpus Christi, a day of immense sacramental importance for the Christian Church.

La conquista de Jerusalén is, in effect, a rather complex *auto sacramental* years before the master of the form, Calderón de la Barca, was to write his first. In its spiraling utilization of the theatrical, the play is on the level of sophistication of the most intricate of works of the Spanish baroque. In the plays of Lope, Calderón, and Tirso there is an emphasis upon the duality present in confused identity. Typical of such plays is Calderón's *El médico de su honra* (The surgeon of his honor) in which a prince, feeling himself to have been wronged, enters a lady's garden at night and engages in conversation with her. She has taken him for her husband in the dark and all three of them are compromised when the husband unexpectedly returns. The husband later enters his wife's chamber at night and is taken for the prince. In both cases she responds to the wrong man, leaving herself dangerously vulnerable. The Franciscan's treatment of Cortés in *La conquista de Jerusalén* is akin to the lady's position in the scenario just described. For as José Antonio Maravall has convincingly shown, the seventeenth-century Spanish baroque theatre had a very explicit political and religious end: the maintenance of the status quo through the reaffirmation of hierarchical authority. The only possible way for the mendicants to use their long association with Cortés to their advantage was both to recognize his transgressions (present him as an infidel) and to convert the transgressors, thereby demonstrating their fealty to the restored secular authority.

What was achieved in performance of *La conquista de Jerusalén*, then, was a convergence of Spanish and Indian attitudes towards maintenance of hierarchical authority. The content of these evangelical plays was definitely Christian but their form was largely dictated by previous indigenous practice. Who converted whom? The Indians may have become good Christians but the Spaniards became, at their theatrical roots, good Aztecs. When the Franciscans adopted Nahuatl as the idiom of the Church in the New World it seems they did more than use a new language. In a manner not unlike that of the Indians who donned the flayed hides of their sacrificial victims, the mendicants got into the skins of the indigenous culture – perhaps more profoundly than even they themselves realized.[65]

CHAPTER 2

Church, colonialism, and theatre in Latin America

By the second half of the sixteenth century the type of Indohispanic theatrical display described in the previous chapter was practically extinct. The mendicant orders, propelled by the certainty of imminent Apocalypse, had carried out their evangelical mission. Their work was stopped in an almost apocalyptic manner, not by some spiritual destruction of the world, but by a convergence of secular forces. Many of the problems the mendicants faced by the middle of the sixteenth century were the direct result of their religious and political success in Latin America. As has been seen, the institution of *patronata real* by the Papacy in 1508 gave broad powers to the Spanish Crown, including the collection of tithes and the right to appoint candidates for all benefices in the American colonies. Due to Cortés' influence, the mendicants were chosen to fulfill such a role. Backed by the Papacy, the Crown, and Cortés, the mendicants' position was one of immense power.

The secular clergy and the laity soon began to arrive in ever increasing numbers, and they resented the mendicants' stranglehold on financial, territorial, and spiritual matters. As early as 1535, Mexico City's municipal council complained to the king that the mendicants were interfering with civil authority by holding prisoners and dispensing justice on their own initiative. Although the secular clergy in the colonies were few prior to 1550, by 1557 their numbers had increased to the point where they were able successfully to petition the Crown to make the construction of any new religious establishments subject to the bishops. The bishops attempted to place secular clerics in mendicant domains and the Crown was forced to restrain them in turn.

By the 1560s, however, so many new priests had immigrated, and so many Creole priests had come through the ecclesiastical universities, that the mendicant orders no longer had a numerical edge within the Church itself.[1] This, coupled with the fact that the European presence in America brought with it a wave of epidemics that drastically reduced the Indian population, destroyed the mendicants' power base. By the end of the sixteenth century the Indian population was 90 percent smaller than it had been at the time of the Conquest.[2] Those Indians who survived no longer remembered the strict prehispanic discipline that had been so advantageous to the mendicants and were, in turn, less likely docilely to accept mendicant authority. With the decimation of the Indian population the friars also lost a powerful weapon they had attained through much labor, the use of Nahuatl. The mendicant-trained artists, composers, actors, and writers who were once turned out by the hundreds from the friars' schools no longer existed.

The mendicants were also attacked by the laity on the grounds that their activities defrauded the Crown of valuable Indian labor. A performance such as *La conquista de Jerusalén* involved many hours of preparation, construction, rehearsal, memorization, and attendance at Mass. As Horcasitas has pointed out, if we accept Las Casas' figure of 80,000 participants, each of whom devoted approximately ten hours of time to the event, the King lost around 800,000 hours of work upon a single occasion.[3] While this was certainly not the principal objection to the mendicant presence, when combined with the more serious political and ecclesiastical objections, the factors were overwhelmingly against the friars. By the end of the sixteenth century the Indohispanic Christian society that had spawned a great variety of enormous theatrical spectacles had died.

THEATRE WITHOUT THE MENDICANTS: ESPINOSO MEDRANO, *EL GÜEGÜENSE*, SOR JUANA DE LA CRUZ

What did the mendicants' decline augur for the seventeenth and eighteenth-century Latin American theatre? To answer this question one must look at the changed composition in the Spanish presence throughout the region. Having broken the mendicants' grip, the secular Church, the Crown, and the laity all strove to enhance their respective positions. The result was a complex administrative system of *virreinatos* (viceroyships) which were, in effect, jointly administered by the royally appointed viceroy and the local representative of ecclesiastical authority. This system was at first only composed of the virreinato of New Spain, founded in 1535, which contained all the territory north of the Panamanian Isthmus, including the Antilles, and the virreinato of Peru, established in 1543, under which rubric fell all the territories conquered as of that date in South America. As time went on the virreinato of Nueva Granada was founded in 1739, which had jurisdiction over the regions corresponding to the present countries of Colombia, Venezuela, Trinidad, Ecuador and Panama. In 1776 the virreinato of Río de la Plata, composed of what are now Peru, Chile, Bolivia, Argentina, and Uruguay, was established.

The theatrical activity throughout these regions was composed, by and large, of ceremonial festivities to mark the arrival or departure of a colonial or ecclesiastical authority, or the death or ascension of a monarch. The plays performed (of both the secular and religious variety) were those of the great Spanish baroque dramatists Ruiz de Alarcón, Lope de Vega, Calderón de la Barca, Tirso de Molina, and their colonial and Iberian imitators. Amidst this imported drama there were instances of indigenous theatrical activity. One such instance was a *Loa* written by Antonio Fuentes del Arco (?–1733) that was performed in 1717 in Santa Fe to celebrate the suppression of a tax on the herb *mate* as it flowed from Paraguay to Buenos Aires. Possibly the only play ever to be inspired by a purely economic event, it was performed during festivities to honor the city's patron saint.[4]

Another is *El hijo pródigo* (The prodigal son), by Juan Espinoso Medrano (1632–1688), also known as El Lunarejo, an Indian raised by a Spanish priest. This is a didactic *auto sacramental* on the theme of the prodigal son. The son (Cristiano) leaves his father's house and enters the world accompanied by *Uku* (The Body) and *Huaina 'Kari* (Youth). Followed throughout by *Diopsa Simin* (God's Word), who continually exhorts him to return to the fold, Cristiano engages in gluttony, debauchery, and lust until Youth abandons him and, destitute, he becomes a pig herder for *Nina Quiru* (The Devil). Miserable, he sees the error of his ways, repents, and God's Word escorts him back to heaven.

Thematically, the play's message is direct and reinforced by the little homilies God's Word directs to the audience after each failure to convince Cristiano to accompany him. Each homily warns the audience that a similar fate awaits them if they stray from the true path. Dramatically Cristiano's servant Uku is a pure *gracioso* of the type found throughout the Spanish baroque. Theatrically, the piece is liberally sprinkled with musical and dance sequences quite similar to what we know of pre-Columbian spectacle. Originally written in Quechua, the play's language is both popular and poetic. As Arrom has observed:

In the work of Espinosa Medrano, then, we are given all the sumptuous twisting of the baroque and the vigorous simplicity of folklore. It's as if the *mestizo* aesthetic has been broken apart to give to each his own: to the Spaniard and the Creole a piece reminiscent of the lavish ornamentation of the altars and pulpit in Cuzco Cathedral, to his indigenous compatriots, an *auto* which would make them think of the painting of the Virgin Mary hanging in that same Cathedral, depicting her as an innocent indigenous maid, her innocent locks tucked beneath a straw hat, carrying in her dark arms a meek little llama.[5]

What Medrano gives us, then, is a play that combines the elements of Spanish presence, religious teaching, and indigenous performance practices seen in the mendicant evangelical theatre, but in eighteenth-century terms. The emphasis now appears to be not upon the act of conversion itself, but upon the use of the theatre to reinforce the primacy of God's word for the Spaniard and the Creole – those who already believe – and link the indigenous spectators to the religious content through association. If the indigenous maid is the Virgin Mary, then the indigenous population is already included as a part of the miracles performed by the Church, and the favored position of the Church is made plain by the rich surroundings in which the picture of the indigenous maid-as-the-Virgin Mary would be hung.

While such a theatrical transaction follows a format akin to that of the actor-as-Quetzalcoátl seen in indigenous performance, the ritual transformation is no longer necessary. Espinosa Medrano is an Indian, a member of the indigenous culture spoken to, but having been raised by a Spanish priest, speaks as a member of the dominant culture. There is already a certain amount of distance between the author and his audience. Since the association between the indigenous maid and the Virgin Mary is being made by means of a performance, there is also a certain amount of distance between the performer representing the role and the indigenous spectator perceiving it. Performer and spectator are no longer one as in the Aztec ritual and there are now other players, the Spaniard and the Creole, whose presence must be taken into account. There is a disjunction in the work of Espinosa Medrano between what the Church wants to achieve and the audience it needs to reach in order to accomplish its mission. As we have seen before, the indigenous population's own mentality and understanding of performance is being used to manipulate that population. It is only with the appearance of liberation theology and liberation theatre in the twentieth century that both the exercise of religion and the practice of performance are returned to the people themselves, thereby creating an entirely new and particularly dynamic political force. One that will use the Church and the theatre for self-generated, not externally imposed, ends.

A more direct connection to indigenous concerns than that depicted by Espinosa Medrano can be seen in the anonymous piece *El güegüense*, a seminal work in Nicaragua that was repeatedly performed from the sixteenth to the nineteenth centuries. The play was written in a mixture of Nahuatl, Mangue, and Spanish, and incorporates a great deal of comic wordplay and dance as the Governor Tastuanes attempts, and finally succeeds, to bring a notorious trickster, *El güegüense*, to heel. The numerous dances interspersed throughout, the repetition of phrases in a formal manner akin to the *Rabinal Achí*, and the continuous action, all point to strong indigenous influence. *El güegüense* himself is a marvelously vital character who uses satire and burlesque to make fun of civil authority.

As with Fuentes del Arco's play, there are also Spanish characteristics such as the names of the characters: *güegüense* is a Nahuatl word – *huehuentze* – hispanicized, which means a venerable old man, and *Tastuanes* is a pejorative term that makes fun of the governor's rank. In addition, there is the presence of numerous archaic Spanish words, references to Spanish customs, money, products, cultural habits, and, of course, the political institutions satirized.[6]

That satire, in fact, is a precursor to the tremendous social, political, and theatrical upheaval that will characterize the late eighteenth and early nineteenth centuries as Latin America begins to assert its independence from Spanish colonial rule. Such a desire for independence first finds its expression in the Mexican insurrections of 1692, the Cuban tobacco planters' rebellions in 1717, and those of the Paraguayan village communities from 1717 to 1735. Added to these rumblings towards the end of the eighteenth century were the new liberal ideas beginning to filter through to the colonies. As we shall see, the nineteenth century brought about distinct changes in Latin America's relationship to the Spanish empire. Where both the *conquistadores* and the Church perceived Latin America as an area to be exploited for either material or spiritual gain, nearly two hundred years of Spanish presence in Latin America was to create a significantly changed landscape. Madrid was far away and successive generations of Creole descendents of the original Spanish colonizers came to see themselves as Latin Americans. Rape of, and inter-marriage with, the indigenous population also created a large *mestizo*, or mixed-race, population that maintained a connection to its Indian roots. What this meant was that the nineteenth-century wars of independence were motivated by a strong feeling of Latin American and indigenous sensibility. Such a historical progression is in marked contrast to the history of colonization and wars of independence in North America where the indigenous population was virtually exterminated and there was relatively little inter-marriage between European settlers and the indigenous population.[7] Where the revolutionary war against Britain in 1776 was largely an economic rebellion by one faction of Europeans against another, the Latin American independence movements that began in the late eighteenth century were the products of disagreements about economic autonomy, but also between inhabitants of what were quickly becoming two distinct cultures.

While not the first theatrical indication of this upheaval, the work of one of Latin America's greatest writers and first female playwright, Sor Juana de la Cruz (1648?–1695?), is of great importance for the way in which it demonstrates the beginnings of this change in colonial sensibilities in the seventeenth- and eighteenth-century Latin American drama and theatre.[8] Over the course of her life Sor Juana accomplished a prodigious amount. As an educated, articulate, independent female within the highly conservative, masculine environment of the Church, Sor Juana's very existence made a forceful political/religious statement by placing in question the infallibility of the patriarchal institution. What is germane here, however, is her work for the stage. For an American of the time her dramatic output is rather impressive. She wrote eight *loas*, three *autos*, two *comedias*, two *sainetes*, and a soirée piece.[9] Probably her best-known *auto* is *El divino Narciso*. *Loas* were short dramatic prologues, frequently panegyrics to the playwright or production's sponsor, which preceded the *auto*. Their purpose was not only laudatory but also to predispose the audience towards a favorable reception of the longer piece. The *Loa* to *El divino Narciso* not only incorporates all the themes discussed so far, it also makes its own distinct contribution to the development of the Latin American theatre.

First published in 1690, the *Loa al Divino Narciso* begins with a *tocotin*, or indigenous dance, and is interspersed with music and dance throughout. Its opening consists of a ceremonial paean to *El Dios de las Semillas* (The god of seed), a thinly veiled Huitzilopochtli who *Occidente* (the West) and América worship. They are joined by Religión and *Celo* (Zeal) who, horrified at the Devil's work they see before them, insist that the Indians worship the one true God. The Indians refuse and war breaks out. Just as Celo is about to kill América, Religión intervenes, saying she wants him alive in order to convert him. This she proposed to do by means of the performance of the *Auto del Divino Narciso*.

It is at this point that the dialog takes on a character not found in the earlier Franciscan drama. There follows a discussion between Celo and Religión concerning the propriety of performing before the Court in Madrid, the rude, rustic drama that anything written in America must be. Religión answers that her *Auto* is the product of faith and, therefore, dignified enough to be shown before the king and queen. It is, in addition, a presentation of an abstract and thematic nature and can, therefore, travel.

What we have here, then, is both territorial and spiritual conquest being effected by means of a theatrical performance that, on the one hand, incorporates indigenous techniques of dance and music like the friars did, while it, on the other hand, seeks to be incorporated into the mainstream of Iberian discourse. There seems to be a strong case being made here (albeit by an acculturated Mexican) for the intrinsic worth of Mexican arts and letters in the larger world, or, put another way, an incipient nationalism. In a certain limited sense a case could be made for Sor Juana's work here as a precursor of contemporary liberation theology. Where the "preferential option for the poor" places the Church firmly on the side of the downtrodden masses, Sor Juana is speaking for the underclass of her time, the Mexicans, insisting that the Church act upon their behalf. This is further emphasized by the reasoning that the *Auto* presents abstractions. Such reasoning is an abstraction in itself, and to the contemporary European, a highly evolved system of thought. If the Mexicans can utilize it, they must be worthwhile. It is also, simultaneously, an explicit understanding of the nature of theatrical representation. The characters in the *Auto* are not themselves, but abstractions of ideas which illustrate a theological or moral point and are thus useful in the process of converting both the Indians and other viewers alike. Sor Juana utilized her religious vocation, and the privileges that it guaranteed her with the government, to reach a level of educational sophistication virtually unheard of for a woman of her times. She also used her position as a platform for asserting the beginnings of Mexican nationalism.

By skillfully manipulating the privileges afforded by her position within the religious hierarchy, Sor Juana was able to write a *Loa* which, by introducing openly subversive ideas, challenged the Spanish conception of the Mexicans. The Spaniards' success in cementing their control over the mass indigenous population after the Conquest can be attributed, in large part, to the way in which the mendicant orders successfully subverted Aztec authority through the use of evangelical theatre. The wars of independence that succeeded in overthrowing Spanish colonial authority also, as we shall see, made excellent use of the theatre to reach their goals. Such aims owed their focus, in large measure, to the work of another religious order, the Jesuits, towards the end of the eighteenth century.

THE JESUITS AND LATIN AMERICAN NATIONALISM

From the very beginning of its presence in Latin America the Jesuit order focused primarily upon scholastic education. It founded a network of schools and universities whose graduates increasingly assumed their roles in local government, the judiciary, and the Church. By the eighteenth century Jesuit influence over intellectual and cultural discourse was extraordinary and that influence, especially in Mexico, began to take on a particular emphasis: pride in Latin America of and for itself. The educational innovations introduced by the order were profound. They began to give great weight to the study of Greco-Latin cultures and languages, to champion the value of indigenous Latin American culture, gradually to relax the strict adherence to scholasticism, to teach that the king's authority was not divinely rendered but the result of the will of the people, and actively to cultivate a sense of nationalism. Gabriel Méndez Plancarte has stated in the introduction to his *Humanistas del siglo XVIII* that

their attitude towards the colonial regime is, naturally, one of distance and, one could almost say, of alienation. They speak of "the Spaniards" as if they were talking about foreigners, not compatriots. However, they do not feel themselves to be Indians either, nor do they dream of an impossible return to the Aztec empire. What are they, then, and to which country do they belong? They are, and want to be, nothing more nor less than Mexicans.[10]

The Crown's reaction to such subversive teachings was quick and decisive. On June 25, 1769 Charles III ordered the expulsion of all Jesuits (the majority of whom were Creole) from his domains in New Spain. The colonial rulers used Charles' decree as the basis for declaring their absolute authority. The Viceroy Marqués de Croix issued the following declaration:

since His Majesty has decreed those disobedient or remiss in cooperating in carrying out his desire to have incurred his Royal indignation, I find myself obliged to use the utmost rigor or military force against those who, in public or in secret, exhibit such a motive in conversations, meetings, assemblies, small groups, or spoken or written discourse. Let it be known that now and in the future the subjects of the great monarch who occupies the throne of Spain were born to keep quiet and to obey, not to conjecture about or to express an opinion concerning the highest matters of state.[11]

Charles III was also responsible for a series of administrative reforms designed to strengthen industry and commerce. The number of vessels sailing between the New and Old Worlds increased enormously and with them came faster and more reliable mail service. This traffic inevitably brought with it an influx of European ideas as well as the publications of such writers as D'Alembert, Rousseau, Diderot, Montesquieu, Adam Smith, Newton, Leibniz and others. Copies and translations of these writers' works began to circulate clandestinely throughout the colonies. This ferment of economic and intellectual activity, when coupled with the Jesuit humanistic teaching, the pride in Latin American culture they fostered, and the growing resentment against the Church and colonial rule, led to a series of unsuccessful rebellions throughout the region. There were revolts in Venezuela from 1749 to 1751 against the abusive behavior of the Compañía Guipuzcoana; indigenous uprisings in 1750 in Peru; militia revolts in Catamarca and La Rioja in 1752, in Tucumán in 1754, and in Salta and Jujuy in 1767. The year 1765 brought Indian rebellions throughout the Yucatán; the Nueva Granada communities repeatedly revolted between 1779 and 1781; and the swansong of Indian uprisings, that of Túpac-Amaru, occurred between 1780 and 1781. While none of these rebellions was ultimately successful, they laid the groundwork for the wars of independence soon to come.[12]

THE COLISEUMS: THEATRE AS A POLITICAL SPACE

Increased economic activity, the wealth it generated, and the nationalistic pride it engendered, led to a period between 1752 and 1802 during which huge, lavish theatres were constructed from Mexico City to Santiago de Chile. These theatres were almost always initiated by the highest civilian authority, both as a means of demonstrating his status and to satisfy the growing demand for certain kinds of entertainment that incorporated the new forms of discourse being introduced into the region. It was here that the Latin American theatre, originally closely linked to the Church through the mendicants' evangelical work, came into increasing conflict with the current ecclesiastical hierarchy. The ecclesiastical response to this burgeoning theatrical activity became a point of contention between the Church and the civil authority. On the one hand there was Juan Palafox y Mendoza, bishop of Puebla, who saw the theatre in the following way:

Tertullian himself refers to two notable cases that occurred during his times when two Christians entered the theatre. While they were there the Devil entered one of their bodies, and that individual left the theatre possessed. Exorcizing himself later in Church, he asked the common enemy how he had dared to enter the body of a Christian, and the Devil responded: "Constanter et justissime quidem feci, in me lam inveni" (Since I found it in my jurisdiction, it was my right to do so.) As if to say, once you enter my theatre you become my subject, because I am in command there and everything within it is my property.[13]

On the other hand, Viceroy Vértiz justified his approval of a theatre in the following terms:

I have also allowed, after several consultations, the performance in public theatre at the annual rent of two thousand pesos to benefit the foundlings. But I have also attentively ensured that whatever defects that could corrupt the youth or create a public scandal were cleansed ... the theatre, so refined, is not only judged by many politicians to be one of the best schools for behavior, language, and general urbanity, but it is also needed in a city such as this lacking in other forms of public entertainment.[14]

The theatre's proper place in the teaching of moral propriety was what was at issue between the ecclesiastic and secular authorities. As the late eighteenth and early nineteenth centuries continued, the theatre increasingly became the preferred arena for political discourse. This was true both for those yearning for independence from strict obedience to what they now perceived as a foreign power, and for those who strove to maintain, or impose, their authority throughout the colonies.

Towards the end of the eighteenth century the political and military governor of Montevideo, Antonio Olaguer y Feliú, in an attempt to offset by means of harmless diversion what he perceived as the potentially negative effect of the new ideas being introduced into the region, ordered the construction of a theatre. Due to a shortage of funds, as well as the umbrage taken by the City Council who had not been consulted regarding his decision, the project languished until Olaguer y Feliú's successor, Manuel Cipriano Melo y Menses, arrived. Melo borrowed 4,000 pesos from the funds earmarked by the Infantry Regiment, guaranteeing them by mortgaging several pieces of his own property. By this means, the Casa de Comedias opened in 1793. Its first performers were a troupe imported from Buenos Aires who presented a repertoire of Spanish plays.[15] From its inception both the governor and the *cabildo* or city council tried to control the theatre and the political space it represented. At first the governor refused to allow the council admittance to performances. When they finally did gain entrance, the governor insisted that each actor bow to him upon entering. The outraged council, demanding equal respect, took their case to the *audiencia* in Buenos Aires, which ruled in the governor's favor. Undaunted, one councilman traveled to Spain and persuaded the *Consejo Supremo* to declare that the governor's jurisdiction over the theatre was null and void since it belonged to the people and their elected representatives.[16]

The concept of theatre presenting a space for the realization of political ends was evident elsewhere as well. Although the struggle for independence from Spanish rule of Chile was initiated in 1810, independence was not achieved until 1818, when José de San Martín dealt a decisive blow to the Spanish army at the battle of Maipú. While Spanish authority was broken between 1810 and 1813, the Spaniards returned to power from 1814 to 1817. During this period the governor, Marcó del Ponto, drafted soldiers to perform in the new theatre he ordered built as a means of extirpating through theatrical diversion the Chilean yearning for independence. The material Marcó del Ponto had presented in his theatre was a Spanish repertoire of *sainetes* and Golden Age *comedias* by dramatists such as Agustín Moreto. His attempts to quell the independent spirit were unsuccessful, and Chile's first president, Bernardo O'Higgins, filled the ranks of the nation's first theatre company with Spanish prisoners of war. One of these, a Colonel de la Torre, was a theatre fanatic and enthusiastically instructed the other prisoners in the fine points of acting.[17]

This military expertise upon the boards seems to have continued into the mid-nineteenth century, when a group of William Walker's soldiers witnessed the demise of their North American filibusterer leader, who had proclaimed himself president of Nicaragua, reintroduced slavery, and attempted to conquer all of Central America. Vanquished, they found themselves released and penniless. By performing songs, dances, and dramatic sketches, they managed to raise enough money to buy themselves passage back to California in 1857.[18] From the performances of *El güegüense* to the Sandinistas' use of street theatre during the 1979 revolution, and the work of Nicaraguan popular theatre groups today, whose performances have led to the removal of a number of corrupt or inefficient government officials, the dividing line between Nicaraguan theatre and politics has constantly been blurred.

Another instance of theatre linked to political ambition, this time in Cuba, was the Gran Teatro Tacón, built at the beginning of the nineteenth century by the governor whose name it bears. Desiring to build the most impressive theatre in Latin America, Tacón levied a seventeen peso tax on every slave imported into Cuba. The money collected, according to contemporary records with their marked tendency to overstate the theater's grandeur, not only enabled him to construct a theatre containing 4,000 seats and 150 boxes, but left him sufficient funds to build the first railroad across the island and erect drinking fountains throughout the capital.[19] The introduction of African slaves into Cuba would affect not only the physical design of Teatro Tacón, but the theatrical content of subsequent performance as well. From the depiction of African tribal rituals and dances to the *sainete* character of the "negrito," the black presence in Cuba was to have a profound effect on Cuban dramaturgy.

Other areas of Central America, so much a part of the military and political "theatre of operations" in the 1970s and 1980s, were no strangers to theatre of a political hue in the early 1800s either. In 1814 independence-minded citizens in El Salvador elected a majority of municipal officials, but the captain general of Guatemala (under whose jurisdiction El Salvador fell at the time) threw out the results and appointed a mayor, providing him with a corps of helpful volunteers. The angry citizens determined to capture the mayor and install their own representatives. To provide a cover for this "palace coup" they announced that a performance of a Spanish play entitled *Más vale tarde que nunca* (Better late than never) would be performed in the mayor's house during the New Year's celebration. The plan was for a number of soldiers and citizens, disguised as actors, to seize the mayor during the performance. One of the conspirators, however, confessed his role to his priest, who informed the captain general. The captain general schemed to allow the play to proceed, seize the conspirators in the act, and execute them immediately; but his plans also became known and the play was canceled. The captain general, wishing to assert his control, only increased the number of those who opposed him by coercing the population into attending a performance of the proposed play the following week. Spanish control was ended without bloodshed in 1822.[20]

The Church was hardly immune from this type of theatrical–political involvement, as one final instance from Venezuela shows. From 1835 to 1855 an amateur acting troupe in Zulia used the proceeds from its performances for restoration of the Church of San Juan de Dios. After the work had been completed a new priest was appointed to lead the parish. When he learned the source of the funds for the restoration he proceeded to demolish all of the recently completed portions of the Church. The mendicants' work in New Spain, which had substantially increased the folds of the faithful through theatrical activity, had been thoroughly forgotten.

The interaction, if not outright tension, between the theatre and political and religious authorities discussed so far was the direct result of the confluence of intellectual and economic forces that characterized nineteenth-century Latin America and laid the groundwork for activity of a rebellious nature. The primary standard-bearers of such rebellion were the neoclassically oriented, journalistically formed, and politically astute Creole playwrights who saw the theatre as a potentially powerful weapon in their push for Latin American independence. While, as has been mentioned, these writers were familiar with European ideas, it is important to recognize that those ideas were, more often than not, adapted to serve the Latin Americans' own needs. Their most pressing need was for independence, and the European whose ideas best served that desire was Rousseau.

ROUSSEAU, NEOCLASSICISM, AND LATIN AMERICAN INDEPENDENCE

Rousseau's ideas were disseminated in Spain and the New World as early as the 1750s by means of both French and Spanish editions of a Jesuit periodical called the *Journal de Trévoux*.[21] In 1762 José Clavijo y Fajardo (later the protagonist of Goethe's *Calvijo*) published his *El pensador* in Spain. In it Clavijo adopts numerous of Rousseau's contentions in both the *Social Contract* and *Emile*, idealizing the American Indian and proclaiming the superiority of the tribal over the European society. *El pensador* was extremely popular in both Spain and Spanish America, where it spawned many imitators. The Inquisition banned Rousseau's works throughout the Spanish-speaking world in 1764 but it was already too late. Although many of the Church's most eloquent ecclesiastics turned their wrath upon the Genevan, his ideas were too entrenched, and the Inquisition's powers already so weakened, for their oratory to have much effect. The first Spanish work to advocate openly Rousseau's theories was a novel by the Jesuit Pedro Montegón entitled *Eusebio*. Eusebio is an orphaned Spanish boy of noble birth who is shipwrecked off the Maryland coast at the age of six and rescued by a Quaker family. Clearly modeled after the *Emile*, Montegón's work carries little weight as a novel but it is highly important as an educational treatise and was widely read throughout the Spanish-speaking world.[22]

This journalistic and literary dissemination of Rousseau's ideas greatly contributed to the rebellious ardor of the Latin Americans. Traces of his influence can be seen as early as 1781 in Chile, when two Frenchmen, Vergue and Gramuset, and a rich Chilean descendant of Spanish nobility, José Antonio Rojas, were arrested on charges of conspiracy against the colonial authorities. The evidence introduced against them included a constitution largely based on Rousseau.

The preamble is devoted to a general defense of a republic, while its provisions include the recognition of natural rights as a basis for laws; abolition of slavery, elimination of social distinctions; the distribution of land in equal portions; and government by a senate composed of members chosen by the citizens, among whom the Araucanians [an Indian tribe] were to be numbered. After the triumph of the projected revolution, an army was to be formed; free commerce established; and fraternity of races insisted upon. The Spanish officials were to be dismissed with courtesy, and the ports to remain open to Spanish boats. While Vergue has been credited with its authorship, the manuscript records of the case give ample proof that the author was a member of a monastic order.[23]

The Spanish edition of the *Social Contract*, published in 1799, was read throughout Spanish America, greatly contributing to Bolívar's formation of his life-long goal of Spanish American independence.

In addition to the impact Rousseau had upon the political ideas of the Creole elite, he also influenced that community's idea of the theatre through the huge popularity of his *scène lyrique*, *Pygmalion*. Even though Rousseau's work was completely prohibited in Spain, this piece, in which he sought the combination of speech, movement, and music in an attempt to achieve dramatic perfection, crossed the Pyrenees to an enthusiastic reception. Probably first performed in the French theatres established by Aranda, Charles III's prime minister, for the Court's enjoyment, *Pygmalion* also entered Spain through an Italian translation made by an exiled Spanish Jesuit, Manuel Lassala, and published in 1783. It was subsequently published in a verse version of a prose translation of the Italian text in 1788, and was the first piece of Rousseau's writings to be published openly in Spain. *Pygmalion* created a vogue for what were called *melólogos* or *unipersonales* (monologues) throughout Spain and Spanish America. While of dubious literary or theatrical quality, the *unipersonales* were of great importance for the Creole writer's conception of the theatre as a political and educational forum.

One such writer was José Joaquin Fernández Lizardi (1776–1827), who was born in Mexico City. Known by his pen name, El Pensador Mexicano (The Mexican Thinker), Fernández de Lizardi wrote two monologues: *Unipersonal del Arcabuceado* (1822) and *Unipersonal de Don Augustín de Iturbide: Emperador que fue de México* (1823). The first is the brief lament of a 21-year-old soldier as he awaits execution for murder. While Fernández de Lizardi supports capital punishment imposed as a deterrent, he makes it clear that the soldier's actions are due to the failure of the state, the Church, and society in general, which have contributed to his delinquency by failing to educate him, and providing him only with examples of hypocrisy and fanaticism.

The second monologue gives us the deposed Emperor Iturbide lamenting his demise. Fernández de Lizardi makes Iturbide into a mouthpiece for liberal ideas who (complete with footnotes provided by the playwright) attacks the Church for its cozy relationship with tyrants, and himself and his former advisors for their contemptuous and cavalier treatment of the wishes of the mass of the people. The piece ends with Iturbide's decision to become a spokesman for the wonderful seed of independence that has begun to flower in Mexico. The play is vaguely reminiscent of Seneca in tone and style, as the deposed emperor sits before a table upon which lie his mantle, crown, and scepter, expounding about the lessons his experience has taught him, but is more indebted for its structure to *Pygmalion*, even though Fernández de Lizardi discards Rousseau's attempt to achieve a harmonious whole of word, gesture, and music.

In all of his published writings, whether appearing in any of the seven newspapers he founded, his poetry, novels, or works for the theatre, Fernández de Lizardi was both a reflection of his times and a literary visionary. Jefferson R. Spell has written of him:

In Lizardi's pamphlets are found the germs of all the reforms carried out in Mexico during the past century [nineteenth], as well as indications of others carried out in the future. He advocated a republican government of popularly elected representatives by universal suffrage, including that of women; and insisted upon the most efficient form of municipal government that would keep watch over public health and protect and regulate commerce, industry and public events. In terms of religion he proposed freedom of choice, the transfer of all Church lands to the State, legislation against clerics in political jobs, and the abolition of the Inquisition, the ecclesiastical tribunals, and ecclesiastical tariffs and tithes. He attacked Papal infallibility, celibacy, perpetual vows, and childhood baptism, and proposed that all religious ceremonies be conducted in Spanish so that the masses could understand them. He insisted, above all, that the Church submit to temporal power. The social reforms he proposed were no less radical. He considered it fundamental that a republic should abolish large estates, distribute the land to the poor, and ensure decent wages for laborers...He advocated obligatory education in government schools for all, the abolition of corporal punishment, and supplying free books and clothing to those pupils in need...He asked for justice for all, both rich and poor, and proposed penal reform that would make it possible for prisoners to be educated.[24]

Another of these writers is José Maria Heredia (1803–1839), whose life and work Rine Leal has characterized as the point at which Cuba

entered the nineteenth century. Considered the first politically
engaged Cuban writer, Heredia is the precursor of Cuban romanticism and the essayist tradition that culminates with José
Marti.[25] Virtually all of his dramatic work, with the exception of
Eduardo IV (Edward IV; 1819), *El campesino espantado* (The frightened
peasant; 1820), an agreeable little *sainete* about a peasant's confusion
and ill-treatment in the big city, and *Los últimos romanos* (The last
Romans; 1829), a neoclassical drama about the fight for power after
Caesar's death with obvious parallels to contemporary Cuban
tyranny, are translations of a variety of French and Italian
playwrights primarily dealing with classical themes. It was Heredia's
clear intent to utilize these plays for political ends, namely Cuba's
freedom from colonial rule. He openly attacked the tyrannical
Fernando VII in the prologue to his translation of a French play
about the Roman Emperor Tiberius (published 1826 or 1827):

This is my first and last dedication to a monarch. I do not believe that I can
be censured for adulation since I dedicate the tragedy *Tiberio* to a king of
whom I am a sworn enemy, the Spanish tyrant. There is, in effect, no one
who deserves such an obeisance better than you since such large analogies
exist between your character and that of the monster who terrorized and
oppressed Rome. Tiberius had Germanicus killed. You wished to do the
same to your father in 1807. Tiberius maintained with insolent frankness the
despotic authority left to him by Augustus. You, perjurer and coward,
ruined the liberties of a people who pardoned you and were foolish enough
to trust in your faith. Tiberius authorized denunciations. You established
military commissions and the Inquisition. Tiberius lived in the most
scandalous debauchery. You---Tiberius spilled his enemies blood. You have
bathed in the blood of those who gave you liberty, the crown, and even your
life...Tiberius left the throne to a monster even more senseless and
barbarous than himself. In your successor the Spaniards may find another
Caligula![26]

The use of theatre for potential political benefit is stressed even
earlier in Chile when, in 1799, a Spanish merchant named José Cos
e Iriberri petitioned the Santiago city council to allow him to build
a permanent theatre in the capital. According to Durán Cerda,
"[Cos e Iriberri's petition]...abounds...in examples proving the
theatre, through its wise maxims, to be a political and moral
influence, and a molder of good taste, necessary elements for a
population beginning to structure its social life.[27] Cos e Iriberri also
delineates neoclassicism as the proper dramatic style with which to
achieve the ends he has stated:

there is no need to have recourse today to those extravagant compositions of times past (that is to say, the baroque theatre) that, since the illusion presented was not done with propriety, neither delighted the eyes, nor left the slightest wholesome impression...Nor is it necessary to have recourse to those dramas written by unrestrained talents who, not observing the unities of action, time, and place, destroy all verisimilitude, corrupt literature and foster and perpetuate bad taste; nor to those plays full of exalted love affairs in which a father's vigilance is ridiculed and scandalously fooled by a bold young man and his astute confederates.[28]

Such a view of the theatre is made even more explicit by Fray Camilo Henríquez (1769–1825), clergyman, playwright, politician, and journalist, who published an article in 1812 in which he stated:

I consider the theatre to be purely a public school, and in this sense it is irrefutable that the dramatic muse is a great political instrument...Among dramatic productions tragedy is the most proper for a free people, and the most useful in the present circumstances. Now is the time when the stage should be filled with the sublime majesty of Melpomene, breath noble sentiments, inspire hatred for tyranny, and move all towards republican dignity. When is it more courageous or more magnificent than when it is imbued with the justice of our cause and the people's most sacred rights! When more interesting than when moving us with the memory of old calamities. Ah! then our Tears won't be shed for nought, their fruit will be hatred of tyranny and execration of tyrants.[29]

Born in 1769 in Valdivia, Chile, Henríquez was sent to Lima when he was fifteen to study in a school run by the Order of San Camilo de Lelis, also known as the Order of Buena Muerte (Good Death). Under the tutelage of a number of Spanish friars cognizant of more advanced philosophical ideas than those current in Latin America at the time (Henríquez would be denounced in 1802 for reading the *Social Contract* in its original language), Henríquez became a novitiate in 1787 and entered the order in 1790.

Throughout all this work Henríquez maintained an abiding interest in the uses of the theatre. In 1817 he joined a number of other intellectuals in forming the *Sociedad del Buen Gusto de Teatro* (The Society for Good Taste in Theatre) "whose object is to promote the improvement of our theatrical exhibitions, by procuring original works, translating the best foreign ones and adapting selected old ones, in order to ensure that the theatre will be a school of manners, a vehicle of enlightenment and a political organ."[30] The Society of Good Taste in Theatre was similar in its constitution to the Academy of Good Taste founded in Spain in 1749, which melded the characteristics of the French *salons* such as the Hôtel de Rambouillet with the institution of the literary academy.[31] Where the Academy was highly aristocratic in membership, the Society was composed of the colonial elite. While the Academy was dedicated to reforming Spanish literary taste, which it considered retrograde in relation to the cultured literature of France, the Society's aims in reforming the Latin American theatre were much more expressly political. It turned to France for guidance as well, but that guidance was found in the hopes and aspirations generated by the French Revolution as they could be effected in Latin American terms, and the colonial elite believed the theatre to be the best forum for promulgating such ideals. They called for the elimination from the theatre of all plays that failed to measure up to the Society's standards, and Henríquez, who had been an unflagging opponent of censorship, suddenly subscribed to it in order to achieve the society's didactic ends.

The pervasive nature of the theatre's role as a political force can be seen by the peripatetic activities of the nineteenth-century Chilean actor, director, and playwright Luis Ambrosio Morante (1755–1837) in Uruguay and Argentina. Born in Montevideo around 1782, Morante was already organizing his own company and producing a season in Buenos Aires by 1803. He first made his mark as a playwright committed to political theatre in 1812 when his play, *El 25 de Mayo*, was performed in Buenos Aires in celebration of the Revolution's second anniversary. Unfortunately, this first piece of indigenous theatre to be performed in the independent Argentina has been irretrievably lost. In 1817, Morante's play *Cornelia Boroquia* was performed at the dedication ceremonies of the *Sociedad del Buen Gusto del Teatro*. Although now lost, it caused a furor when it was ferociously denounced by the inquisition and the press, creating a serious confrontation between the pro-Hispanic, clerical forces and the liberal, anti-Hispanic constituency.[32]

Morante continued his theatrical crusade for an independent America with his play *Túpac-Amaru* in 1821. In it Morante reworks historical accounts by Garcilaso de Vega and others about the Inca Túpac-Amaru's rebellion against the Spaniards in 1780. While some of the characters are well drawn, the play's major motive is to support South American independence movements and all else is subordinated to that end. In 1824 he once more incurred the Church's wrath when he produced a play called *El falso nuncio de Portugal*

(The false nuncio of Portugal) in a manner designed to ridicule the papal nuncio, Monseñor Muzzi, who was in Chile on a diplomatic mission from the Holy See. Morante performed the title role, imitating Muzzi right down to his missing eye. He entered the stage with a long train of clergy, dispensing benedictions to all.[33] With this play, and a piece called *El Aristodemo* (The Aristodemocrat; 1823) by Miguel Cabrera Neves that portrayed the philosopher Polignesto attacking the Pope concerning matters of religion, Morante succeeded in sharply dividing public opinion as well as greatly increasing his ticket sales. The public flocked to see Morante, arms held aloft, end the play with the words, "People of the world,/ Here you see the tyrants who oppress you,"[34] which reflected the liberal climate of the times – one in which Muzzi's diplomatic mission met with deeply seated resistance.

All of Morante's productions described, especially *Cornelia Boroquia*, *El falso nuncio de Portugal*, and *El Aristodemo*, demonstrate the way in which the theatre's view of the Church had changed radically since Cortés' arrival on American soil. Where the mendicant evangelical theatre had attempted to convert the indigenous population to Christianity through the use of performance to effect a complex integration of that population into the mysteries of the Church, Morante's performances now employ the theatre to ridicule the Church. To a large extent this reflects the different character of the Church in each instance. Franciscan millenarianism led to evangelical activity bent upon saving the indigenous Americans by incorporating them into the Kingdom of God. The Franciscan's belief in the impending apocalypse also meant that by saving the Indians an even greater state of salvific grace would redound upon the European missionaries themselves and, by extension, all of Europe. As has been seen, however, the Church's composition in Morante's day was far from the mendicant's apostolic fervor. When the secular church broke the mendicant orders' hegemony over the Americas it did so by means of a direct alliance with the Crown. That alliance brought about a distinct shift in the Church's attitude towards Spain's colonial possessions. While the mendicants definitely sought to convert the indigenous population for their own ends, religious such as Bartolomé de Las Casas also expended considerable energy in defending the Indians from abuse. The secular church demonstrated no compunction against abusing its indigenous flock, an attitude that carried over into Morante's day. Both the Crown and the Church expected the populations of their Latin American colonies to fulfill the demands of the empire with strict obedience. The Latin Americans bridled against such paternalism and Morante skillfully exploited this view of the Spaniards as colonial oppressors and the Church as their handmaiden in his performances.

Three final playwrights belonging to the politically oriented, neoclassically inspired theatre of the time deserve mention. They are the Colombians José Fernández Madrid (1788–1830) and Luis Vargas Tejada (1802–1829), and the Uruguayan Juan Francisco Martínez (dates unknown). Like Fernández de Lizardi, Heredia, Henríquez and Morante, these writers turned to indigenous subject matter. They idealized the American Indian, utilizing "civilized" noble savages to press their case for an end to colonial rule, and producing plays of a rather undramatic and didactic nature whose worth cannot be judged by their theatrical quality but, rather, by the manner in which they reflected and contributed to the contemporary social upheaval. The only example of any lasting merit is Fernandez Madrid's five-act tragedy, *Guatimoc* (*c.* 1824–1825). *Guatimoc* deals with Guatimoc's (Cuatehmoc) last days as Aztec emperor, when he hid the sacred treasure and attempted to flee Tenochtitlán in order to regroup and revenge himself upon the Spaniards. Well conceived and well executed, the play clearly seeks to inflame the patriotic fervor of its Colombian audience by depicting the Mexicans as noble souls fighting to protect their land, and the Spaniards, with the exception of Cortés, as consummate evil. Fernández Madrid's relatively sympathetic treatment of Cortés is curious here. He is given a number of soul-searching speeches in which he debates the justice of his actions towards the Aztecs. Perhaps his presence is meant to indicate that Spaniards of conscience could force the removal of colonial rule if they so desired. It may also be an implicit acknowledgment of the fact that Fernández Madrid, and the educated colonial elite of which he is a part, would not have existed but for Spanish conquest and rule.[35]

Concurrent with this type of politically oriented, neoclassically inspired theatre created by and for the educated portion of the population with liberal ideas, there was also a significant amount of theatrical activity of a more popular nature. Utilizing dance, song, and satire, it found its expression in Mexico, Cuba, Argentina, Uruguay, and, above all, Chile. Frequently at odds, if not in outright confrontation, with neoclassical theorists of the period, this more popularly oriented theatre was to help lay the foundation for the effectiveness of the more socially engaged theatre to come.

In Mexico this tendency was represented by the great popularity of the *sainete* form. Largely influenced by the plays of the Spanish playwright Ramón de la Cruz, these plays were brief satirical sketches of local customs and professions, liberally sprinkled with songs. Looked upon with great disdain by the neoclassical tragedians because of their lack of superior models for behavior, they enjoyed great popularity with the general public, which saw itself reflected in the idiom and the actions of the characters depicted. These works were often performed between the acts of a more soberly conceived piece of writing, and were often, in fact, the only reason that the public bothered to attend the stodgier neoclassical performances.[36]

In Cuba the popular tendency was the result of the mixture of vestiges of the indigenous *areito*, a semi-dramatic form employing elements of costume, dance, music, and religious and social rites, and the African cultural forms brought to the island by the imported slave population. The slaves' tribal, ritual dances, utilizing song and dance of a magico-religious character, were codified by the Spanish authorities, who only allowed them to be performed publicly on Three Kings' Day (Epiphany), January 6. Until 1884, when they were prohibited, the Cuban Epiphany celebrations were composed of a series of processions in all the population centers on the island. Slaves and freed blacks jointly celebrated their Afrocuban religions by costuming themselves as gods and goddesses and dancing and singing through the streets. The Spanish perception of this activity would give rise to the "negrito" of the later *costumbrista* theatre. Such a character was similar to those appearing in North American minstrel shows. Played by whites in blackface, the "negrito" was a means of caricaturing and ridiculing black social customs and forms of speech.[37]

This popular *costumbrista* theatre, while very different in style from the neoclassical tragedy of the period, frequently shared similar goals. Its purpose was not merely entertainment; it also sought to teach a moral and, often, political lesson that could be easily grasped by its audience. The first of these pieces to be performed in Argentina was an anonymous *sainete* entitled *El amor de la estanciera* (The rancher's daughter's love) written some time between 1780 and 1795. In it there is a dispute over whom the daughter, Chepa, should marry: a local rancher or a rich Portuguese nobleman. She is at first disposed to wed the nobleman but changes her mind when he pulls a gun on her father, who is opposed to the match. The entire family grabs farm implements and beats the Portuguese into submission. Humiliated, he is forced to cook and serve the young couple's wedding feast. The piece ends with everyone singing and dancing in celebration. With its broad characterizations, colloquial dialog, and use of local customs, the *sainete*'s obvious purpose is to celebrate Argentine country life. In the depictions of the young rancher and the Portuguese noble are found the seeds of the later *gaucho* and the Cocoliche clown of the subsequent Creole circus.[38]

The figure of the *gaucho*, in fact, becomes the symbol of Argentine and Uruguayan independence, reaching a literary apogee in the poetry of the Uruguayan Bartolomé Hidalgo. The character that gives rise to Hidalgo's refined verses, however, is the result of a combination of forces directly affecting the *gaucho* that last from the mid-seventeenth century to the mid-nineteenth century. Those forces are the *gaucho*'s response to the pressures brought to bear upon him first by the colonial authorities, then by the fight for independence and civil war, and, finally, by the institutionalized urban government that attempts to regulate his life. The image produced is of the *gaucho* as the individual and rebel *par excellence*. He is characterized by a fiercely rural lifestyle, the picturesque nature of his speech, and larger-than-life personal exploits. Whether battling the colonial authorities, the local caudillos, or the ranching oligarchy, the *gaucho* continually demands justice against the arbitrary exercise of power, and acts in proud, insolent silence.[39] The *gaucho*'s demand for justice and his refusal to be dominated link him in spirit to the later liberation theatre and liberation theology. The goals shared by all three are similar. The primary difference is that, unlike the twentieth-century conceptions of liberation found in communal (whether religious or theatrical) action, the *gaucho* operates alone.

The figure of the *gaucho* is prominent in another anonymous piece of theatre from Argentina called *El detalle de la Acción de Maipú* (The Battle of Maipú detail), written in 1818. This delightful *sainete* describes the Battle of Maipú in which San Martín repulsed the Spanish forces and freed Chile from colonial rule. The story is told by a *gaucho* soldier, Juan José, returning home from the action. Using comedy, colloquial dialog, well-drawn characters, song (the *Cielitos* of Bartolomé Hidalgo), and dance, the play effectively conveys the excitement the Argentinians themselves must have felt upon hearing the news. Unlike a great deal of the neoclassical drama dealing with similar themes during the period, *El detalle de la Acción de Maipú* is eminently playable. It is possible to see in it the seeds of the later socially engaged, peasant-oriented theatre that draws upon source material from the peasants' own lives to help them recognize and find the means to deal with their oppressors.

This type of popular theatre was most vigorous in eighteenth- and nineteenth-century Chile. Once again a mixture of dance, music, and dramatic sketches, the form began in Chile when a Spanish musician named Antonio Aranaz, formerly orchestra leader for the Teatro de la Ranchería in Buenos Aires, journeyed to Santiago to assume his post as choir master in the cathedral. Discovering that the post had been given to someone else, Aranaz turned his performances of the new *tonadilla* form into a profession. Based on popular song and dance forms, the *tonadilla* mixed rural and urban musical elements to create a new form of musical folklore. With colorful lyrics filled with vernacular expression, the *tonadilla* became a sharp weapon for satirizing public affairs.[40]

While Santiago had its own ornate theatre, built in the late eighteenth century, it was extremely expensive to run. As a result, a large portion of the city's theatrical activity took place beyond the theatre's walls. Performances frequently occurred in the patios of private homes, and some intrepid souls began to erect stages in the city's inns. One of these was Ambrosio Gómez del Valle, who rented the largest building in the Jesuit Colegio and converted it into a site for gaming and theatre. When the first independent government came into power in 1813 Gómez del Valle's operation was shut down as a hotbed of anti-republican sentiment, causing its enraged patrons to smash the place to smithereens.[41]

At the same time the fight for independence, by breaking the hold of the Iberian morality prevalent in colonial times, caused a veritable explosion in the popularity of the *chinganas*. These were inns, restaurants, and cafes bubbling with nightlife and imbued with the republican spirit, where Creole singers accompanied the traditional Chilean dances then in vogue. The leaders of this explosion were two women, Ña María Rutal and Ña Teresa Plaza, who created a vibrant scene described by Samuel B. Johnston, a North American visitor, in the following way: "Sunday night is commonly spent in the theatre, which is always full of people on that day. The actors are always mulattos or of mixed caste, they perform in the open air, ordinarily in the patio of an inn, and the more clowns the better."[42]

The character of the dramatic pieces performed in the *chinganas* must have been very similar to the pieces described by another visitor, the British merchant Samuel Haigh, in 1818:

Much has been said about the great influence of the clergy, in South America, amongst all classes of the people: but, as a proof that they are not held in such very great reverence, I shall make an extract from my common-place book, written on 29th June, 1818, when the piece alluded to was presented in Santiago.

The plot is very simple, and I dare say founded on fact. A priest, who is confessor to a lady, falls desperately in love with her, and she returns his passion. The husband knocks at the door whilst they are in conference, the priest hides himself until she contrives some excuse to send the husband out again; however, as he would soon return, she dresses up the priest, in the interim, like the image of a saint and makes him stand on the table. On the husband's return, he discovers his wife kneeling to the image, and is delighted with her piety. The image, as he thinks, representing a saint of a very superior order, he also asks a boon of it, upon which the priest tells him to have a procession and take him to his convent. The man runs out and returns shortly after with his neighbors, for the purpose of carrying the image in procession: they sing and perform all the rites requisite for the occasion, when the alcalde of the district, attracted by the noise, enters and discovers the imposture, he immediately exposes the priest, who, by way of recompense, gets a sound cudgelling from the mob. Such is the outline of a piece that I actually saw represented after a grand procession-day.

I shall now give a specimen of Spanish farce, which I also witnessed. A sportsman appears in quest of game, with a lady, supposed to be his wife. They each kill a bird, and very naturally sit down together to prepare for a meal; she has the diligence to pluck the birds, and he goes out for a time. A wild Indian appears who wishes to gain the lady's good graces, he is *doing the amiable* in as civilized way as possible, when the husband returns and immediately shoots the gallant, upon which exit the lady. The sportsman, not knowing what to do with the body, at length places it in an upright and fantastical position and goes away. The dean then enters, and, observing that the Indian does not pay him any respect, gives him a kick which causes the body to fall. The priest thinks he has killed the savage, but he reconciles himself by saying that he supposes he is gone to the devil, as he was not a Christian; upon this, the curtain falls and so ends this precious morceau.[43]

Where the early mendicant theatre clearly taught that retribution would strike all those who failed to observe respect for the Church and its laws, these pieces present the Church's representatives as buffoons. Even discounting Haigh's Protestant bias, it is evident that these pieces were highly irreverent, comical farces that flouted all the conventions the colonial authorities had held most sacred. Haigh's diary entry is evidence of the cylindrical nature of Latin American theatre history traced here. The mendicant evangelical theatre utilizes the power of performance in order to undermine the status of the Aztec hierarchy. Here the power of performance reflects the newly found republican spirit of independence by using theatre to undermine the status of the recently defeated colonial hierarchy. Time and again in Latin America the theatre takes on such a liberating role.

The boisterous and, at times, dangerous atmosphere of the *chinganas*, with their gaming, drinking, occasional knife-fights, and satirical performances, brought them into direct confrontation with the new republican authorities as well. Those authorities, led by men such as Camilo Henríquez and Andrés Bello, saw the *chinganas* as a threat to civic peace and a travesty of what the theatre should represent. Bello, the great Venezuelan humanist, literary and theatre critic, and founder of the Chilean university system, wrote of the *chinganas* that:

Everyone knows the type of spectacles that are offered the public in these nocturnal reunions where the shadows and the mixture of all classes of people stimulate the gradual relaxation of morality, to the point where the habit of attending them opens the door to insensitivity and soon to corruption. There the voluptuous movements, the lascivious songs, and the insolent witticisms wound the sensibilities of our tender youth with a vehemence... There is no longer any honest diversion taking place in these locations, which the police, no matter how hard they strive to shrink the limits of their operations, will never succeed in doing since no amount of vigilance is sufficient to cut off immorality's resources.[44]

The republican government certainly tried to "cut off immorality's resources" by issuing strict guidelines regarding the *chinganas'* operations. An official decree in 1824 created a licensing system for the establishment of *chinganas*, limited the area of the city where they would be legal, reduced their hours of operation, and created a special squadron of seasoned troops with the authority to levy severe fines against drunks, gamblers, and knife-fighters, or anyone caught singing indecent songs.

The *chinganas* fought back, appointing one of their own, a *chinganero* named José Romero, to speak for them in an attempt to amend the law. Romero based his defense on the necessity for a society to have at its disposal a means of indulging in certain pleasures so as to mitigate the effects of its citizens' behavior. "In every cultured country," he wrote, "the inns, cafes, and other public meeting places are an individual occupation that shelters and protects the government. They fulfill a social function. There do the artisans and laborers not permitted to enter establishments for superior classes unite."[45] The *chinganeros* carried their offensive to another realm as well. They erected stages and performed *sainetes* that imitated and ridiculed the behavior of the lowest classes, with the object of reforming their worst vices.

While Bello's views of the *chinganas* are in keeping with his neoclassical predilections concerning the teaching role of the theatre, he and others like him refused to see that the *chinganas* were often carrying out the reforming intent of the neoclassical theatre in their own way. What was, in fact, beneath all of the polemics regarding the *chinganas'* morality, was a clash of social classes. On the one hand was the cultured liberal elite, builders of the coliseums and proponents of the neoclassical theatre; on the other hand were the lower classes, who fled from the boring, moralizing, neoclassical tragedies in search of a more popularly oriented, though no less sentient, form of entertainment. Where the liberal Creole elite used the theatre to undermine Spanish colonial authority and further the cause of Latin American independence, the *chinganas* used the theatre to undermine the authority of the new Creole government. The Franciscans had introduced theatre in the New World as a means of subverting Aztec rule and civilization. Now the nineteenth-century theatre, greatly influenced in both form and content by the work of the Jesuits, became the battleground on which different social classes attempted to settle their differences. As the mendicant evangelical theatre had laid the groundwork for the neoclassical use of theatre for educational purposes, so too did the neoclassical theatre, through its desire to reform social customs, lay the groundwork for the theatre with an interest in social change that was to follow in the late nineteenth and twentieth centuries. Such a popularly oriented, politically engaged theatre found its beginnings in the coliseums, the satirical *costumbrista* theatre, and the *chinganas* of the 1800s.

CHAPTER 3

Homegrown empire: the contradictions of an emerging region

If the early nineteenth century Latin American theatre can be characterized as the period in which popularly oriented theatre such as that found in the *chinganas* and *costumbrismo* began to blossom, then the later half of the century and the early twentieth century is the period of its full bloom. The popular theatre of this epoch began in the circus ring and ended in diverse modes dedicated to libertarian ideals. As it had been since Europeans first touched American soil, the primary conflict that affected society throughout the region was access to and ownership of the land and its resources. The ruling Creole elite, who had used Rousseau's exaltation of the tribal life to justify their right to autonomous rule, were now the very ones to turn upon those whom they had once championed. They now saw the rural life as an impediment to their access to the resources contained in their hard-won territory. Empire was now made at home, by Latin American hands, and the theatre both reflected and resisted its demands.

The Creole attitude towards the Indians and indigenous culture in general was the direct result of the desire to do away with Spanish domination over their own activities while maintaining their own domination over the Indians. While the Latin American wars of independence found their rhetorical impetus in the French Revolution and the revolutionary war in the United States, the newly independent states maintained a feudal social structure and an oligarchical form of government. For these reasons, although the beginnings of these independence movements can be discerned around 1820, it was not until the twentieth century that forces intent on changing the feudal and economic legacy of Spanish rule began to achieve any real power. Once the initial exhilarating impact of independence had worn off, the newly independent, politically unstable republics underwent a series of internal power

63

struggles characterized by dictatorships and *coups d'état*, battles over national boundaries, and foreign armed intervention. Examples of this kind of progression can be found in the Rosas dictatorship in Argentina (1829–1832 and 1835–1852), the way in which both Puerto Rico and Cuba pass directly from Spanish to North American hands; or the case of Mexico, which, over the course of thirty-three years, suffered through the imposition of an empire, five constitutions, two federalist and two centralist governments, wars with France and the United States over territory, and a dictatorship.[1]

What occurred as a result of this historical progression was a Latin American society that was profoundly split between two classes. On the one hand was the indigenous population and on the other hand the Creole. Mexico, where the indigenous population numbered 4 million out of 7 million inhabitants yet was severely limited in its access to public life, can be seen as an example of one aspect of this bifurcated society. The dual character of the intellectual Creole elite has been best described by Alejo Carpentier:

From the very beginning the American Creole displays a dual preoccupation: that of defining himself, his own particular idiosyncrasies, and that of demonstrating, both for himself and for everyone else that, despite being Creole and despite living far from the great intellectual and artistic centers, he knows what goes on in the rest of the world and possesses the necessary information and understanding to utilize techniques that have born such excellent fruit in other locations. This is the cause of his desire " to be up-to-date."[2]

This bifurcation of Latin American society is further exacerbated by the immense wealth accumulated by the Creole land-owning elite in the nineteenth century through events such as the discovery of gold in Chile, or businesses such as meat exportation from Argentina. Two different cultures were created: one the dominant urban class with its eyes upon European culture, the other rural and in the majority, directly involved in a traditional way of life that European culture had not penetrated. With slight modifications this type of rigidly divided social structure can be found throughout Latin America at the turn of the century and is directly reflected in the forms of theatre and drama that arise throughout the region.

Another factor in Latin American history of the turn of the century is the ever present shadow of the United States. As George Black demonstrates in his fascinating study of popular perceptions of

Central American and the Caribbean, *The Good Neighbor: How the United States Wrote the History of Central America and the Caribbean*, before the Civil War the southern states looked to the Caribbean for its potential value as a new slave empire. Years later, having exhausted its own frontier, the United States turned its expansionist tendencies southward with the Spanish–American War in 1898 and the subsequent seizure of Puerto Rico and Cuba. While the impetus for the Spanish–American War had been provided by the lurid and xenophobic depictions of Spanish rule by Pulitzer and Hearst's newspapers, removing the hateful Spanish

did not mean that the local population itself was any more suited to the task. Even lower than Europeans in the hierarchy of capable self-government were the blacks and mulattoes who inhabited the region. Illustrators of the day showed Spain as a stage villain, all black cloak and twirling mustachio. Cuba was a slender young woman – the kind who gets tied to railroad tracks. And the native population was portrayed as squalling, watermelon-eating imbeciles and infants – transplanted southern blacks, in other words, or "pickaninnies," a word derived from the Spanish *pequeño*, for little child.[3]

These images out of melodrama and minstrel shows, with varying degrees of overt racism, have persisted to the present day. The 1989 US invasion of Panama was accompanied by print and telegenic images of Manuel Noriega as a rabid dog, a pit-bull whose fighting spirit the marine corps would quickly neutralize. Extensive reports following the invasion detailed the supposed voodoo artifacts uncovered in Noriega's home. Such a fascination with what the national consciousness sees as taboo, the exotic and vaguely erotic nature of Latin American sensibility, is another reflection of the puritanical ethics embedded in US culture and with which it has consistently viewed Latin America. The invasion of Panama, as well as countless other interventions since 1898, reflect, as Louis Hartz wrote, the seemingly unshakeable belief that American moral rectitude can solve any problem.[4] From road-builders to election monitors, the presence of US citizens will provide the necessary technical fix for Latin America's ills. The Latin American popular theatre rejects such a paternalistic attitude, whether it is European, North American, or Latin American in origin, and provides us with a clear critique of imperialistic aspirations from the late nineteenth century onward.

The new popular forms with distinct national characteristics that began to emerge around the mid-nineteenth century started this trend towards examining the class structures that were created as the colonial yoke was thrown off. These new forms reflected the opposition between the new Creole elite now in power and the masses. Given the legal benefit of certain rights in the new constitutions written throughout the region, the great majority of people were, in fact, as disenfranchised as they had been under Spanish rule. As elsewhere in the world, popular forms of entertainment provided both a means of venting frustrations and partially assuaging the harshness of daily existence. The popular form that was to have tremendous importance for the future Latin American theatre was the circus.

THE CIRCUS AND THE DEVELOPMENT OF A LATIN AMERICAN DRAMA

The circus, or at least elements of it, has a long tradition in Latin America dating back to the period before the Conquest. Bernal Díaz del Castillo (one of Cortés' officers) tells us that Moctezoma had two dwarf clowns in his court, and the chronicles speak of the "Volador" ceremony, a feat still done in the northern part of the State of Veracruz. In it a number of men climb a tall pole, attach a rope to their ankles, then dive off headfirst towards the ground. The rope gradually unravels swinging out in a circular arc around the central pole, in a variation upon the maypole idea worthy of the most death-defying trapeze artist.[5] Itinerant circus performers were common throughout the region from the beginning of the eighteenth century. Called *bubulús* in Río de la Plata, they were puppeteers, tricksters, acrobats, jugglers, minstrels and their concubines, usually led by a clown, and were often given shelter by the monastic orders and the Jesuit missions in exchange for diverting their parishioners.[6] These performers were, by the mid-nineteenth century, presenting their public with a mixture of circus, puppetry, and melodrama that, in Mexico, included short pieces on religious themes performed in the circus ring before or after the circus itself. The Mexican clowns were also poets, competing in the composition of verses to thank their public for its attention. One of the most successful of these was a clown named José Soledad Aycardo (dates unknown), who composed and performed such pieces as *El hijo pródigo* (The prodigal son) and *Las Cuatro apariciones de la Virgen Guadalupana* (Four appearances of the

Guadalupe Virgin; published 1918) in the circus ring and later moved from the sawdust to the stage, becoming widely acclaimed among actors of the nineteenth century.[7]

In his move from the circus to the stage Aycardo anticipated by twenty years the same movement by José J. Podestá (1858–1936) in Argentina. Podestá, who was to revolutionize the Argentinian theatre with his performance in the serious title role of *Juan Moreira* (1884/1886), first gained enormous success as a clown called "Pepino 88." Enrique García Velloso has described Podestá's performance in the following way:

He was not the type of clown who gets knocked around, nor the tumbler who says arbitrary and incoherent things, but a strange character dressed in an excessively ornamental fashion who carried on a conversation with the ringmaster concerning contemporary events. At times this was done in such an exaggeratedly serious manner that there sprang from his excess satiric hilarity or the mordant sarcasm of a terrible child with indirect reference to a political figure, frequently a spectator at the circus, who was the first to applaud the clown's witticisms... In addition, he performed songs that he himself composed and that gained astonishing popularity throughout the Republic.[8]

Podestá's abilities as Pepino 88 were the same ones that would enable him to inaugurate the *teatro gauchesco* and the Argentinian national theatre tradition in 1884. Both Pepino 88's sarcastic references to political figures and the *teatro gauchesco*'s depictions of mythic characters based upon the reality of *gaucho* life reflected the lives and beliefs of Podestá's audience back at themselves and they responded enthusiastically. During Maximilian's reign in Mexico the circuses found it increasingly difficult to find spaces in which to perform. Like the Chilean *chinganas* before them, they were forced to perform in the patios of inns surrounded by their public while other spaces were made available to French, English, and Italian pieces promoted by the Bourbon government attended only by those who wished to curry favor with the regime and largely ignored by the common people.

CUBAN POPULAR THEATRE: THE *TEATRO BUFO*

Concurrent with the growth of these popular forms on the Latin American mainland, and following a similar progression from itinerant performances outdoors to permanent indoor theatres, was the emergence of the Cuban *teatro bufo* or "clown theatre." This was a popular form that was markedly Cuban in idiom, characters, and themes, as opposed to the operatic, romantic works whose performance was encouraged by the colonial elite. The product of a curious mixture of influences, the *teatro bufo* began by building upon the elements of music, parody, dance, caricature, and satire found in the North American minstrel shows that toured the island between 1860 and 1865. To these elements the Cubans added the *negrito* figure, as well as other vernacular types.

They created a mulatto-colored stage that produced a populist ideology, literary and joyful in opposition to the opera, the "culture" and the closed circle of the privileged. Their characters are popular to the extent that they represent majority sectors of the population, their language is domestic, common, comprehensible by all, their themes are small precisely because the country's destiny is not in their hands. Marginalized from History, they present the story of the men without history, nourishing it with a vernacular taste and sensibility that is a faithful sketch of a dispossessed class.[9]

At one and the same time the *teatro bufo* reflected the prejudices of its audience while it made noises about social protest and lightly criticized the colonial administration. The *teatro bufo* began in 1869, in fact, as another arm of the Cuban independence struggle with the events at the theatre Villanueva.

On January 21 a popular *bufonero* named Jacinto Valdés shouted "Long live Céspedes" (the general commanding the Cuban insurgent forces) before singing a song. The colonial authorities fined him 200 pesos and gave him a severe reprimand, putting forth the story that the actor had been in his cups when he made the offending remark. Word quickly spread and the following night a special benefit performance for "some insolvent ones," in reality the revolutionary forces, was announced. The theatre was covered with flags, women arrived wearing the national colors, their hair defiantly swinging loose, and with single stars emblazoned on their dresses. Valdés at one point in one of the pieces performed gave the line "Long live the sugar cane-producing land!" and the audience responded with repeated shouts in praise of a "Free Cuba." The colonial troops surrounding the theatre took this as their signal to act and, rushing the theatre, fired indiscriminately upon the audience. Those who did not flee were massacred. Valdés, along with many other *bufos*, escaped to New York, returning in 1879 to take up their place as a constant irritation to the colonial administration. Towards 1895, however, the *teatro bufo* began to decline until, by 1900, it had degenerated into purely pornographic revues that held their audience with gross jokes, racist vignettes, and social chauvinism.[10]

TEATRO MAMBÍ/TEATRO COLONIAL

The day after Valdés fled from the Villanueva a small newspaper called *La patria libre* (The free fatherland) published a dramatic poem by a sixteen-year-old named José Martí (1853–1895) called *Abdala* (published 1869). With it Martí gave birth to a new current in the Cuban theatre, the *teatro mambí*, that was to pursue the *teatro bufo*'s early inclination towards social protest and criticism while the *bufoneros* themselves sank into vulgarity. *Abdala* is a one-act verse drama clearly designed to inspire patriotic defense of Cuba. Abdala is a Nubian commander who, over his mother's objections, battles the invading Arabs at the cost of his life. In character and intent *Abdala* is similar to the neoclassically inspired dramas of the late eighteenth and early nineteenth centuries. What distinguishes Martí's work, however, is his use of a black hero to press the cause for independence. This was a significant step in Cuban social perception, for it meant that the *negrito* butt of *bufonero* jokes was now capable of leading the forces for independence, and of presenting a revolutionary social critic. The *teatro mambí* was to continue to put forth this anti-slavery, anti-racist attitude throughout its existence, embracing the attitude of the insurgent forces who suffered hardships in the Cuban jungle.

An Irish-American journalist named James O'Kelley, who interviewed the insurgent leader Carlos Manuel de Céspedes in 1873, described an actor's performance that he witnessed in the jungle camp:

He was a colored man and a mixture of minstrel and comedian. He performed sketches of life in Free Cuba, taking all the parts himself... [and] a series of comic sketches of all the various types of *mambises*. His portrayal of them was so natural, although with a slight hint of exaggeration, that no one present could stop laughing. Neither the defects nor the failures of some of the spectators were pardoned in his satires, one of them depicting a convoy searching for food near the advancing Spanish troops. The man's nervous excitement, due to his awareness of the danger he was in and his terror of giving himself away to some hidden Spanish soldier, his precipitous flight and abandonment of his bag of provisions, were all done with such mastery that they would have been a triumph on any stage. When I inquired about the actor's background, I learned that he had been a clown at some time in the past.[11]

From O'Kelley's description this actor can be seen to have been a descendant of the *griot*; a kind of story-teller, mime, minstrel, and clown brought over on the slaveships from Africa. Unlike his ancestors with their fawning attitude, however, this man used his position to present a type of performance that, like that of clowns from the European Durov to the Uruguayan José J. Podestá's creation, Pepino 88, offered a biting critique of those in authority.

This description of a performance in the jungle leaves no doubt that a form of *teatro mambí*, albeit closer to the circus than the stage, was present under the Spanish rule. The majority of the *teatro mambí*, however, was written, performed, and published in exile due to the simple fact that the colonial administration would not tolerate its presence. With the *teatro mambí* in exile or in the jungle, the non-*bufo* Cuban stage was left to foreign companies presenting lyric opera or pieces designed to exalt the colonial regime. One of the latter was a one-act musical comedy called *El gorrión* (The sparrow; 1869) that was based on an extra-theatrical episode that took place on the island in 1869 and, as so often in Latin American theatre history, provided more spectacle than anything present at the time in the traditional theatre spaces. The sparrows were peninsular birds brought to Cuba by the Spanish and came to be associated in the popular mind with colonial rule vs. the Cuban *bijirita* or "warbler," a bird that preferred to die rather than live in captivity. Newspapers published satirical verses on the theme of the *gorriones y bijiritas*, a dance became popular by the same name, and both Spaniards and *mambises* christened vessels with the name of their respective bird.

Such was the atmosphere on Holy Thursday, 1869, when a volunteer in the 7th Spanish battalion found a dead sparrow outside the walls of the captaincy general. Believing the poor *gorrión* to have died from fasting on the religious occasion, the soldier took the bird back to his barracks where a beautiful coffin was constructed and a subscription started for the cost of burial. The *gorrión* duly received all military and religious honors. He was attended by the wives of the spanish colonial authorities led by the military dictator's wife. They prayed for the bird who had died at his post "like a good Spaniard." Since the sepulcher into which the bird would be laid (an allegorical rendering of a silver tree with two *gorriones* in it and one, dead, at its feet) was not ready by the end of the ceremony, the bird was paraded in a funeral cortege through the streets of Havana. From there the hapless *gorrión* was converted into a symbol of colonial rule and was passed in state through the streets of Cárdenas, Matanzas, and Guanabacoa. In Guanabacoa a second *gorrión* was added to the first, this time the victim of a vile murder perpetrated by a cat, which the colonial press termed to be probably "a laborer." The cat was detained, tried by a military court, condemned to death, and given extreme unction by a priest. Just before the sentence was to be carried out, the cat's owner, an individual above suspicion, explained that his cat, although definitely a rat-catcher, had strong Spanish sentiments and the cat was set free.[12] This singular display of colonial sympathy, with all of its absurd extremes, is a measure of how threatened the colonial regime felt itself to be by the insurgent forces. As so often in Latin American history, political and religious action demonstrated its theatrical nature. *El gorrión*, the musical piece mentioned earlier, became a huge popular success, spawning an entire series of pro-colonial theatre pieces that used the symbolic character of the *gorrión* and the *bijirita* to play upon audience emotion.

ARGENTINA AND THE *ORGANIZACIÓN NACIONAL*

Back on the Latin American mainland, the development of the popular theatre was of a different order from that of Cuba. Although both currents began with clowns and circuses, the mainland variety proved to have a much greater influence upon Latin American theatre as a whole. This was largely the result of different circumstances, for the mainland countries broke the colonial hold much earlier than their Caribbean neighbors. The years after independence show a period in which various constituencies battled for power over the newly autonomous territories. Nowhere was this more evident than in Argentina, where after independence was won in 1816 civil war broke out, culminating in the Juan Manuel de Rosas dictatorship of 1829–1852. Rosas' defeat at the battle of Caseros in 1852, and the promulgation of a new constitution in 1853, began a period known in Argentinian history as the *Organización Nacional* (National Organization). It was a time of violent changes, especially in political and economic orientation. The country's prolonged period of isolation was broken and it turned to the outside world for models: Britain in the political and economic spheres, and France in the artistic and cultural spheres.

The vision of Argentina as granary and cattle ranch for the world was formed and with it the necessity for new hands to carry it out. Contemporary Argentinian leaders such as Domingo Faustino Sarmiento saw the country as a vast desert that needed to be cultivated, and Juan Bautista Alberdi stated that "to govern is to populate." From such sentiments came the so-called *aluvión immigratorio* (immigrant flood) facilitated by the provisions of the 1853 constitution that assured the security of all able-bodied men who wished to work the land. Its framers clearly were thinking of the vast regions inhabited by indigenous tribes, and "desert campaigns" were unleashed against the Indians to open up the land for cultivation and ranching. The end result was a human wave of immigrants that descended upon Buenos Aires from all corners of the globe. With their dreams, their desires, and their dialects, these immigrants created, seemingly overnight, a new social order that would find its eventual expression in 1916, when the radical leader Hipólito Yrigoyen came to power. For the moment, however, as in so many cases of mass migration throughout history, only a few of the newcomers managed to achieve their goals. The vast majority were caught up in a cycle of frustration, disillusionment, and failure. It was from the clash of this new class of immigrants with the traditional Argentinian populations that the popular theatre was to derive new characters and concerns.[13]

JUAN MOREIRA AND THE TEATRO GAUCHO

The flood of immigrants brought an influx of itinerant performers as well. In search of commercial opportunity, these performers, and above all the European circuses, were added to the previously existing Latin American popular forms. The sheer number of circuses, both foreign and *criollo*, operating in the Río de la Plata region during the mid-1800s is a testament to their vitality and popular appeal. It was the combined talents of a foreign and a creole circus that created the first piece of Argentinian national theatre. The two circuses were, respectively, the internationally acclaimed Circo Humberto I led by the Carlo brothers, and the Circo Scotti-Podestá led by the Podestá. These circuses frequently included sentimental pantomimes on heroic or novelistic themes which were performed in the ring between attractions. The Carlo brothers came up with the brilliant idea of basing a pantomime on the enormously successful novel by Eduardo Gutiérrez (1853–1890), *Juan Moreira* (1884/1886), as the centerpiece of their farewell performance in Buenos Aires. Gutiérrez himself enthusiastically undertook to adapt the novel for the circus ring, but all concerned felt it important for the hero to be played by a creole actor and the Carlo brothers' circus was composed completely of foreigners. The role was offered to the Uruguayan José J. Podestá who not only accepted, but brought his circus with him. Its creole performers gave a more authentic flavor to the new pantomime.[14] With *Juan Moreira* the *teatro gaucho* was born and with it many of the themes, conventions, and concerns that would mark, in one way or another, the subsequent Latin American theatre into the twentieth century.

What was *Juan Moreira* and what did its performance signify for the development of the Latin American theatre? The answers to these questions operate on many different levels, and in order to have a solid grasp upon them it is necessary to return to the eighteenth century and *Juan Moreira*'s antecedents. Those antecedents are found in two different places: the colonial *sainetes* such as *El amor de la estanciera*, *El detalle de la acción de Maipú*, and *Las bodas de Chivico y Pancha*; as well as the *gauchesca* poetry that finds its earliest expression in the work of Bartolomé Hidalgo. While the *sainetes* offer a much more superficial view of the world than the later *gaucho* theatre, they deal with the same characters and their struggles to make a living off the land in the face of antagonistic forces that would remove them. The influence of the *gaucho* poetry, as first expressed in Hidalgo's *Diálogos* and *Cielitos Patrióticos*, was much greater on *Juan Moreira* than its theatrical precursors.

Gauchesca poetry can be seen to go through three distinct phases dating from after the Revolution in 1810 to the time of its decline in 1885. Each phase represents the political and social ideas of the moment, as well as the passion with which those ideals were pursued. Bartolomé Hidalgo writes about the *gauchos* and their exploits in the wars of independence. His work reflects the spirit of their rebellious response to authority, and their hatred of the Spanish who imposed it, while celebrating their victories for the nation. Hilario Acasubi, whose work represents the second phase in *gauchesca* poetry, writes about the *gaucho* life during the Rosas dictatorship. Unlike Hidalgo's poetry, which has a marked national character where all join in battle against a common enemy, Acasubi's individuals reflect the intense internal battles between the federalist and the unitary forces. His sympathies are clearly with the unitary forces and he sings praises to their patriotic efforts against the tyrannical Rosas regime. The final phase of *gaucho* poetry, and the best known, is that represented by José Hernández' work *Martín Fierro*. Hernández' poem is in two parts and treats the lot of the *gaucho* pressed into service in the campaigns to clear the Indians out of the frontier areas in order to open up the land for cultivation and ranching. The poem's first part deals mainly with the *gaucho* as a persecuted figure, constantly pursued by the political and military authorities who want to use his legendary fighting abilities against the Indians. In response, the *gaucho* deserts and rises up in resistance to their attack on his historic independence. The second part of the poem reflects the changing Argentinian political and social reality, and speaks for the *gaucho*'s assimilation into the national life – an assimilation that requires the discarding of a now sterile stance of individualism, and the forging of a new consciousness of what it means to live and work with others for the good of society.[15]

It was against this backdrop of *gauchesca* poetry that Eduardo Gutiérrez wrote his novel *Juan Moreira*, which appeared in a newspaper called *La Patria Argentina*, in 1879. The serialized novel, as represented by such authors as Sue, Dumas, Dickens, and Conan Doyle, first appeared in France in the first half of the nineteenth century. The result of advances in journalistic technique and the social situation of the industrial Revolution, such novels had to be structured in such a way as to maintain suspense and reader interest between installments. The solution was frequently the creation of larger-than-life heroes whose exploits were eagerly awaited by their readers. While conceived of in fictional terms, such novels had the direct political and social effect of diverting reader attention from the drudgery and danger of daily life. Censured by those who wished to make reading into a means of education and social amelioration, the serials were also championed by poets and philosophers such as Nietzsche and Lautréamont, who saw a metaphor for the state of the universe in their mythic heroes. It would take Dickens to utilize the form to attack the very conditions that the sponsors of the early serializers sought to maintain.

Gutiérrez' novel can be seen as the direct result of the enormous changes affecting contemporary Argentinian society. His audience was composed of the new creole sectors and the emerging immigrant masses, all of whom were searching for a means of forging a new national identity. One of the places where they found it was in the figure of the *gaucho*, a proud, brave, individualistic, and xenophobic character around which a national consensus could be formed. Gutiérrez' original source was the historical figure of a ruffian for hire, bodyguard to Adolfo Alsina, who was killed by the Buenos Aires police in 1874. From the bare facts of his life, Gutiérrez created the legendary character of Juan Moreira, who, as a consequence of his social marginalization and arbitrary treatment by the authorities, is forced into a life of crime, producing a fatalistic personality that some see as demonic.[16]

Analogous to the North American Western, Gutiérrez' novel describes the hard-working, humble Moreira, who, wanting nothing more than a good life for his wife and son, suffers a series of humiliations at the hands of a deputy mayor who covets his wife. When a man to whom Moreira has lent a large sum of money denies the debt and is supported by the deputy mayor, the affront to Moreira's honor compels him to kill them both. Disgraced, Moreira begins an outlaw life that turns him into a living legend who, though generous to the poor and good-hearted, singlehandedly fights off provincial patrols, Indians, soldiers, Buenos Aires police, and hard *gauchos* until a battle in which he is overwhelmed by force of numbers and a bayonet in the back.

Gutiérrez' writing vividly describes Moreira's outlaw life, although at times it reaches maudlin excess in its treatment of the *gaucho*'s despair. The author's sympathies are quite evidently with the *gaucho*, who, as a class, are persecuted and oppressed, forced into military service on the frontier, their land and women taken from them by provincial officials. Clearly seen by the authorities as little more than cannon fodder, efficacious only for ridding the countryside of marauding Indians, these men of the country are depicted by Gutiérrez as possessing extreme nobility as well as purely human failings.

When approached by the Carlo brothers of the Circo Humberto I with their proposal to adapt *Juan Moreira* for the circus, Gutiérrez pared the action of the novel down to two acts of five and seven scenes each that made full use of the scenic possibilities of the circus. A platform was erected in the center of the ring where the interior scenes were played, while outdoor scenes, and the party/dance scenes were performed in the ring itself with full participation by horses, dancers, and musicians. This type of theatrical arena spectacle, reminiscent of such mendicant spectacles as the *La conquista de*

Jerusalén, was later lost when the piece's great popularity made movement to a traditional stage feasible.[17] The original production in 1884 was conceived by the Carlo brothers as a farewell performance before they returned to Europe. The Podestá circus returned to its itinerant life in Latin America and it was not until two years later that José J. Podestá decided to remount the production. It was this new staging that was to prove so important for the development of the national theatre, for, upon returning to his hotel after the performance, Podestá was greeted by its French owner, M. León Beaupuy. Beaupuy congratulated him on the quality of the pantomime but added that it was a pity that what was intimated in mime and gesture was not spoken. He suggested that with dialog the piece would produce emotion comparable to that of the classical theatre.[18] Podestá enthusiastically pursued the suggestion by excerpting portions of appropriate dialog from Gutiérrez' novel. The resulting adaption met with phenomenal success.

This new adaptation discards all but the most essential scenes of Gutiérrez' tale. The last two scenes were played out in pure action with, one would assume, appropriate adlibbing. The style of performance seems to have been much more realistic than seen theretofore on the Argentinian or Uruguayan stage. A Spanish actor, José Valero, who saw a performance in 1888, wrote a letter to Podestá containing the following observations:

Your method of performing is very different from that of other theatres. In ours, for example, only the leading characters, and occasionally the secondary ones, speak, act, and move. In yours everyone is doing something and nobody gets in anyone's way. In the *pulpería* [type of general store], I saw people playing cards at one table and chatting at others. At the counter people drank while further away some guitar players stroked their instruments, and the owner waited on everyone, all maintaining their roles...even your dogs are artists who know what to do and when!...You make fiction seem truth. When you fight, one wants to scream. Enough!...In the end, one who sees a spectacle such as this for the first time with all its coarseness, its language to which the ear must become accustomed, its naturalism and the enthusiasm with which you perform realizes why the audience feels for, and gets caught up in, a performance![19]

The only changes made to the novel for the circus performance were the use of picturesque character types – such as the Cocoliche clown – an insistence on approximating the *gaucho* dialect, and a few effective (albeit rather melodramatic) pieces of staging such as when

Moreira leaves his family for the last time and his son stumbles after him, arms outstretched crying "Tata, tata!," the colloquial term for father.

When the Podestá Circus debuted their new pantomime with dialog in 1886 in Chivilcoy they were performing for an audience lacking the sense of decorum that inhibited certain types of behavior in the Buenos Aires theatres. The provincial audience recognized themselves in the language, attitudes, and actions of the characters. They joined them both in body and in spirit, as demonstrated by anecdotes about the peasant who jumped into the ring to fight alongside Moreira and the girl who, feverishly enamored of the *gaucho* character, insisted that she had conceived a child by him. This type of popular reaction and participation was lost as *Juan Moreira*'s popularity drew it into the theatres of Montevideo in 1889 and Buenos Aires in 1891. The exigencies of performing on a proscenium stage meant that many of the innovative scenographic elements of the circus ring had to be discarded, and the new "cultured" bourgeois audience emphasized the distance from, rather than their common heritage with, the characters of the pantomime. Although *Juan Moreira* was to spawn a new generation of *gaucho* works and to provide José J. Podestá with a long career on the stage, its enthusiastic reception by the Buenos Aires theatre community marked the beginning of the end of the *teatro gaucho*.

The play *Calandria* (1896), by Martiniano Leguizamón (1858–1935), the last *gaucho* theatre piece of merit, was the break between the *teatro gaucho* and its popular audience. Leguizamón wrote his play especially for the Podestá and gave it to them with the sole condition that it be performed in a legitimate theatre, not the circus ring. While the play certainly possesses its own intrinsic worth – especially in terms of its delightful dialog and able manipulation of dialect – its primary interest comes from its place in the development/demise of the *gauchesco* drama. By insisting that the Podestá perform the piece in a regular theatre rather than the circus, Leguizamón removed the *teatro gaucho* from its original audience and imposed quite different demands upon the form that are evident from an examination of the text. To begin with, the constant fighting that characterizes *Juan Moreira* is absent from *Calandria*. Calandria, whose name means a kind of lark and refers to his desire for freedom, mocks his enemies rather than killing them. The majority of the play consists of vibrant dialog, not action, laced throughout with song. In the play's denouement Calandria, outnumbered and disarmed is pardoned and revealed to have been the subject of a *burla* himself when his captors are shown to be his friends in cahoots with the local authorities. The end result is that Calandria pledges to become a hard-working *criollo*.

As can be seen from *Calandria*'s content, by moving into the theatre the *gauchesco* drama plays to a very different audience from that of the circus ring. Its audience is now much more aristocratic: the educated and artistic elite with its own highly formulated view of aesthetics. The raw violence of the *gauchesco* is discarded as Leguizamón writes for this new audience. His aim (like that of José Hernández in his book *Instrucción del estanciero*) is to advocate the *gaucho*'s incorporation into the new social order, rather than his persecution by it. What he in fact accomplishes, at least in formal terms, is a much more effective destruction of the meaning of the *gaucho* lifestyle. Calandria's pardon only allows him a measure of liberty on the ruling order's terms. By becoming a *criollo trabajador* he is integrated into the social order more effectively, and in equally a subservient role as those *gauchos* pressed into service along the frontier.

CITY VERSUS COUNTRY

Leguizamón's *Calandria*, and the general trajectory of the *teatro gaucho* traced here, is an example in theatrical terms of the opposition between the rural and the urban sensibility, of the gradual dominance of the city over the country and the life that it represents that marks this period in Latin American history. Raymond Williams has ably demonstrated this conflict as it is represented in English literature and its antecedents. The country's subservience to the city is a direct result of the progression of agrarian capitalism to industrial revolution to imperialism, and can be seen reflected in the literature of various societies throughout the centuries. In Theocritus the pastoral landscape is constantly nearby, just outside the city and surrounding it. The languorous life of Hesiod's Golden Age is a mythic memory in contrast to the contemporary conception of, and admiration for, labor's necessity. By the time of Virgil's *Georgics* a marked ideological transition has occurred and the countryside is now Arcadia, that land of leisure to which one retires in the imagination. There is a parallel progression in English literary and social history, where the development of towns in the Middle Ages is an aspect of the new agricultural order. The towns become important first as markets, then as financial and administrative centers with a concomitant ideological transition in literature. This can be seen in dramatic literature as early as the 1620s with Philip Massinger's *The City Madam* and *New Ways to Pay Old Debts* and their emphasis on the increasing commercialization of the countryside, to the Jacobean and Restoration comedy of manners, where problems of love and marriage reflect a society increasingly concerned with issues relating to the ownership of land. Sir Giles Overreach is a consummate example of the lust for wealth and ambition of the city vs. the honest, worthy country character of goodman Humble.

The social consequences of agrarian capitalism were an extraordinary improvement of the land and an increase of wealth in the hands of a few. Many were dispossessed and became subject to attack by vagrancy laws designed to force the landless into wage labor and do away with the possibility of free mobility as represented by "sturdy rogues" or free laborers.[20] A discussion of English agrarian capitalism in the context of Latin American theatre history is not as far-fetched as it might seem for the political–economic model adopted in the Río de la Plata region during the *Organización Nacional* was English, and its social effects can be seen reflected upon the stage through the *teatro gaucho*, the *drama rural*, and the *grotesco criollo*. While such terms are specific to the Argentinian theatre, similar movements are discernible in the theatre development in other areas of the region as well.

The end of the nineteenth century in Argentina brought not only an influx of 3,300,000 European immigrants over a period of less than sixty years, it also brought a gigantic infusion of foreign investment. By 1889 40 percent of the United Kingdom's foreign investment was in Argentina in areas such as railroads, public services, ports, gas, telephone and electrical lines, and banking, all of which directly contributed to the development of agriculture at the expense of ranching and, with the establishment of an incipient industrial sector, the creation of urban means of employment. The growing importance of urban centers can be measured by the population explosion in Buenos Aires. The city leapt from a population of 187,000 in 1869 to 1,576,000 by 1914.[21] British investment in Argentinian agriculture was not only a means of accumulating great wealth, but also a necessity if the empire was to survive. The nineteenth-century British industrial revolution, with its concentration on urban manufacturing centers, meant that Britain's own agriculture was shunted aside and distant lands became the United Kingdom's rural areas. As those lands became organized into the financial and administrative network of the empire, new rural societies captivated the English imagination. Kipling, Maugham and the early Orwell's tales of plantation life, the constant commercial transactions that rule Conrad's stories and analogous to the kinds of social, political, and economic structures created in Latin America in the late nineteenth and early twentieth centuries. Those structures, however, were frequently in conflict with the still existent structures of the Spanish empire implanted long before throughout the region.

The *conquistadores* were not colonists but soldiers, and their dreams of El Dorado, of wealth won through conquest, led them to relegate the task of cultivating their new-found fertile lands first to the Indians and then to imported black slaves. They looked upon the South American plains as a gigantic range in which cattle multiplied magically. The herd of horses abandoned after the failed attempt at founding Buenos Aires and the seven cows and a bull brought by the explorer Goes from Paraguay were the foundation of wild herds that roamed the plains. There they were managed by the Indians and the *conquistadores'* descendants, the *gauchos*. Both Indians and *gauchos* saw the range as held in common, and were easy prey for those absentee landlords with the wealth and political connections to obtain deeds to the land the *gaucho* inhabited. Like the victims of enclosure in Britain, the *gaucho* was considered a vagrant by the nineteenth-century authorities (as we have seen in *Calandria*) and was forced to choose between a life of persecution or a position as a wage laborer for the new owner of the land he had once roamed freely. With the "immigrant flood" and the movement of the *gringo* (foreigner) into the plains, the land was parceled off into areas enclosed by copperwire fences, the new colonists obeying Sarmiento's order: "Don't be barbarians, put up fences!"[22]

As has been seen, the *teatro gaucho* reflected thematically certain aspects of this drastic change in lifestyle. Technically, the *teatro gaucho*, in its initial circus format, mirrored its thematic concerns. The spectators recognized themselves in the itinerant performers, and knew the stories performed by heart, vitiating the need for extended sociological analysis. What gave the circus performance its vitality was the innocence of its audience that participated in the story wholeheartedly, seeing its own destiny in that of the preindustrial hero. At the other end of the scale were the established city theatres, inheritors of European culture who, with marked delay, offered their audiences all the innovations of neoclassicism, romanticism, naturalism, and realism. While the intelligentsia had some familiarity with Ibsen, Hauptman, Zola, and Sudermann, the Buenos Aires audience's taste turned more towards Echegaray's romanticism, Bretón de los Herreros' *costumbrismo*, and López de Ayala's social realism than towards the sort of innovation Antoine was introducing at the time in the Théâtre Libre.[23] The concerns of these two theatrical currents – the cultured and the popular, the city and the country – mirror the bifurcated social structure following independence and were gradually to be joined in the late nineteenth and early twentieth centuries as Latin America became integrated into the political–economic system of the modern world. With this integration came a perception of the Latin American countries as, if no longer European colonies, countryside to the European (or North American) city. This perception was widely disseminated, upheld by the Latin American bourgeoisie convinced of its provincialism, and fought against by a large body of writers who utilized *costumbrismo* and the *drama rural* to celebrate Latin American customs, language, and history.

FLORENCIO SÁNCHEZ AND THE *DRAMA RURAL*

The most eloquent spokesman of this newly combatative group of writers was Uruguayan playwright Florencio Sánchez (1875–1910). Sánchez can be seen as the first of a new breed of Latin American playwrights that appears in the early twentieth century. Highly educated themselves, they do not withdraw into elite enclaves like their neoclassically influenced predecessors, but apply their more extensive knowledge to popular concerns. Like Che Guevara many years later, these writers make common cause with a range of the population from which they themselves do not spring. Ideologically, Sánchez was profoundly influenced by anarchist thinkers such as Kropotkin, Bakunin, Gorri, and Malatesta, and, in his self-appointed role as a worker's journalist, placed himself at the forefront of the various labor struggles in the Río de la Plata region in the early 1900s. Theatrically, he was aware of the innovations of Ibsen, Zola,

Becque, Giacosa, and Bracco, but attempted to wed their realistic and naturalist technique to his concern for an accurate portrayal of the Argentinian national character and the progress of the society as a whole.[24] The play of his that best presents this mixture of ideological and theatrical concerns is *Barranca abajo* (1905).

Barranca abajo (Over the precipice) is generally acknowledged to be Sánchez' best work and one of the masterpieces of Argentinian dramatic literature. The play demonstrates the overriding theme of the *drama rural*, that of the honorable, hard-working, peaceable *criollo* displaced by the ever-widening sway of the city and authority. Don Zoilo, having lost his *estancia* (ranch estate) to Juan Luis in a lawsuit, is permitted to continue living on his former property together with his wife, their two daughters, and his sister. Having suffered the outside world's blows, he is now laid siege to by the members of his own family. His wife, his sister, and one of his daughters all revolt against the solitary life he wishes them to lead. The daughter throws over a *buen criollo* for her father's enemy, Juan Luis, and Zoilo's sister pursues the local authority figure, Comisario Butiérrez. His other daughter is the only one to defend Zoilo, but she is sick with consumption and persecuted by the other women, who are jealous of the favoritism Zoilo shows her. When the consumptive daughter dies, Zoilo allows the other women to leave. The play ends as Zoilo is about to hang himself.

Sánchez is clearly drawing parallels between his *criollo*, Job, and King Lear. Zoilo rails against God with all the force of Lear's anger on the heath and is as unable to comprehend what he has done to deserve his fate as is Job. While the work does not really reach either Shakespearian or biblical power, there are a number of moments of true pathos and Zoilo's last line, as he tries to fling the noose over a beam and gets it caught in a bird's nest, is a masterstroke: "By God... A man's home is destroyed more easily than a bird's nest!" That line, combined with the title, synthesizes the main thrust of the play and, indeed, many of the playwright's central thematic concerns. A forceful critic of works such as *Juan Moreira* because of what he saw as their false mythification and mystification of the *gaucho*, Sánchez offers a much more complex world in *Barranca abajo*. At first victims of the legal machinations of the encroaching immigrants, some *criollos* learn to play the paper game of deeds that allows them to dispossess their neighbors under the force of law. The *gaucho viejo* Zoilo represents the last bastion of a type of stubborn agricultural producer who has refused to make himself into a local power figure and now lacks either the economic means or the political connections to ingratiate himself with the new local authorities. Sánchez rounds out the *drama rural* by portraying the destructive effect the corrupt system has upon the creole family until don Zoilo (as performed by José J. Podestá) is left completely alone, defeated as a man and as an institution.[25]

The twentieth century had arrived and with it came an explosion of urban centers throughout Latin America. The Río de la Plata region became a huge commodities shipping center and a cosmopolitan city that was the first link between Latin America and Europe. In such an atmosphere artistic focus shifted to a larger range of subject matter that included urban concerns and an examination of inner psychology within that framework. The theatre began to gaze not upon the *gaucho*'s plains, but upon the city banks, those border regions that were the natural transitional areas for the river of immigrants flowing into the city from the countryside, and from countries far away. This new urban theatrical consciousness can be seen repeated in national settings as diverse as Peru, Mexico, and Chile, but is nowhere as marked as in Argentina.

THE "IMMIGRATION FLOOD" AND THE EMERGENCE OF THE *GROTESCO CRIOLLO*

Between 1871 and 1920, 4·5 million immigrants arrived in Buenos Aires. The great majority of them were Italian, followed to a lesser degree by those of Spanish extraction, and a smaller percentage of other nationalities. Two-thirds of the new arrivals were men, and the average age of both sexes ranged from twenty to thirty years old. Such a demographic breakdown led to the extreme facility with which people married across ethnic lines as well as frequent clashes of social customs.[26] When the tradition of labor militancy the immigrants brought with them from Europe was added to the city's rapid industrialization, Buenos Aires saw an unprecedented period of social strife and change. A variety of popular theatre forms imported from Spain including the *zarzuela*, the *género chico*, and the *sainete* sprang up to deal with the new social reality leading, in the end, to the development of a distinctly Latin American form, the *grotesco criollo*.

The *género chico* was a Spanish form under whose rubric fell a number of short pieces including operettas and revues, and which presented various recognizable character types familiar to its audience. One of the most successful of these works, and typical of the form, was *La Gran vía*, which premièred in Madrid in 1889. A series of boulevard sketches depicting life on Madrid's central avenue, La Gran vía, it was quickly transferred to Buenos Aires with suitable adaptations of character and dialog to fit the new milieu. The social exigencies of the audience's daily lives, however, soon led to an abandonment of the *género chico* in search of theatrical forms that would communicate in addition to entertaining. To fulfill this need, a new form that combined the ground-breaking use of national idiom was first presented in the circus by the Podestá, with the urban popular forms to create the native *sainete*.

In his *Tesoro de la lengua castellana o española*, Sebastián Covarrubias y Orozco defines the term *sainete* as deriving from *sayn*, which refers to "the offal of any animal, ... from the Latin sagina or saginae, and referring to the marrow, brains, or other treat (called a *sainete*) falconers gave their birds in order to retrieve them. The word came to refer to the tasty morsels brought to the master of the house by the cook, in order to whet his whistle before drinking."[27] In the theatre such "tasty morsels" were, at first, the brief pieces performed between acts dealing with popular types, language, and ambience such as Lope de Rueda's *pasos* or Cervantes' *entremeses*. In the eighteenth century the term *sainete* became specific to the works of Ramón de la Cruz, which were one-act pieces dealing with contemporary customs. The Buenos Aires immigrant lifestyle, with its characteristic slums and tenement houses, led to a further modification of the *sainete* form that reflected the incredible confusion of idioms and customs familiar to its audience.

Its characters are the immigrant and the *criollo*, its settings the tenement and the slum. The huge amount of humanity that the society is experimenting with assimilating, finds its life in the theatre in the *sainete*. People recognize themselves in it, learn from it, identify with it, and convert it into a phenomenon of such magnitude that its popularity has not been equaled until the present day.[28]

Luis Ordaz has characterized this Argentinian *sainete* as containing three different currents: the investigatory and entertaining *sainete*, the *costumbrista sainete*, and the *sainete* as a form of mass communication. All three forms reflect the tremendous change the city was experiencing, as well as the ambitions of an incipient middle class. The first type of *sainete* explores the actions of a wide variety of character types, as reflected in the interaction of immigrant and *criollo*. Formulaic and frequently melodramatic, ending in a duel, death, or suicide, these pieces nevertheless investigate and interpret the various courses of action open to their audience under similar circumstances. The second type of *sainete* is uninterested in investigating the situations its audience finds itself in, but rather in reflecting them back to that audience. This type of *sainete* operates under a rigid moral code that seeks to maintain the status quo. The third type of *sainete*, and the most important, is that which uses the form as a means of mass communication. Seeking a social politic that enables its members to feel part of a community while maintaining their individual characteristics, the audience of this type of *sainete* turns to the theatre as a place where all the anguished contradictions of daily life can be exposed without their customary masks. For these spectators the stage offered a forum for presenting unmasked the truth about their lives with the possibility, although channeled into severely limited courses of action, of salvation.[29] It is from this last current that the creators of the *grotesco criollo* such as Francisco Defilippis Novoa and Armando Discépolo spring. These playwrights, each in his own way, pursue the mixture of theatrical, religious, and political concerns characteristic of Latin American theatre from its inception to the present day.

THE *GROTESCO CRIOLLO*

In her definitive book on the subject, *El grotesco criollo : estilo teatral de una época*, Claudia Kaiser-Lenoir has characterized the central concern of the *grotesco criollo* as the social seen *vis-à-vis* the individual. Within the context of the early twentieth-century Buenos Aires milieu and its particular political and economic interests, the individual's position is seen not as an inherent condition but the result of a specific social order leading to unjust treatment and alienation. It is for this reason that all of these works end in their characters' total failure to achieve any of their aspirations. Such failure represents a direct attack upon a social order that so reduces a man's dignity that, unable to support the tension, he rebels in a (not necessarily conscious) affirmative gesture of his own humanity that removes him from that order, negating, invalidating, and denouncing it. All of this is achieved by the *grotesco criollo* through comic means. Unlike the comedy of the *sainete criollo* that focused upon the ridiculous nature of those who sought to escape from the established order, thereby reconfirming and perpetuating it, the *grotesco criollo*'s focus is upon the ludicrous nature of those who continue to adhere to a system that destroys them. Such a form of comedy derives its power from our dual response to it. While we laugh at the characters who actively pursue incorporation into a social order that denies and deforms them, we simultaneously experience a profound sense of unease before a condition that is unspeakably sad.[30]

The word "grotesque" or "grotesco" comes from the Italian "grotta" or "gruta" deriving in turn from the Latin "crypta" referring to a subterranean vault. Its first use to describe an artistic movement was towards the end of the fifteenth century, when excavations in different parts of Italy revealed an ancient form of ornamental painting. Vasari, the sixteenth-century Italian painter and architect, described the paintings in the following way: "The 'grotesscos' are ridiculous, licentious paintings the ancients used to adorn holes or hollows where nothing else would do. Represented in them are all manner of monsters that, whether due to natural caprice or the fantasy that such artifice engendered, are outside of any of the rules of representation." In Spanish the word *grotesco* has resonances of the ridiculous, the extravagant, and the comic, in addition to its ultimate derivation of a subterranean cosmos, an interiority as represented by a cavern.[31]

According to Kaiser-Lenoir, the *grotesco* finds its theatrical antecedents in elements of the *commedia dell'arte*, with its use of masks and its emphasis upon comedy, satire, and caricature, the *Sturm und Drang*, and in Victor Hugo's romanticism (as laid out in his preface to *Cromwell*), which, in its aspiration towards the sublime must divest itself of the inhuman, deformed, and monstrous world of nocturnal fantasy. The closest parallel to the *grotesco* in European theatrical tradition is to be found in aspects of Pirandello's work, with its emphasis upon the true depiction of the self; and in the aesthetic deformation of Valle-Inclán's *esperpento* world. While Pirandello's naked masks and Valle-Inclán's concave mirror both, in very different formal ways, tend towards a conflation of the external and internal worlds of the human being, the *grotesco criollo* embraces that dichotomy. The grotesque nature of its characters is the result of the constant battle between their interior beings and the external world that denies their existence.[32] The best examples of the form can be found in the work of Francisco Defilippis Novoa and Armando Discépolo.

DEFILIPPIS NOVOA

Like his contemporary Florencio Sánchez, Defilippis Novoa (1889–1930) began writing as a journalist with libertarian ideals. Unlike Sánchez, whose theatre is informed by a mixture of a desire for anarchistic community and a belief in progress derived from Comtian positivism both applied towards building an Argentinian national theatre, Defilippis Novoa's theatre is informed by a deeply Christian sensibility (prefiguring in many ways contemporary liberation theology) and a discovery of expressionism. Where Sánchez' models were Ibsen, Becque, and Zola, Defilippis read Kaiser, Toller, and Sternheim.[33] As we have seen with Sánchez' dramaturgy, these writers did not simply imitate European techniques and trends. Their plays reflect, on the one hand, the specifically Argentinian conflict between city and country and, on the other hand, the complex immigrant culture of Buenos Aires. Defilippis Novoa's own peculiar vision of this densely packed together humanity can be seen in his two most important works, *María la tonta* (1927) and *He visto a Dios* (1930).

María la tonta (María the idiot) is a *via crucis* in a prologue, four acts, and six scenes, leading to the thematic statement: Love. To love one's fellow human being is the only path to salvation. In the manner of the German expressionists, the work is presented in a series of scenes containing strong biblical symbolism and allusion, characterized by a tone of ironic comment. We follow María la tonta and an old woman through their painful existence upon the earth. María is revealed to be, or possess within her, the Virgin Mary, and the old woman is revealed to be, or possess within her, Mary Magdalene. At the beginning of the play María gives birth to a still-born child. When she refuses to leave the hospital without her child, she is tricked into taking a bundle of rags with her in its place. Later she kills a man who threatens the "child."

We follow the women through numerous stations of the cross such as: "The Stable in Bethlehem"/The jail where María gives birth; "the three Kings"/The hospital where she is given the rag doll; "Herodes"/The street where she kills; "Via crucis"/An interlude in which she is led away a prisoner as our conscience speaks to us;

"Pilate's Judgment"/The sanatorium where police, journalists, doctors, the Church, and the judiciary combine to pass judgment on the women; and the culminating scene called "The Ascension", in which Christ descends from the cross and joins the two Marys to plead for the human race before God. While the play lacks the dynamism of the German expressionists, it more than compensates for that lack by a pervasive feeling of both mystery and anguish somewhat akin to that found in San Juan de la Cruz' poetry. Defilippis Novoa's central theme here is clear: Love equals fraternity, justice, and happiness. If the world fails to heed this message it will meet with destruction.

What distinguishes Defilippis Novoa from the early evangelical theatre is his central thematic insistence upon equality. That insistence also links him directly to contemporary liberation theatre and liberation theology. The evangelical theatre sought to impose Christianity through Pedro de Gante's bullying and baptism by mass aspersion. Franciscan millenarianism led to mass conversion. If that conversion was initially superficial, it was felt that proper guidance and teaching (as provided by the Franciscans themselves) would bring about a more profound understanding. This relationship is one in which the mendicant possesses the truth and doles it out by degrees to the childlike indigenous population. In contrast, contemporary liberation theology departs from the fundamental belief that all interpreters, not only the clergy, are capable of discerning biblical truth as it relates to their own lives. Christian base communities, therefore, work upon the basis of consensus not command. Liberation theatre is created in a similar fashion. It departs from a fundamental belief that no single participant's point of view is uniquely privileged in the theatrical exchange. The input of all participants, whether audience member, actor, or playwright, is equally valid and the performance is not dictated by a single perspective, but created through the consensus of the various points of view. Where Defilippis Novoa's message of love is a clarion call, a warning to his audience to avoid destruction, the liberation theatre attempts to construct models for a new society within its own methods of production.

Defilippis Novoa's other important work is a fascinating play called *He visto a Dios* (I have seen God). The playwright subtitles it a "modern mystery," seeming to consider it an expressionist work. Luis Ordaz, however, characterizes the play as a fundamental work in the development of the *grotesco criollo*. That seems more apt, since the play is much more concerned with character development – utilizing some expressionist elements to that end – than it is with the broad thematic strokes designed to convey certain ideas in expressionism.

The central character is an avaricious Italian pawnbroker named Carmelo Salandra, who lives in Buenos Aires. Utterly devoted to his son Chico, Carmelo is cruel to everyone else, cheating them or treating them disdainfully. When Chico, a good for nothing who lives off his father's largesse, is killed under mysterious circumstances, Carmelo cracks. Drunk one night, he mistakes his assistant Victorio for a vision of God. Victorio takes advantage of the happy coincidence gradually to fleece Carmelo of his money. When Chico's former girlfriend Nuncia, whom he had impregnated and abandoned, and her father Gateano attempt to cash in as well, Carmelo's tenant, the Bible Seller, destroys their game.

The Bible Seller is a mysterious figure who rents a corner of a room from Carmelo and bears a marked resemblance to Christ. He is the only person, other than Chico, in whom Carmelo ever shows any real interest. When the Bible Seller unmasks Victorio, Carmelo is nearly destroyed by the loss of his God. The Bible Seller nurses him back to health, whereupon he forgives his deceivers and gives his business to Victorio and Gateano. Counseling Nuncia to rear her child lovingly, Carmelo then departs to look for God on his own, to see him in his own heart.

Technically, the play utilizes the large shadows and broad angles of expressionist scenography, and the deformed characterizations and language of a Valle-Inclán *esperpento*. There are a number of scenes that could be quite powerful visually, especially the mirror images of Chico's dead body lying on the floor and Victorio's live body lying unmasked in the same position. Thematically, the play continues Defilippis Novoa's central concern with love as a motivating force in the world, converting Christian forgiveness into an internal, personal forgiveness. While Victorio and Gateano begin to fight over the spoils that Carmelo has given them, Carmelo undergoes an internal struggle with his own nature: the cruel, avaricious man society has made of him. Carmelo discards his deformed self, forgiving his son, Nuncia, and the world by forgiving himself. The entire experience has given him the strength not to need an external God in order to survive.

Dickens created a new kind of novel that, both formally and

thematically, was part of the city's emergence as the dominant social form in nineteenth-century Britain. As Raymond Williams has pointed out,

This way of seeing connects with his moral naming of characters: Gradgrind, McChoakumchild, Merdle. But it connects also in a less obvious way with a kind of observation which again belongs to the city; a perception, one might say, that the most evident inhabitants of cities are buildings, and that there is at once a connection and a confusion between the shapes and appearances of buildings and the real shapes and appearances of the people who live in them.[34]

In a similar fashion there is a strong suggestion throughout *He visto a Dios* that everything outside this dark little corner of the world is threatening. The city impinges upon the lives of the new immigrant class and, unless they take some action, take some sort of control over their existence, it will deform them into a reflection of the dark structures they inhabit.

ARMANDO DISCÉPOLO

The characters of Armando Discépolo (1887–1971) inhabit this world as well but, while Defilippis Novoa uses his individuals to reach for a universal vision of the world, Discépolo's dramaturgy is located in an investigation of the problems and ambience of the immigrant class. For this reason Discépolo's work is the height of the *grotesco criollo*. Defilippis Novoa and Discépolo wrote at nearly the same time and shared the passion for anarchist thought and Christian generosity that seems to have been the intellectual currency of the times. Where Defilippis Novoa was profoundly influenced by the German expressionists, Discépolo began his career as an avid reader of Dostoevsky, Andreyev, and Tolstoy, later becoming Argentina's foremost director of Pirandello's works. His own plays are quintessential *grotesco criollo* utilizing external character masks as the burlesque manifestations of internal anguish. The two plays of his that best reflect this are *Mateo* (1923) and *Stéfano* (1928).

Mateo tells the sad tale of Miguel, the driver of a horse-drawn hansom cab who finds himself in dire economic straits due to the advent of the automobile. In order to pay off his debts he borrows money from an undertaker named Severino. When Severino refuses Miguel's latest loan request and demands immediate repayment of all the previous loans, Miguel is forced to use his horse and cab for a robbery – a sideline that Severino also "undertakes". As they are about to make their getaway an automobile horn frightens Mateo, the horse, who refuses to move. A mad chase ensues in which horse and cab are overturned and Miguel escapes long enough to present Severino with the ruin of his loanshark and robbery enterprises.

The grotesque elements reach their peak in the play's final scene, when Miguel tells Severino the news while beating him with a wooden shoe and destroying his clothing. At the scene's end the police pound at the door and arms yank Miguel from the stage. The grotesque is also evident in the behavior of Miguel's sons. One of them, in training to become a boxer, does nothing but exercise throughout the entire play. The other comes home in a chauffeur's uniform as Miguel is fleeing the scene of the crime, driving the last nail into Miguel's coffin by adopting the profession that has pushed him to his ruin. The play's title is also significant, for by titling the play with the horse's name – a character who never appears onstage – Discépolo juxtaposes the loyal animal's many years of loyal service to the mechanistic, corrupt world Severino and the automobile represent. That world enters and runs roughshod over Miguel's life, destroying all the values that Mateo as character, friend, and provider represents. In the final scene, as is so characteristic of the *grotesco criollo*, Miguel lashes out, reasserting his humanity by destroying Severino.

In *Stéfano* Discépolo presents us with a more technically mature example of the *grotesco criollo*. The title character was once a prize-winning composer whose parents sacrificed themselves in order to pay for his education. Never having completed his great opera, he is now a broken, middle-aged man employed as a trombone player in a municipal orchestra. During the course of the play Stéfano, unable to hear his part anymore, loses his job with the orchestra and his disciple is hired in his place. The loss of his job is the catalyst for the gradual revelation of the suffering that cuts through his entire family. Its victims are his parents, his wife, his children, and, most of all, himself. The play's epilogue is a masterly episode scored like a small symphony. In it Stéfano's son Ernesto repeats the exact words about ideals and art that Stéfano spoke to his parents at the same age, while Stéfano plays an imaginary violin. Then, in the midst of mutual recriminations, Stéfano sits down to write a poem (Ernesto is a poet) while his younger son, Radamanés (who constantly dreams of and plays at being some sort of savior such as a fireman) sits on his couch-

bed crying "I'm dreaming! I'm dreaming!" In response Stéfano falls
to his knees calling to Esteban "Sing. All this pain for a single verse.
Is life worth so little?" and then begins to bray like a goat.

The grotesque elements here again come not so much from
external causes as from the internal deformations of character that
manifest themselves in external characteristics coupled with the
almost expressionistic settings. Costumes, make-up, set elements, and
character traits are constantly exaggerated, underscoring the internal
contortions of the main character, who must reach a point of
complete desperation, suffer a complete stripping away of all of his
defenses, before he can see. The biblical imagery Discépolo uses, such
as Radamanés' claim that he should have been named Salvador
(Savior), and his continual apocalyptic dreams of things falling apart
and invading insects he must fight are hardly accidental. But when
coupled with Stéfano's increasingly animalistic behavior, their
resonance is not so much of the scriptures – although they certainly
refer to them with the final scene a parody of the lamb led to
slaughter – as to psychological torment that becomes physically
palpable. Stéfano's degeneration is both comic and horrorific as we
laugh at his absurd behavior and feel his pain.

The *grotesco criollo* speaks to a new kind of audience in Latin
America. Its concerns are distinct from those of the *género chico* or the
circus audience because the Argentine social structure itself has
changed. The tremendous surge of immigration, rapid industrialization, the accumulation of wealth and the creation of new forms of
economic disparity in the urban setting; all lead to the creation of
new characters, themes, situations, and forms of expression in the
Argentine theatre. While the means of expression have changed,
however, the social position of a Miguel or a Stéfano in the new social
order is quite similar to that of a Don Zoilo or a Juan Moreira in the
old social order. Society treats all of these characters not as human
beings but as elements to be exploited. Excluded from active
participation in social and political life they find themselves lacking
a firm identity and, unable to find a rational alternative to their
increasing sense of marginality, they cry out in pain.

The Latin American theatre that has been traced in these pages
has from the outset been an instrument of opposition to existing
authority and the social order it represented. The *grotesco criollo*, in its
presentation of the violent contradiction between the moral precepts
of the social order and the profound crisis of personal identity that

order caused, presents a dialectic critique of the existing system and is part of the oppositional line that has been traced here. It was the theatrical product of the progression from the optimism of the mid-nineteenth century, as embodied in the governmental policy encouraging immigration, to the beginning of the twentieth century, when that great social experiment foundered beneath the weight of its own contradictions. The end of that progression finds its major symbol in the Argentinian context in 1919 in the events of the *semana trágica*, in which hundreds of metal workers were massacred. The beginning of the twentieth century was to see the theatre being used as a means of popular political expression throughout the region. As such it was part of a long tradition of Latin American popular theatre reflecting and helping to reform the social reality.

CHAPTER 4

Religion, politics, and theatre: the twentieth century and the return of ritual

The beginning of the twentieth century in Latin America brought with it not only new theatrical forms such as the *grotesco criollo*, but also a return to a mixture of politics, religion, and theatre more akin to that present after the Conquest. Theatre was seen as a catalyst for change in the existing societal order. This was most evident in Mexico, where the Mexican Revolution greatly affected the form and content of the theatre, and the course of Mexican education in the early twentieth century. The repercussions of Cortés' greeting to the twelve Franciscans at Tenochtitlán continued to reverberate throughout Mexico several hundred years after the Conquest.

Cortés had arranged for the mendicant presence in order to cement his political position both in the New World and at home in Spain. Alliance with the Franciscans would not only keep the Indians in check, but would also provide a spiritual and theological basis for controlling the worldly aspirations of the Spanish colonists, the royal officials, and the Court of Spain. The Twelve accomplished their task so well that, due to the *patronato* system, the Mexican Church was effectively integrated with the colonial government and, even after independence, its financial and political reach remained strong. The Church's political machinations greatly reduced its moral credibility in the eyes of those nominal Catholics who supported nineteenth-century liberal movements and, as we shall see, led to the violent anticlericalism of the Mexican Revolution and the subsequent Cristero rebellion.

The Franciscans' highly successful combination of Christian symbolism with Aztec spectacle as an armament in their evangelical arsenal after the Conquest meant that Christian influence, whether welcomed or battled against, has been a nearly universal presence in Mexico ever since. During the Conquest and the War of Independence images of the Virgins of Guadalupe and the Remedies were

94

carried into battle by both sides and were frequently awarded
military degrees after successful campaigns. The Mexican Father
Miguel Hidalgo y Costilla started the fight for independence at his
church in Dolores, Guanajuato, with the cry "Long live the Virgin of
Guadalupe and death to bad government!" The Royalist army
carried banners with the image of the Virgen de los Remedios, which
had been brought with the Spaniards to Mexico during the Conquest.
Both Virgins attained the rank of general during the War of
Independence.

When either side got a banner away from the other with the "enemy"
Virgin on it, it was shot like a traitor. During the ten years of fighting, the
people did not dare to have an image of the Virgin of Guadalupe in a niche
outside for fear of being shot by the Royalists. But after the Insurgents won,
their Virgin had more influence than ever. Now her image is seen
everywhere – in churches, chapels, in niches on bridges and houses, even on
liquor bottles; it is reproduced in paint, stone, metal, glass.[1]

The summary executions of religious symbols bears a marked
resemblance to the ritual "Flowery Wars" engaged in by the Aztecs
to propitiate the Sun god, and that were appropriated by the
Franciscans in such mass theatrical spectacles as the *La conquista de
Jerusalén* for evangelical purposes.

While a combination of religious and military activity was a part
of Mexican history throughout the first quarter of the twentieth
century, religious spectacle of a theatrical nature persists to the
present day in villages scattered throughout Mexico and the
southwestern part of the United States that was once Mexican
territory. These are plays of a religious character performed by
villagers with no formal training who enact and improvise from a
predetermined scenario. Such scenarios tend to fall into four different
types: portrayals of biblical stories from both the Old and New
Testaments; dance-dramas (the most famous of which is probably
the *Dance of the Moors and the Christians*); reenactments of the
Crucifixion of Christ; and those plays that depict religious events in
the New World such as the miraculous appearance of the Virgin of
Guadalupe.[2] Of all of these types the Nativity and the Passion plays
were the most popular. Barker describes the common Nativity play as
follows:

In addition to their common theme of the pilgrimage of the shepherds to
Bethlehem, most of these plays have one or more episodes in which the Devil

attempts to break up the procession. In most of them, also, it is the Archangel Michael who finally vanquishes Lucifer and leads the shepherds safely to the Holy Manger. Although the plays vary in their recital of the events connected with the Nativity, almost all of them end with the adoration scene in which the shepherds present their humble gifts to the Christ child.

Similarity of plot in many of the Shepherds' plays is paralleled by similarity of characters and lines. Besides the Devil and St. Michael, many of the plays feature a hermit, not too holy to be tempted, a gluttonous shepherd named Bato, and his coquettish wife, Gila, and a lazy and crusty old shepherd named Bartolo, who provides comic relief. The various episodes of the plays are introduced by quatrains sung by the *letra*, or chorus; the passage of time between episodes is indicated by the singing of the *caminatas*, or marching songs.[3]

In terms of the continuity of indigenous practice mixed with Christian forms, perhaps the most interesting of these religious dramas is the Passion play called *Las tres caídas de Jesucristo* (Jesus Christ's three falls) as performed in Ixtapalapa, DF, Mexico. For the most part it is a fairly straightforward dramatization of the Passion beginning with Caiaphas and Herod's decision that Jesus' death is the only way to remove the threat to their rule, and ending with the Crucifixion and Resurrection of Christ. Unlike some of the other folk dramas, this play is not a scenario, but a fully fledged script. While the opening scenes are heavily expository and static, the dynamism of the events that it chronicles and the inherent conflict they contain gradually create dramatic interest. The day after the play's performance is completed, Saturday of Holy Week, the Ascension is depicted in the San Lucas parish church by the simple recourse of raising Christ's image, superimposed over some white and gold cardboard clouds, above the altar in such a way that the strings that support it cannot be seen.

The most interesting aspect of this play, however, is the way in which the person portraying the part of Jesus is required to go into seclusion thirty days before Holy Thursday, when the play begins. During that time the actor is to "dedicate himself to the practice of spiritual exercises, which will serve to prepare him, and to contemplate deeply, with all proper spiritual absorption and respect, the role he is about to play." The actors who portray the two thieves, Dimas and Gesta, are also kept in seclusion, but only for the fifteen days prior to Holy Thursday. During this time period all three actors received simple, Spartan meals.[4] This ritual purification of the three actors is reminiscent of the ritual purification of the actor portraying the role of Quetzalcoátl in the annual Aztec festival for Quetzalcoátl.[5] While *Las tres caídas de Jesucristo* presents us with nothing approaching the conflation of the matrix of actor/character/audience present in the Aztec festival – the actors playing Jesus Christ and the two thieves are not actually crucified – there is an association of the actor with the character portrayed. In order to portray that character the actor must be set apart so that he can attain a purified state that is distinct from that experienced in daily life. The play already deals with material from the holy scriptures, and by introducing the purification ritual it becomes a sacred rite. What we are seeing here is the end result of the early evangelical theatre after it had retained the spectacular and transformational aspects of ritual performance and had wedded them to Christian theological and political concerns. The sacrificial aspects of the ritual have been removed but the performance still carries a transformational character. As in the Aztec festival of Quetzalcoátl, the ultimate purpose of *Las tres caídas de Jesucristo* is convergence of the community in worshiping the god.

Similar in conception and execution to *Las tres caídas de Jesucristo* is the version of the Passion performed annually at Milpa Alta, DF. The Milpa Alta play dramatizes the events of the Passion as well, the differences being the inclusion of scenes within the church itself (rather than completely at sites in the open air scattered about the village), the frequent interpolations of various sermons appropriate to the scene being played, and the substitution of an image of Christ for the actor/priest playing the role at a certain point in the story. The text itself seems less dramatic and, as the interpolations of sermons demonstrates, more didactic than other Passion plays. There are also numerous times when Falvio, servant to Pilate sent to observe the events, speaks directly to the audience in anachronistic passages from the later scriptures describing what will happen to those who denied the Messiah at the time.[6]

This play presents us with a further step in the evolution of Mexican ritual performance. Here the actor portraying Christ is an actual priest, supposedly virtuous enough to dispense with purifying rites, but even the priest is seen as an inadequate substitute for the god, who is more fully represented by his iconographic image. The evolution from the sacrificial offering of the actor/god Quetzalcoátl to the highly symbolic crucifixion of an iconographic representation of Christ demonstrates that ritual performance, in this instance at least, has moved further and further away from a direct impact upon the actors involved and reached the level of abstract theological representation.

While folk performances of religious dramas dealing with biblical subjects can contain, as has been seen, elements of indigenous forms and presentation, the majority of them seem to have more in common with medieval European cycle plays. As in the medieval drama, content is drawn from the scriptures and even the interpolation of comic characters appears to have come about in a similar fashion. There is another Mexican theatrical presentation, however, that seems closer to both the indigenous spectacle and carries the potential for the evangelical purposes of a colonial offering such as *La conquista de Jerusalén*. This is the so-called "theatre of masses" that took the methods of religious folk drama and tried to reorient them towards an understanding of Mexican history and the possibilities for progress informed by the goals and ideals of the Mexican Revolution.

TEATRO DE MASAS

Official governmental interest in the *teatro de masas* was the natural outcome of the Mexican government's approach to education after the Revolution. At the beginning of the twentieth century more than 70 percent of the Mexican population was illiterate and the majority of schools were run by the Church, which was frequently more interested in religious instruction than comprehensive education. The Porifio Díaz dictatorship, itself more interested in the economic and political strength of the nation than its schools, did little to challenge the Church's hegemony over education. Allowing the Church free reign in educational matters was, in fact, a relatively painless way for Díaz to ensure Church support in other areas.

The Mexican Revolution permanently changed governmental attitudes towards education. The 1917 Constitution guaranteed the right to a free primary education and, in 1920, President Alvaro Obregón named José Vasconcelos, an idealist with a messianic approach to education, Secretary of Public Education. Obregón's successor, Plutarco Elías Calles, a former schoolteacher, proclaimed the institution of universal public education. Calles' "socialist" schools were bitterly fought by the Church and the Cristero rebels, who often left public schools bathed in their teachers' blood. The populist presidency of Lázaro Cárdenas extended the reach of public education by requiring each industrial and agricultural firm in the nation to maintain a school for its workers' children. This edict increased the number of public schools to 1,500, all under the control of the Secretary of Public Education.

There was a backlash against this secular system of public education in 1940 when President Manuel Avila Camacho appointed Octavio Véjar Vázquez as Minister of Public Education. Vázquez not only overturned previous governmental decrees that forbade religious instruction in public schools, but he maintained that all education must be based upon religious principles. The pendulum swung back to a point between the two extremes in 1944 when the new Minister of Public Education, Jaime Torres Bodet, conciliated both sides by proposing to concentrate on eliminating illiteracy and on teacher training.[7]

In 1921 the Secretary of Agriculture and Economic Development authorized the construction of a regional open-air theatre by Rafael M. Saavedra in San Juan Teotihuacán.[8] Using the traditional religious dramas as a springboard, Saavedra produced plays that were a combination of didactic scenes and popular diversions.[9] The works presented included "a choreographic representation of native industries, a rhythmic pantomime of daily tasks in saddlery and blacksmithing" and a "mime about the life of slavery lived by the Indians on the cane plantations in the State of Morelos." Saavedra himself described the latter work as follows:

Humbly dressed, their faces soiled, tired, a little drunk, the cane workers leave for work accompanied by their wives, driven by the foreman who, pistol at his belt, whip in hand, keeps an eye on them and flogs them, threatening them with the loss of their salaries if they do not work harder. This is followed by a series of evolutions full of color and scenic power, depicting the work done on the plantations until the foreman touches a wreath and takes a doll made out of corn paste – that symbolizes food – in his arms, and presents it to the dancers, who fall to their knees around him.[10]

Saavedra's theatre was soon taken over by the Secretary of Education and was abandoned when Saavedra himself moved on to other interests; but he had provided the model for the mass spectacles to come.[11]

In 1929 a gigantic open-air theatre with 9,000 seats was constructed at the Centro Social Deportivo para Trabajadores "Venustiano Carranza." One of the first pieces performed in this theatre was *Liberación* (Liberation) by Efrén Orozco Rosales (1903–1973).

Orozco Rosales has said that his greatest concern in writing the play was "to make the Mexican people more conscious of their great tradition so that they would be able to identify themselves with that which was theirs and feel proud of the fact that they were Mexicans."[12] *Liberación* is nothing more nor less than a dramatization of Mexican history from the founding of Mexico City to the early twentieth century. The piece calls for a cast of 1,235 people, who perform against a "schematic representation of the Valley of Mexico."[13] Largely a hieratic display with the occasional interpolation of phrases spoken in unison by the gigantic cast, *Liberación* attempts to focus on the most important moments of Mexican history. In its progression from the Conquest to the Cacicazgo (the period after French intervention was ended, when urban aristocrats and rural caciques, with clerical and military support, took advantage of the confused political situation to steal land and increase their economic and political power) the play presents the events leading up to the Mexican Revolution and Mexico's final liberation. In its use of spectacle, battles, and music *Liberación* resembles the mendicant evangelical theatre. While Orozco Rosales' play does not end with a mass conversion through baptism, as does *La conquista de Jerusalén*, the triumph of the Revolution is presented as a secular form of salvation for the Mexican people. This salvation is the result of a reorganization of society in which the meek and the humble are vindicated for all their years of suffering and afforded proper respect for the contribution to society. That reorganization is the direct result of the *mestizaje* (mixture) that has characterized Mexican history. The mixture of Spanish and indigenous bloodlines translates into the mixture of various classes necessary to create the revolutionary society. *Liberación* seeks to demonstrate the vitality of this new Latin American society and, in a symbolic display containing numerous ceremonial aspects similar to the Catholic mass, to confirm the Revolution's viability in the eyes of the faithful.

Orozco Rosales wrote a series of these plays for the *teatro de masas*, including *Tierra y libertad* (Land and liberty; 1933), a gigantic pantomime about the Mexican Revolution that presents the innovation of short dialogs made possible by hidden microphones, *Creación del Quinto Sol* (Creation of the Fifth Sun) and *Sacrificio gladitorio* (Gladitorial sacrifice), written in conjunction with Carlos González and first performed for the Twentieth Lions Club Convention in 1935. *Creación del Quinto Sol* depicts the sacrifice of the Aztec gods

Tecusitecatl and Nanaoatzin, who threw themselves into fire, creating a new sun and moon in order to save the world from darkness. *Sacrificio gladitorio* presents a dramatization of the Aztec custom of permitting their prisoners to engage in single combat with their warriors. In this case the prisoner wins and is given the hand of one of the Court ladies. The whole performance ends with a lavishly costumed display of various aspects of Aztec life and requires 3,000 actors in all for the three sections.[14]

The only one of these plays besides *Liberación* that I have been able to locate is Orozco Rosales' work, *El mensajero del sol* (Messenger to the sun), presented in 1941 in honor of the Second Inter-American Travel Congress and the Fourth Pan-American Highway Congress. It was another massive open-air performance requiring 1,400 participants and depicts the annual Aztec ceremony in which a "Messenger to the sun" was sacrificed in order to maintain the sun's light and heat. Against the shadow of war in Europe Rafael Molina Betancourt, Secretary General of the Organizing Committee of the Inter-American Travel Congress, introduced the story of *El mensajero del sol* as one that demonstrates "the ideal of a new and better humanity, [which] will be summed up in just one phrase, which transcends our emotions: 'Save America!'"[15]

Each one of these plays rejects colonially imposed history and resuscitates Aztec nobility of spirit as the foundation upon which the nation's new life after the Revolution should be based. Where the folk-religious drama moves closer to the forms imposed upon indigenous ritual practice by the evangelical Church, the *teatro de masas* recaptures the indigenous rituals themselves, utilizing them as a moral foundation for the new regime. At the same time, however, these plays put forth the notion that the people must be guided by the revolutionary government. The paternal authority of the Church is replaced by that of the regime and the attitude towards its people exhibited by the PRI (Institutional Revolutionary Party) in Mexico to this day is already in place.

While the series of works described present the peculiar spectacle of supposedly consciousness-raising works for the Mexican populace being patronized by international business and trade organizations, in the 1940s the Mexican government determined that this sort of spectacle could have educational benefits, and the Department of Public Education began to produce performances of its own. In 1944 it produced an Orozco Rosales piece called *La bandera nacional* (The national flag), which utilized close to 4,000 actors and told the history of the national flag. In 1945 the Department produced a piece called *Siembra* (Sowing time) written by Orozco Rosales in collaboration with Waldeen and Julio Prieto. The play attacks illiteracy, showing the illiterate as dominated by personifications of evils such as poverty, hunger, alcoholism, witchcraft, and general misery. The school-teachers in the play fight to free the people from these tyrannical oppressors by planting the "seed" of learning.

Where the mendicants saw themselves as tilling the land in the New World in order to prepare the soil for salvation, Mexican history presents a picture of the revolutionary government approaching education with apostolic fervor. The mendicants' millenarianism led them to practice certain theatre forms designed to support mass conversion and to undermine Aztec authority. The twentieth-century Mexican government also saw itself as living on the cusp of a new millennium. Where the mendicants insisted upon the salvific powers of Christianity, the Revolutionary government preached a secular gospel that had to be followed to attain a state of grace. Both brands of millenarianism found it necessary to convert masses of people to avoid apocalypse, and in both cases those masses of people were of indigenous descent. The "language of gestures" Cortés and the mendicants had employed during the Conquest as a means of subduing and converting the indigenous population finds its parallel in the "language of gestures" employed by the revolutionary government to effect its educational goals. Nearly 400 years of European presence in Mexico, however, meant that certain gestures were now well understood. Communication was based upon new relationships and was of a different order. While the Franciscans did witness the gradual dismantling of their powerful position in the New World, they never were present at the final apocalypse they had predicted. With its educational policies, however, the revolutionary government unleashed its own battle of Armageddon. That battle was once again the reflection of the ever present tension between city and country in Latin America, and its fields of combat were the schools, the Cristero Rebellion, and the theatre. To comprehend this conflict it is necessary to understand the crucial role played by one man mentioned in this brief summary of Mexican educational history, José Vasconcelos.

VASCONCELOS AND THE CULTURAL MISSION PROGRAM

Obregón's appointment of the philosopher–educator José Vasconcelos to the post of Secretary of Public Education completely transformed the face of Mexican education. Vasconcelos approached his new role with apostolic fervor and missionary zeal. His role, he said, was to "preach the gospel of the mestizo by trying to impress on the minds of the new race a consciousness of their mission as builders of entirely new concepts of life."[16] He saw his duty as "saving the children, educating the youth, and redeeming the Indians" by sending them "teachers who would imitate the action of the Catholic missionaries of the colonies, sent among the Indians, who did not, as yet, know the Spanish language."[17] In order to carry out this ambitious task, Vasconcelos fostered the creation of the Cultural Mission Program, which led to the notion that every school was a "House of the People." In all of this, as had been the case with the colonial missionaries, theatre played a large role.

While Vasconcelos exhorted his teachers to carry out a "holy crusade for civilization," and preached "that the intellectual [must] cleanse himself of his pride, learning the hard, simple life of the men of the people," these missionaries brought not Christian doctrine, but the doctrine of Social Revolution.

With Vasconcelos the revolutionary byword became "to educate is to redeem" – not from sin, but from ignorance, not to rewards in the hereafter, but to sanitation and to a better and more fruitful earthly life. This was what the new secular religion promised. Its emphasis, despite its religious trappings, was of this world. It was material; it offered here-and-now happiness.[18]

During the Revolution two battle cries were heard on the lips of the revolutionary forces. The first was "Tierra y Libertad" (Land and Liberty) and referred to the desperate need for land reform that persists throughout Latin America today. The second battle cry was "Tierra y Escuelas" (Land and Schools), and its demand of education for all reached into the remotest regions of Mexican territory. When the Mexican Revolution came to an end in 1920, however, there were few rural schools and the only teachers' training colleges were completely oriented towards education in an urban environment. The Cultural Mission Program was founded both to select and to train rural teachers, and to devise a curriculum suitable to the rural environment.

The first Cultural Mission was formed in 1923 and included six teachers in the fields of rural education, soap making and perfumery, tanning, agriculture, music, and physical education and nursing. While the overall composition of the mission teams changed over time the arts, and theatre in particular, remained an integral part of everything they did. The first six missionaries were to travel to the rural Indian communities, live with them long enough to be able to report upon their educational and cultural conditions, and then propose methods of training and school organization.[19]

The missioners [*sic*] were, at one and the same time, teachers, supervisors, administrators, research workers, and philosophers. They were sent into the field to promote a cultural revolution, but the only financial support they received was in the form of their salaries... the objectives were the economic rehabilitation and cultural advancement of the rural populations. To accomplish these objectives rural schools were organized as community centers to work with adults as well as children. During the day and the regular term the schools worked with children, but in the evenings and during vacations classes and programs were held with adults. In this way the Mexican rural school accepted a social mission and became known as the "house of the people."[20]

The Cultural Missions aimed to improve the economic well-being, health and sanitation, homes, nutrition, and cultural conditions of the rural communities. This task was accomplished, however, not by imposing solutions brought by the *misioneros*, but by stimulating the people themselves to take action and utilize their own intelligence and resources. The *misioneros* were the facilitators, not the dictators of action. Unlike the mendicants who utilized indigenous forms primarily for the parallels that could be drawn between them and those of Christianity, replacing Aztec authority with Christian authority, the *misioneros* encouraged the population to discover ways in which their own daily practices could provide solutions to the problems they confronted.

One of the most effective educational tools utilized by the *misioneros* was the theatre. In 1930 a *misionero* conceived the idea of using theatre to educate the people in his village about the danger of the alcoholism that was widespread in the community. He wrote a one-act play and, together with his students, constructed a small open-air theatre. Building the theatre and rehearsing the play proved to be so successful in terms of providing the participants with recreational opportunities other than the local bars that the idea of theatre as a force for social change spread rapidly throughout the country. In the next two years 3,500 to 4,000 open-air theatres were built in rural communities. Many of these theatres used a wall of the village church to form the back of the stage.[21]

Whether consciously or not, these revolutionary missionaries were repeating many of the same methods used by the evangelical theatre after the Conquest. As has been discussed in an earlier chapter, the Church in the New World created the new architectural form of the "capilla abierta" or "open chapel." The open chapel gave out onto a large courtyard (*atrio*), modeled upon that of the Aztec temples, and provided an ideal setting for a theatre audience.[22] The Catholic missionaries, at first lacking the ability to converse with the indigenous population in their native tongue, employed theatrical technique and the preexisting artistic ability of the Indian population to convert that population to Christianity. Hundreds of years later the *misioneros*, lacking conventional educational resources in rural communities, frequently confronted by a population that spoke no Spanish, seized upon the artistic ability of the descendants of the colonial Indian population as a means of converting that population to the social doctrine of the new revolutionary government.

While the methods the *misioneros* used were nearly identical to those of their religious forebears, the *misioneros* taught a totally secular doctrine that focused upon temporal, not spiritual, well-being. Cook relates a conversation with the chief of one Cultural Mission in which he describes the content of the type of plays performed.

I've just finished writing a play that will be performed the day the open-air theatre is inaugurated. It's called: *If you're not rich at 30, at 40 you're an ass.* We've performed two other plays already: *Land and Schools* and *What the teachers do*. From the play's title you can see that it deals with presenting the social work that the teachers perform. I took the theme from the life of this very community, its customs, its ideals, its language and even its social and moral flaws, in order to give a rich lesson on stage, one that will reach the people's heart. The rural teachers will be the actors, along with some of the people from the village.[23]

M. Concepción Becerra de Celis (1906–1973), in her book *Teatro y poemas infantiles*, gathers together fourteen pieces dealing with social injustice and the steps the Revolutionary government is taking to rectify it. Her short, heavily didactic plays present such subjects as an investigation of "landlordism," a paean to May Day, and a dramatization of Lázaro Cárdenas' speech announcing the nationalization of the oil fields. In her introduction Becerra Celis writes:

> Let us create class consciousness in our theatre. Let us present works that discomfit and move, let us present themes that show the equality that will be found in the life of the future.
>
> This is a revolutionary task that the teacher must carry out ... We have to educate our children to do and to speak. Social struggles call for articulate and convincing men.
>
> Many of our workers wanted to speak, to explain what they felt at assemblies or demonstrations, but a strange complex, the result of their unpreparedness, prevented them from doing so.
>
> So let us properly prepare our children by converting dramatization into a scholastic means of artistic expression.[24]

In 1938 Armando List Arzubide (dates unknown) published a series of brief, didactic plays designed to teach Mexican history from the revolutionary perspective. One of these plays, *Visión de México* (Mexican vision), is described by List Arzubide as an "attempt at theatre for the masses." He comments that "The entire reconstructive vigor of this theatre is based on the value of the gesture, on attitude, and on the scenic whole." In effect, the piece is a gigantic pantomime of recent Mexican history involving large crowd scenes and an Invisible Voice that narrates the gestural action. The play takes us from Porfirio Díaz' dictatorship in 1907, through the beginnings of labor militancy, the military campaigns of Práxedis Guerrero, the Flores Magón brothers, Madero, and Zapata; Madero's assassination by Huerta; and the final joining together of workers, peasants, and soldiers against Huerta's treachery to safeguard the revolution. Comparable in its processional and symbolic character to the evangelical drama, List Arzubide's play presents the figure of the wounded labor organizer Lucrecia Toriz, who periodically crosses the stage carrying the workers' flag like the French symbol of Liberty. In a procedure reminiscent of the Inca ceremony of purification Zapata and Huerta's troops both make salutations to the front, right, and left upon entering before unveiling their respective plans of Ayala and San Luis. Due to its primary reliance on symbolic gesture and pantomime rather than dialogic exposition, *Visión México* is quite effective in conveying the sweep of Mexican history in a highly theatrical manner.

Alongside the presentation of didactic dramas of this type based upon the people's daily lives, the Cultural Missions also actively promoted the revival of indigenous music and dance as a means of encountering a national heritage uncorrupted by colonial influence. While the plays that Becerra Celis anthologizes, and those described in other sources, are of poor artistic quality, the Cultural Mission Program was not dedicated to the creation of a Mexican regional theatre network, but to the empowerment of rural communities. By carrying out such an endeavor the Cultural Mission Program can be seen as a precursor to the work of contemporary Latin American theatre professionals such as Alan Bolt, whose Nicaraguan National Theater Workshop also emphasizes the resurrection of indigenous dance, music, and theatrical forms as a means of breaking the cycle of colonial repression by affirming pride in popular forms. In both cases theatre, and the arts in general, are seen as a tool to be used in creating a strong, healthy community. Neither one nor the other can be evaluated on the viability of the plays produced. It is the process, not the product that is of ultimate importance.

The Cultural Mission Program, as Vasconcelos conceived it, was to be a force for eliminating the colonial structures and attitudes that led to repression of the rural communities. This would be done by incorporating these rural, largely indigenous populations into the social fabric of the larger nation, inculcating them with the ideals and goals of the revolutionary government. While such a program was well-intentioned, it is clear that it could be seen as simply the substitution of one kind of authority for another. Instead of colonial administration and Christian doctrine, the Indian peasants were given revolutionary authority and socialist doctrine. As the Nicaraguan government discovered when it attempted to integrate the Miskito Indian population of the Atlantic Coast into the national socio-political system following the 1979 revolution, misinformation about the population's history and cultural attitudes, as well as the way in which government officials perceive those attitudes, greatly affects the success of any such program. Used to autonomy over their lands and affairs, the Miskitos responded to governmental intrusion by forming their own *contra* military organizations.[25] The literature reflects a similar tendency to run roughshod over the indigenous populations they were ostensibly trying to aid on the part of the Mexican revolutionary government as well.

Hughes describes some of the problems encountered by the Cultural Mission Program among the Popolocas Indians in Veracruz. Isolated for centuries, used to their traditional ways, speaking only their indigenous language, the Popolocas refused to accept the health-care advice of the Missions' nurses. The nurses complained that in spite of the fact that gastrointestinal diseases, water-borne diseases, parasitosis, malaria and tuberculosis were rampant among the Popolocas, Indian men forbade their wives and daughters from attending literacy classes taught by a male instructor even though no female literacy instructors were available.

The solution of the problem depends, in the opinion of the supervisors of cultural missions in the Popoloca area, upon teaching the people Spanish and integrating them into the national life and culture. The success of a program of Spanish teaching among these peoples, however, depends on the solution of their socioeconomic problems, since their ignorance and antipathy result in large part from prolonged isolation. Before much headway can be made, therefore, roads and other means of communication must be extended into the Popoloca area. As a consequence of these factors, it has recently been agreed that the basis of all education among the Popolocas should be Spanish teaching, so that the process of assimilating the Indians can be accelerated...The Popolocas are typical of isolated and retarded Indian peoples in many parts of the country. They are the peoples most in need of the services of the missioners [*sic*], but to-day because of language barriers peoples of this sort generally do not participate voluntarily in the cultural mission program.[26]

While the cultural insensitivity and racist language of the last paragraph cited conceivably reflects more the opinion of the UNESCO author than that of the Cultural Mission Program itself, the supervisor cited by Hughes displays a similar contempt for Popoloca culture and looks upon the rapid assimilation of these people into "national life and culture" as their only hope for salvation. Toor cites one rural population's response to an offer of federal help:

The Municipal President of Putla, Oaxaca, summed up their reasons for not wanting schools to a Federal School Inspector, as follows:
    "I shall tell you why we do not want to learn to do the things you do and teach in your schools. In your cities the majority of the people have gone to school. What they learned there must be very bad, because many of them lie, take what belongs to others, betray their friends, stab a man in the back, and it is seldom they are ashamed of their acts.
    You are well acquainted with our laws, so you will know that what I am saying is true. If we tell you that we are your friends, it means until death; the same is true when we hate you. But we are incapable of betraying friends

as you do. Here we kill one another like men, face to face, and murders are
never pardoned...

This village is poor but healthy. Don't hurt it by making it like your places
because it will lose its health, freedom and happiness. If you love our people,
don't teach them anything; don't make them lose faith in their beliefs as I
did when I served the priests of a large church.[27]

Intelligent and articulate, this man is clearly cognizant of his
community's needs. His plea for allowing the villagers to retain their
faith untarnished reflects the power of the rural Church in certain
areas of the country. Vasconcelos' revolutionary educational crusade
brought the Mexican government into direct conflict with the
Catholic Church and its rural constituents.

THE BATTLE OF ARMAGEDDON: CHURCH RESPONSE
AND THE CRISTERO REBELLION

Since the founding of the religious schools by the various mendicant
orders after the Conquest, education had been one of the main pillars
of Church power. It perceived secular education as an infringement
of its own historical prerogatives and actively fought against it.
Cultural missionaries and rural teachers were attacked, some killed,
by parishioners whose impetus for action came from weekly sermons
against the state schools. The Church attacked public education
primarily by threatening to excommunicate parents who sent their
children to the public schools. At the same time the Church continued
to operate and expand its own educational system.

Alongside Vasconcelos' new national, revolutionary school, the
Catholic clergy promoted the Church school as the basis for its work
in the social sphere. For this reason the conflicting goals of the
Catholic Church and the Mexican Revolution were most evident in
education. The Church determined that state education would
create a "revolutionary child" who would be free of all religious
influence. To fight such an invidious creation Catholic educational
policy developed a dual approach. Its immediate goal was the best
possible education for Catholic children within the confines of the
revolutionary government. Its second, and much more important,
goal was complete clerical domination of all education in Mexico.
The second goal represented the Church's ultimate aim and as such
put it on a collision course with the Mexican government. The
Revolution's demands for a completely secular, anti-religious system

of education were entirely antagonistic to, and completely incompatible with, the demands of the Catholic Church. The extreme nature of the policies of both sides left no room for compromise.[28]

The revolutionary government's attitude towards the Church's role in education and society was more than the application of idealistic battle cries. It was also a continuation of the historic state response to the Church in Mexico. As the Spanish crown had attempted to control the Church through the *patronato real*, so had the nineteenth-century Bourbon regime tried to subjugate the Church to the modern state. The Mexican revolutionary government was continuing this age-old battle. The wars of reform in 1857, 1867, and 1876, the anti-clerical provisions of the 1917 Constitution, the persecution of the Church and the resultant Cristero Rebellion between 1926 and 1938, can all be seen as the result of the conflicting interests of the Church and the state.

The Church challenged the revolutionary government not only in the educational sphere, but in the social realm as well. Even before the Revolution, the Church, through the efforts of Catholic Social action, was speaking the language of social change:

The worker, in return for this terribly exhausting labour, receives between 18 and 25 centavos a day, which is paid partly in seeds and partly in cash, and even with these low wages, there are some landowners who find ingenious ways of reducing them further ... We understand Socialism ... You rich men, there is no other way: either you must open your hearts to charity and reduce the hours of work and increase wages, or you are accumulating hatred and resentment ... and your riches and you yourselves will be buried.[29]

While this emphasis on social works spawned a trade-union movement remarkable for its feminist and proletarian character, its efficiency, activism, and lack of bureaucracy, and a new political party – the Partido Católico Nacional – precursor to today's PAN, the ideological underpinnings of this activity that covered the Revolutionary government's terrain, were quite different from those advanced by the state and its labor movement.[30] As Father Alfredo Méndez Medina, one of the organizers of Catholic Social Action, said,

[Catholic teachings] say to the employer that he should consider the laborer to be his powerless brother and treat him with charity. They say to the worker that he should respect his boss as a superior, for all authority comes from God; that the poor must love the rich; and that they must mutually respect each other's legitimate rights; that the industrial worker must respect the property of the capitalist, who must, in turn, respect the personal dignity of the worker; that the artisan must work with honor...; that the capitalist must pay him a just salary.[31]

This accomodationist stance between labor and management gained adherents among the faithful and threatened the power base of the state trade-union movement, gaining the Church the enmity of Luis Morones, its leader.

All of this came to a head in 1926 when the Calles government, in addition to its offensive against religious education, ordered the deportation of foreign priests and compulsory registration of the native clergy, in order to give the government power over designating which priests would be placed in which churches. The Mexican Episcopate responded by declaring a strike: the suspension of all religious services as long as the Calles decrees remained in effect. Tensions increased, leading to the beginning of guerrilla warfare between the religious forces and the government in 1926.

As Meyer has observed, "It was a colonial war, carried on by a colonial army against its own people, and followed the course of all wars of this type: the harshness of the repression, the execution of prisoners, the systematic massacre of the civilian population, scorched earth, looting, and rape; all left in the wake of the Federal troops the germ of fresh risings."[32] While the Mexican military displayed an almost rabid desire to defeat the Cristeros, misunderstanding of the degree of their popular support, geography, and numbers – the federal army never had a numerical superiority of more than two to one – made a guerrilla war unwinnable in the field. It was only the indefatigable efforts of the US Ambassador to Mexico, Dwight W. Morrow, and the change of presidents from Calles to his former Minister of Government, Portes Gil, in 1928 that made a settlement possible.

With that settlement the Church entered into a *modos vivendi* with the government in which it agreed to register its priests if, in return, the government allowed it to carry out religious education within Church property, and to the Church's right to petition the government for the change of laws. Although Portes Gil promised amnesty for those Cristero soldiers who voluntarily surrendered to federal troops, many of those who did so were summarily executed. While the settlement was bitterly denounced by militant Catholics as nothing more than surrender, since 1929 Church schools have operated openly under the convenient fiction that they are private and secular. What the long struggle has meant for the Mexican Catholic Church in general is that it is one of the least progressive in Latin America, and will probably never again be a major player in the struggle for social change in Mexico.[33]

The Mexican Revolution and the Cristero rebellion had strong repercussions for the nature of early-twentieth-century Mexican drama. We have seen how revolutionary ideals affected the Cultural Missions' open-air theatres, and the *teatro de masas*. In addition, aristocratic antipathy for revolutionary principles can be seen in the upper-class commercial theatre embodied by the Comedia Mexicana. In the sort of plays presented in the Comedia, however, political questions are largely secondary to the melodramatic investigation of the personal problems of these plays' characters. There was another type of drama as well that, more vibrant in its presence, developed out of the Mexican *drama rural* and was used by both sides of the conflict, a particularly Mexican form of revolutionary drama.

As Meyer has observed, when the government labeled the religious rebels "Cristeros" they went a long way towards defining the nature and significance of the conflict: "The persecution of the priest, a revered figure, loved as the dispenser of the Sacraments, who brought about the coming of Christ under the semblance of bread and wine, was resented as a diabolical war against Christ Himself; the persecutor was, therefore, the Devil himself."[34] The infernal nature of revolutionary policies is best reflected in the plays of Francisco González Franco (dates unknown), a fierce partisan of the Church.[35]

The most fully realized of these works is the full-length play *La perfecta alegría* (Perfect happiness; 1938). *La perfecta alegría* deals with the Cristero uprising against the Calles' government, painting the Catholic forces as betrayed by an alliance of the White House, the Jewish (*sic*) Morgan Bank, the Mexican government, and weak Catholic prelates and bishops swayed by Morrow's diplomacy. The purpose of the betrayal is a peace that will be conducive to the ordered functioning of Yankee business in conjunction with their Americanized Mexican associates.

The play centers around the character of Lina, whose husband Manuel is an officer in the Cristero army. Leaving her son and daughter with relatives, she has gone to the mountains, where she lives in a Cristero community that, like the early Christians, has set up a clandestine church in a cave. An Americanized cousin of hers, whose offer of marriage she refused years ago, arrives. Predicting the imminent alliance of forces that will put an end to the uprising, he attempts to persuade her to join him in convincing Manuel that a mine in which he owns the controlling interest should be reopened. When she refuses, the cousin proceeds to turn her husband against her with manufactured stories of her infidelity, and sends her son off to be educated in the United States where, Americanized, he turns against her. The daughter falls ill and dies.

When the peace accords are signed the cousin returns and tries to force Lina to marry him. She is protected by an orphaned Catholic boy whom she has taken under her wing, and by some of the Cristero soldiers who, though wounded, refuse to surrender. One of them smashes his gun to bits and leaps off a cliff. The standard bearer is brought before a firing squad but not before he gives the orphan the Cristero flag. In the final scene Lina and the orphan carry the flag as a tremendous thunderstorm destroys the cave and she cries:

Now, poor orphan, symbol of the Mexican people, sad and unprotected, let us go delight ourselves in the most perfect happiness: the poverty, nudity, hunger, disdain, incomprehension, revilement, desolation, oblivion, infamous betrayal, the full, dark night sung by those great disconsolates Catalina of Siena, Teresa of Avila, and John of the Cross. The horrible, divine solitude, the obscure infallibility of Him on Mt. Calvary...when he saw himself abandoned by all, even his Father in Heaven![36]

The term "the perfect happiness" comes from *Las Florecitas de San Francisco de Asís* where the story of St. Francis' dialog with Brother Leon, "Christ's sheep", is told in which St. Francis says that "the perfect happiness is in all this, if we suffer everything with resignation and patience, because there is Christ's perfect love: there is the supreme pleasure."[37] While the play is extremely verbose at times, it has portions of undeniable theatrical power. The characters of Lina and the cousin are well written, and the final image of a woman stripped of everything and everyone taking an orphaned child under her wing is a good one that would benefit from a less insistent hand. Nomland acknowledges that González Franco's plays have been treated with disdain by the few critics who knew them and ignored by theatre producers. He points out, nevertheless, that many of the plays have been printed several times and remain a potent means of propaganda.[38] Other playwrights, such as Rodolfo Oneto Barenque (dates unknown) and Ezequiel de la Isla (dates unknown), mined the same territory, but none comes close to González Franco's ability.[39]

REVUES, *CARPAS*, AND CANTINFLAS: THEATRES IN AID OF A CAUSE

The counter-revolutionary religious forces were hardly the first in Mexico to employ the theatre in aid of their cause. As early as the late nineteenth century the primarily urban political revue, with its focus on a particular contemporary person or incident, was highly popular. With the turn of the century and the social upheaval of the Revolution, these revues began to take on a distinctly Mexican flavor, utilizing typical Mexican characters, songs, and street slang in order to attack the new revolutionary government of Francisco I Madero in 1911.

Roberto Soto, a revue comedian known for his biting political wit, was a player in one of the most famous incidents in Mexican theatre history, the Soto–Morones feud. Soto bore an uncanny resemblance to Morones, the powerful labor leader of the state trade unions, and he used that resemblance to satirize Morones' passion for large diamond rings and to expose systematically his corrupt leadership. Soto's theatre was frequently closed, only to be reopened again. Censorship of the revues was more a personal affair between the actors and politicians than official governmental policy. As such the actors found that one branch of government could be successfully played off against another and, with the excising of a few offensive remarks, they could easily reopen.

As a largely bourgeois form, the political revue reserved its most virulent satire for the populist regime of Lázaro Cárdenas. Numerous revues branded Cárdenas a communist and blamed him for virtually all of the country's ills. The political commentary of the revues was quickly abandoned when, with the increase in tourism after the institutionalization of the Revolution, the companies discovered they could make more money catering to foreign tourists with elaborate stage shows based on folkloric dances, sketches, and, in some cases, ballets. The kind of populist theatre once found in the revues made its way into a new form, a kind of Mexican *commedia dell' arte*, called the *carpa*.

The *carpas* were groups of itinerant performers who moved their collapsible stages from town to town, setting up in the main square or the middle of a street, and presented a program of song, skits, and comedy that spoke directly to their mixed-class audience. There was a relaxed, informal atmosphere in these performances in which the audience and the performers engaged each other directly, with audience members giving the performers suggestions, and the performers soliciting the audience for money and cigarettes. Out of the *carpas* came the famous comedian, Cantinflas (1911–1993), frequently dubbed the Mexican Charlie Chaplin.

Where Chaplin's comedy depended upon his amazing physical abilities, Cantinflas' comedy was based upon the peculiarly Mexican way of speaking.

Cantinflas impersonates the class-conscious man of the city's lower classes who suffers from an inferiority complex hidden under a stubborn individualism and an affected and meaningless wordiness. His genius lies in the masterful use of this relentless dribble that never achieves a phrase with sense, rather in the style of the English comedian Oliver Wakefield, but endowed with a mad, rascally humor of the most surrealist variety. Typical is the sketch in which Cantinflas plays the labor leader at the head of a delegation of workers who call on the owner of a soap factory, played by Medel. Cantinflas lists the demands of the workers in a florid proletarian speech to which the employer readily agrees, remarking gleefully that the price of soap can now go up. Then the owner, in his turn, continues the conversation by figuring the hours of the year in which his employees do *not* work, deducting Sundays, Holy Days, vacations, Labor Day, time out lunch, time for meetings and so forth, cleverly juggling mathematics to obtain a total of non-working hours that leaves only four days in the year in which the employees work. Cantinflas' heart sinks lower and lower and he ends by asking the factory owner humbly to tell them how much they owe *him* for the privilege of working for him.[40]

Cantinflas went on to a hugely successful movie career where, although his linguistic style was maintained, the class-conscious satire of his earlier stage performances was largely discarded.

While the political revue and the *carpa* both employed revolutionary themes for humorous purposes, there was also a more serious treatment of such themes in the Mexican theatre both before and after the Revolution. The first signs of such a trend can be found in the plays of the novelist Federico Gamboa (1894–1939) at the beginning of the twentieth century. Gamboa wrote three plays: *La última campaña* (published 1894), *La venganza del gleba* (1904), and

Entre hermanos (1924). *La venganza del gleba* (The sod's vengeance) stresses the importance of equality among human beings and is the first to introduce the idea of social justice on the Mexican stage. It portrays a world in which the land-owning aristocracy will either begin to address social inequality in a dignified and benevolent fashion or self-destruct through its own indifference and abusive behavior towards the peasants that sustain the aristocratic lifestyle.[41]

The first plays to truly espouse the underlying principles of the Mexican Revolution were those written by Ricardo Flores Magón (1873–1928). Flores Magón was one of the precursors to the 1910 Revolution. A committed anarchist, he based his political philosophy on what he had seen in his native Oaxaca state as a boy. There in the late 1800s the *ejido* system, in which land was held in common and worked by the community with the produce shared equally, was still being practiced by the peasantry. To this practical example Flores Magón added ideas of Kropotkin, Bakunin, Malatesta, and Emma Goldman, but his own anarchism was firmly rooted in the Mexican context. His policies were, in fact, quite close to those espoused by Emiliano Zapata and his agrarian movement.

The founder of the Partido Liberal Mexicano during the Porfirio Díaz dictatorship, Flores Magón was forced to leave Mexico in 1904 due to his political activities. For the next six years Flores Magón published his newspaper, *Regeneración* (Regeneration), from various venues in the United States, and organized two armed uprisings against the dictatorship within Mexico. Militarily unsuccessful, they planted the seeds for the 1910 Revolution. During the Revolution itself Flores Magón worked to create a true social revolution based upon anarchist communist ideals rather than what he saw as a merge change of political leadership. He was, therefore, opposed to all of the revolutionary leaders who gained power from Madero to Carranza, and remained in the United States. There he was frequently arrested for his political activities and, in 1918, sentenced to a lengthy prison term in the federal penitentiary in Leavenworth, Kansas. He was found dead in his cell under mysterious circumstances on November 20, 1922.[42]

Flores Magón clearly saw the drama as another medium for spreading his message of social change. His two plays, *Tierra y Libertad* and *Víctimas y verdugos*, both published for the first time in 1924, put that orientation into practice. Flores Magón's language is energetic but simplistic. It is basically his propaganda spoken by his characters.

Those characters are the one-dimensional evil representatives of the state, the landowner, the Church, and the union leadership vs. the good, honest, upright anarchist peasant and his ignorant, duped, urban counterpart. Throughout the plays the seeds of revolutionary consciousness are planted by the appearance of copies of *Regeneración*.[43] These plays by Gamboa and Flores Magón are representative of the kind of revolutionary-oriented drama written in Mexico before 1925. Overall, such plays lacked literary or theatrical fluency and depended upon the time-honored Mexican dramatic tradition of the dishonored woman to drive their points across.

INDEPENDENT THEATRES: REVIVAL OF INDIGENOUS SENSIBILITY IN THE THEATRICAL REPRESENTATION OF RELIGION AND POLITICS

From 1925 onward a series of university-affiliated and independent theatre groups sprang up throughout Latin America. These groups were organized in a variety of ways and adopted diverse methods of production, but the essential impetus behind their organization was the creation of a specifically Latin American theatre movement capable of speaking to and for a region still struggling to forge its own identity. Some of these groups, like Teatro de Ulises and Teatro de Orientación in Mexico, were primarily literary and concerned with introducing what they saw as the more advanced European drama onto the Latin American stage. Other Mexican groups turned to the theatre as a vehicle for expressing political and social themes that not only dealt with the events of the Revolution, but also looked at middle-class and proletarian problems from a leftist perspective. One of the playwrights involved in the latter trend was Elena Alvarez (dates unknown).

Alvarez' *Dos dramas revolucionarios* (Two revolutionary dramas; 1926) are more than plays, brief dramatic sketches dealing with class perceptions of poverty. In the first, *Muerta de hambre* (Dying of hunger), a woman and her child are discovered lying on the ground in front of a church. The woman's breasts are exposed and her legs show a good bit of thigh. Both she and her child are in need of a good scrubbing. The piece consists of five scenes in which everyone who passes, including two pious women, two foppish young men, two dirty old men, two ostentatious bourgeois women, and a priest all comment, with greater and lesser degrees of lasciviousness, on the woman's condition. Each of them castigates the disrespect she displays for the church by lying drunk before its doors. Some of the men go so far as to abuse her, the two young men stepping on her breasts to see whether they will express milk or *pulque*,[44] the priest kicking her to get her to move.

It is only in the final scene, with the appearance of a common "man of the people," that the woman receives any help. He determines she is not drunk but faint from hunger, and gives her something to eat. He also upbraids the priest, telling him that he is just like everyone who is rich – they have so much to eat, they cannot conceive of anyone dying of hunger. The man's final words are: "Jesus Christ would not have driven a woman dying of hunger from the doors of his temple."[45]

Alvarez' writing is a simple, direct example of a didactic theatre. Its view of society is crystal clear. Although the dialog occasionally descends to the level of political cant, Alvarez' characters are always interesting. There is nothing trite or stereotypical about the people she creates and it is especially fascinating to see the way their ghoulishness is used to depict society's structural biases. More importantly, *Muerta de hambre* presents a greater sophistication in the revolutionary attitude towards the Church. While clearly anti-clerical, the play's final statement makes a distinction between the institutional Church and Christ's teachings. In its insistence upon Christ's concern for the hungry can be seen a foreshadowing of contemporary liberation theology with its "preferential option for the poor." In her analysis of the social structure that condemns the woman to death Alvarez is engaging in precisely the same kind of analysis engaged in today by the Christian base communities. In both cases the hypocritical behavior and social biases of state and Church are shown to be the very instruments by which large segments of the population are marginalized in direct opposition to the religious doctrine or the social ideology that both institutions preach.

In 1930 a Spanish translation of Erwin Piscator's *The Political Theatre* was published in Madrid. Soon distributed in Mexico, Piscator's theories caught the imagination of two young playwrights, Juan Bustillo Oro (1904–) and Mauricio Magdelano (1906–1986), who founded Teatro de Ahora in 1932. This theatre company lasted only a brief time, but had a profound effect upon subsequent Mexican theatre with its attempt to find a Mexican equivalent of

Piscator's theatre. The Teatro de Ahora performed several works of the two founders, and their own adaptation of Ben Jonson's *Volpone* called *Tiburón* (Shark; 1932).

Both Bustillo Oro and Magdaleno focus on social ills, but Magdaleno presents those ills as a result of the damage caused by foreign exploitation of Mexican resources coupled with how that exploitation affects the indigenous character, making his work of more importance to this study of the development of the Latin American theatre than that of his co-founder. Magdaleno's first play to be performed by Teatro de Ahora was *Pánuco 137* (1932), which premièred at the Teatro Hidalgo in Mexico City in 1932. The play tells the story of the Galván family, Romulo, his wife Cande, his daughter Raquel, his son-in-law Damián, and his compadre Teófilo, in their fight against the Pánuco River Oil Company. The time period is sometime after the Revolution when US businessmen have made various pacts with the Mexican government. In this particular case, oil has been discovered in the area surrounding the Pánuco River and the Pánuco River Oil Company, aided by compliant local officials who view the company's presence as a civilizing influence, force the peasants off their land. The oil company forms a private army, the White Guards, and employs a local thug named *Perro* (Dog) to lead it and protect the company's interests.

Romulo and Damián refuse to sell their land and are simply ignored. The company drills for oil behind the family home and that well, Pánuco 137, proves to tap the richest vein discovered. On the night the family plans to leave, Perro, who has always lusted after Raquel, kills Damián and takes the pregnant Raquel by force. The final scene of the second act portrays these events in a brutal and powerful manner. The enraged Romulo falls upon Perro and is beaten up. When his inert body is carried off, Cande and Teófilo try to protect him and are beaten in turn. At the same time Raquel is dragged, kicking and screaming, into the field by Perro's men. Simultaneously, Pánuco 137 erupts in a geyser of oil.

The third act shows the *gringos* casually breaking their promises of dividends in the company and paying off their Mexican associates in fixed sums. Two young US beauties, sexually aroused by these savage Mexicans, take snapshots and arrange assignations. In the midst of all this Romulo enters carrying a charge of dynamite. When he threatens to blow up the well an oil worker reveals that the charge is empty. Perro's men gun Romulo down, egged on by Mr. Allen, the oil baron, who calls for champagne to wash the bitter taste from his mouth as the curtain descends.

Magdaleno creates three-dimensional characters whose past history is gradually revealed to us. The relationships between his characters are complex and have as much to do with the traditional codes of Mexican society as with the appearance of the North American company. The oil company's appearance, in fact, merely serves to accelerate and exacerbate tensions and conflicts already present between the Mexicans themselves. The foreign company's presence gives the Mexicans license to ignore the traditional boundaries and lines of authority that have previously kept them in check. Although Don Casimiro, the rich landowner who got Perro released from prison to work for the company, tries to stop him from raping Raquel, the company's disregard for anything other than its black gold has stripped Casimiro of the authority he once held. As we have seen elsewhere in Mexican drama, the land is the central issue here. Whoever controls it controls the lives of those who inhabit it. To the oil company the Mexicans are backward, ignorant, worthless, and utterly expendable. As with the Argentinian *drama rural*, the focus is upon the destruction of the rural laborer by the invasion of urban and foreign forces. In its gradual deformation of each of its characters Magdaleno's play also resembles the dramaturgical techniques of the *grotesco criollo*. In both instances traditional familial and territorial relationships and boundaries have simply been discarded, stripping away any sense of identity and leaving only pain.

Magdaleno's best play is entitled *Trópico* (1932) and deals with the story of Cecil Chester Bond, who has come to Mexico from New York as president of the American Tropical Gum Company. He is accompanied by another US citizen, Ben Sunter, who spouts biblical chapter and verse, calls himself a good Quaker, and is scandalized by the Indians' habits and their belief in more than the one true God. The North Americans, aided by compliant Mexicans similar to those in *Pánuco 137*, proceed to take over. Chico Díaz, a rich landowner, essentially forces his daughter Rosarito to become Bond's lover. When Marcelino Contreras, the man Rosarito has loved since they were children, returns and discovers the new situation, he rebels and gathers an Indian army that proceeds to attack and destroy the American Tropical Gum Company's installations.

In the meantime, Bond, alcoholic and suffering from malaria, has become more and more incoherent. At the beginning of the play an old Indian had predicted that the jungle would destroy the company. Bond now claims that his fever is the jungle, the jungle in Rosarito's skin, blood, and kisses, a jungle he wants to consume. At the same time Magdaleno makes it clear that it is the jungle that drives the rebel Marcelino, turning him hard and cruel. When Marcelino is captured, Rosarito finds herself torn between the two men and prevails upon Bond to release him. Humiliated by his release, Marcelino returns for vengeance and Rosarito now pleads with him to spare Bond and her father, revealing that she carries Bond's child. Hurt and disgusted, Marcelino spares their lives and sets the factory on fire.

The play's final scene is powerful. Sunter has sent for Bond's daughter Alma to try and convince Bond to return to the United States. She arrives with two friends, Gloria, a movie star, and George N. Atkinson, her director. They plan to use the jungle to shoot a few scenes for their latest movie, but Atkinson quickly realizes that what is happening around him would make an incredible movie and starts to film clips for an epic entitled *Trópico*. In the final scene Atkinson films Bond sitting on the floor, playing cards and rolling cigarettes Indian style with his Indian servant, while Alma tries to convince him to return with her, and Sunter fulminates against the voluptuous nature and vice-ridden life of the tropics. As Marcelino frees Sunter, Díaz, and Bond and pushes Rosarito away in disgust, the red light of the blazing factory fills the sky and another Mexican collaborator, Juan de Dios, appears. A pompous lawyer with pretensions to high culture, Juan de Dios is covered in ditch reeds and moss from head to foot and moves "like a vegetable form." He says that, fearing for his life, he disguised himself as an innocent vegetable. This vegetable figure crosses the stage as the North Americans run screaming for their planes, and Bond plunges into the jungle (as if into a tunnel, Magdaleno tells us) crying out for Rosarito. His cries echo all over the stage, "a jeering singsong, ending in something that could be a bird's cry or a cackle of laughter."[46]

Although quite distinct from one another in formal terms, Magdaleno's play and the combination of religion, politics, and theatre utilized is similar to that seen in the early mendicant theatre. Where Moctezoma and the Aztecs greeted Cortés and the Spaniards as arriving gods in an effort to fit them into a comprehensible context, Magdaleno's Mexicans greet the North Americans as representatives of a new kind of divine order that will bring economic wealth and civilized well-being. The final scene, with its complex layering of "civilized" and "primitive" cultures, greed, lust, revenge, freedom, death, and new birth – is a phoenix born from the ashes of the blazing factory? – is comparable to the imagistic and associative density of Cortés' greeting to the twelve Franciscans, or the ending of *La conquista de Jerusalén*.

Unable to control the course of events on his own, Sunter, the pietistic representative of *gringo* religion, sends for Bond's daughter Alma, whose name in Spanish means "soul." Her "soul"-full presence as a member of the next generation and, consequently, a force for renovation and renewal, is intended to provide Sunter with an ally in his battle against the tropical forces that are consuming her father. This "soul," however, brings Gloria and Atkinson with her. These two characters are members of that "civilized" world that the Mexicans aspire to, but their profession is one that deals exclusively in illusions, in temporary, and illusory images of life. Confronted with the vitality of the tropics, Atkinson abandons his original, comparably empty, plans in an attempt to capture the density that surrounds him. He films the "inferior" tropics consuming the "superior" representatives of North American civilization.

The tropical presence is shown to touch all of the characters involved and, in doing so, inverts the conceptions of wealth and civilization upon which the majority of the characters have based their actions. Bond was originally the dynamic force whose Tropical Gum Company was to be the medium by which the primitive tropical culture would "bond" with its superior northern culture. By the end of the play he is the one who has "bonded" with the "primitive" culture he came to replace. The tropics are a fever that have entered his bloodstream in the form of his love for Rosarito and she now carries his child, a seed he has planted that binds him to the jungle. Magdaleno shows us how completely Bond has been integrated into the tropical milieu by his actions in the final scene. As Alma and Sunter, the representatives of the culture he has abandoned, attempt to convince him to return to the United States, Bond assumes the actions and attitudes of not only an Indian, but an Indian servant to the white *gringo*. Sitting on the floor, he is now physically beneath all those who surround him, and is taught Indian techniques by a man who was once subservient to him. The master–servant relationship has been completely inverted but, since the Indian servant's previous willingness to perform servile tasks for the *gringo* has invalidated him as a true representative of indigenous culture, Bond has bound himself to another illusion of culture, one that will ultimately flicker and die like one of Atkinson's movies.

In contrast to Bond and the Indian servant, Magdaleno gives us Marcelino, the modern Cuauhtémoc, who forms his indigenous army to drive out the Tropical Gum Company. Unlike his Aztec ancestor, Marcelino succeeds in breaking the grip on power held by the modern *conquistadores*. In doing so, he is shown to be both a strong, capable military commander and a magnanimous leader. He frees his North American captives in the same way that Cortés refused, initially, to put Cuauhtémoc to death, but in doing so Marcelino has paid a much higher price than Cortés ever did, for he has lost Rosarito. By becoming Bond's lover and carrying his child, Rosarito has become a modern Malinche, Cortés' Aztec concubine and interpreter who supplied him with the linguistic key to conquest and gave birth to the first *mestizo* child, thereby becoming a symbol of the foreign rape of Mexico.

While Magdaleno gives us Marcelino as the indigenous warrior whose decisive torching of the factory will wipe out the North American presence, he also gives us the image of Juan de Dios, the lawyer who believed in the superiority of the foreign culture, as "a vegetable form." This Mexican who attempted to deny his link to the tropics is depicted as literally consumed by them. As the North Americans use the technology he so admired to escape, Juan de Dios is returned to an earlier point on the evolutionary chain, he becomes a part of that jungle undergrowth into which Bond himself disappears. The spiraling references to death and rebirth are shown through the depictions of Alma, Rosarito, the fire, and Juan de Dios' (John of God's) reincarnation as a part of the jungle. The entire play shows us the resurrection of the indigenous and tropical sensibility that reasserts its power over the territory the North Americans see as an extension of their empire.

Nomland comments that Magdaleno attempted to create true tragedies, but his work was marred by his propensity for introducing a beautiful young woman whose sexual attractiveness provided the play's catalyst. He criticizes this aspect of Magdaleno's work as falling back upon an outmoded Mexican tradition and observes that Bustillo Oro managed to break free of such traditional plotting to create something entirely new. While I would not disagree with Nomland's analysis, it seems to me that he misses the point.

Magdaleno has taken the traditional bourgeois plotting and turned it on its head, expanding the Mexican societal codes to push them to new levels, and stretching the boundaries of Mexican dramaturgy to introduce new techniques, thereby introducing new visions of the world to the Mexican theatre.

In 1933, the same year that Bustillo Oro and Magdaleno's plays were published, another volume of plays, titled *Tres comedias revolucionarios* by Germán List Arzubide (1898–) appeared. Two of the plays included, *Las sombras* (The shadows) and *El último juicio* (The last judgment; 1930), the one a depiction of Mexico City's working poor, the other a one-act play in which the world's workers unite to put God on trial for their suffering, are not well realized. The third play, however, is a small masterpiece. Entitled *El nuevo diluvio* (The new flood), it is a satiric view of the Revolution. After the flood Noah has set himself up as an ark builder, providing luxurious arks complete with various floors and attached garages for the animals who can afford them. Noah mistreats his workers, all sheep, so that he can suck as much money as possible from the pigs, monkeys, elephants, and other animals who are his customers. The only animal who expresses any dissatisfaction with this arrangement is the rebellious Coyote, who warns Noah that for food, clothing, and shelter the animals will rebel: "There will be another flood, but it will be ours. It already advances like an enormous wave from the east. Remember Noah, I am the one preaching now, construct your ark and tremble, soon it will rain fire and blood."[47]

When the wolves and sheep, led by Coyote, finally do rebel, all the other animals go running to Noah for protection. Following the advice of his brutal foreman, the Dog, however, Noah has been building his arks with inferior materials to cut costs. As the approaching revolutionaries advance singing *The Internationale* the other animals rush aboard a newly constructed ark, trampling the Dog to death in the process. Too weak to hold their weight, the ark collapses killing them all.

The decision to place the play in this sort of fantasy world is an excellent one. It saves the play from becoming merely a didactic tract. The play clearly has a message to teach and presents it forcefully, but the animal characterizations allow List Arzubide much greater freedom for satirical touches. In this fashion the Pig is a banker, the Cow a suffragette, the Rat a philosopher, the Vulture a priest, the Tiger a general, the sheep workers, and so on. The humor employed lightens the political thrust, actually making it much more effective through the creation of a kind of grotesque fairy-tale or bizarre children's story world that delights and makes us more disposed to hear the play's thesis.

Beyond Teatro de Ahora and playwrights inspired by its example, the only early-twentieth-century theatre company to espouse popular values was the Teatro de las Artes founded by the Japanese director Seki Sano. Seki Sano arrived in Mexico in 1939 after having worked as Meyerhold's assistant in the Soviet Union and spending a brief time in New York City. In Mexico he joined with the US ballerina Waldeen to found a theatre school based on Stanislavskian and Meyerholdian aesthetics. Calling themselves "A theatre of the people for the people," Teatro de las Artes produced an eclectic mixture of a number of ballets, dramatizations of novels, and Mexican and foreign plays of a progressive nature. In 1942 they claimed that Teatro de las Artes was born:

free from "mercantilism", from "degenerate professionalism", from the "star system" and from any other defect that has prevented, until today, the healthy development of a genuinely popular theatre in our country. It will be a weapon in the hands of the people, so that they can improve themselves.

The Teatro de las Artes fights the principle of "art for art's sake"; it is essentially: theatre by the people, for the people.

The Teatro de las Artes is a realistic theatre, free from trivial naturalism or realism, as well as from a formalism distant from the people.

People of Mexico! This is your theatre, it represents your aspirations for progress! Give it your encouragement, support it![48]

In addition, Teatro de las Artes founded an itinerant theatre group called Teatro de la "V", shorthand for Caravana Cultural y Artística "Victoria." The Teatro de la "V" performed under the motto "Art in Service of the Democracies" and was formed to support the allied cause in the Second World War by presenting anti-fascist pieces utilizing marionettes, song, and radio throughout the country. Due to scant Mexican interest in the war the Teatro de la "V" quickly folded. Seki Sano left Teatro de las Artes in 1948 to form the Teatro de la Reforma with another American, Luz Alba, and the Mexican actor Alberto Galán. Teatro de la Reforma, however, displayed little interest in political themes, concentrating instead on foreign works.

Such an interest was another trend in Mexican twentieth-century theatre that had begun with the Teatro de Ulises in 1928 and Teatro de Orientación in 1933. This was a trend found, to a greater or lesser degree, in all the countries throughout the region. Attempting to break free of the moribund middle-class drama, these theatres looked abroad, performing works by Lord Dunsany, Cocteau, O'Neill, Lenormand, Synge, and Strindberg, as well as encouraging Mexican playwrights to experiment with new forms as a means of creating a new Latin American dramaturgy. Although Teatro de Orientación produced plays by other Mexicans as well, it did not begin to present that new dramaturgy until it produced those of Alfonso Gutiérrez Hermosillo (1905–1935).

Gutiérrez Hermosillo's play *La sombra de Lázaro* (Lazarus' shadow; published 1945) is of interest both for its technique, and its attempt to introduce a dramatic form of subjective expression into the Mexican theatre. The plot is simple. A rich man, Francisco, marries a young woman, Justina. Justina does not love him, but has been pushed into the marriage by her grasping sister, Engracia. Soon after they are married, Francisco abandons Justina. Engracia then persuades her sister to take a lover and have a child, leading everyone to believe it is Francisco's, in order to consolidate their hold over the estate. Ten years later Francisco, having suffered many hardships, participated in the Revolution, and now a *curandero* (healer), returns. He saves Justina's son from dying of a snake bite, and the estranged couple reveal their secrets to each other. Despite Francisco's willingness to accept her son as his own, Justina feels she has betrayed him and plots to take the child away, leaving the estate in his hands. Before she can do so, Francisco himself leaves.

Gutiérrez Hermosillo's attempts at technical innovation are interesting. The first scene presents a divided stage: one side the actual world where Francisco is returning to his estate, the other side his imagination where he imagines how Justina will receive him. This technique is repeated at crucial moments in the play. In one instance Justina appears to Francisco as a young woman in order to convince him to stay and cure her son, in another Francisco's shadow appears to convince Justina that her son has a better chance of surviving if she waits for the *curandero* instead of taking him to the nearest hospital.

The whole play unfolds against the biblical background of Lazarus' resurrection. There are numerous parallels to biblical events: Justina keeps a candle constantly burning before a picture of the Virgin, and both Francisco and Justina speak of their respective lives in terms similar to those used to describe Christ's journey to Calvary. Francisco has returned in the guise of the *curandero*, the healer, who uses traditional indigenous medicine that employs roots and herbs found on Mexican soil to cure Justina's son of a snake bite. In contrast, it is the conception of honor she has learned from the externally imposed Catholic religion that makes Justina unable to accept Francisco's offer to stay with her and begin life anew. The *curandero* lacks the skill to heal himself and leaves. Lazarus' shadow has come between Francisco and Justina. The shadow's presence manifests itself not only in the sense that Francisco is a Lazarus-like figure who experiences his own resurrection, nor only in the technical use of Francisco/Lazarus' shadow to get Justina to stay and wait for the *curandero*, but also in the sense that it is the tenets of a religion originally alien to Mexican soil that ultimately overshadows and blots out the possibility for healing and reconciliation the *curandero* has created. Francisco's resurrection is less comfortable to live with than the character's own imagination or rancor, and must be fled from. Justina wants to leave Francisco because she cannot offer him a Virgin-like purity; Francisco leaves Justina in order to atone for his previous abandonment of her and to ensure that her son will have the advantage of growing up on the estate. If they were able to lay aside the imposed past and live the restorative present, neither would be compelled to leave.

More innovative is Gutiérrez Hermosillo's play, *La escala de Jacob* (Jacob's ladder; published 1945). In this odd, flawed play a poor man schemes to support himself and his wife, but always fails and is constantly consumed by doubts about his wife's fidelity. The play is lengthy, frequently to little added effect. The most interesting aspects of it are the surrealistic characters and scenes utilized. The entire second act is a dream in which the Man becomes convinced of his wife's infidelity. From the beginning of the play the Man's Subconscious is a separate character, slyly insinuating doubts and fears into his reactions to everything around him. The Subconscious walks through walls, speaks directly to the audience, and, in the dream act, is joined by four doubles. In that act the stage is also filled with four students whom the Man calls his children and who treat him like a God, and an "Affixer" who takes care of arranging the fascinating multicolored rays of "sunlight" that traverse the set, creating a network of rays of light from floor to ceiling. In the final act the Man awakens to find his wife's dead body as his Subconscious says to him "So much the better. Now no one else will have the woman you loved" as the curtain descends.

The biblical reference of the title and the epigraph from Luke 23:29, "Because soon the days will come when you say: Blessed are the sterile," is rather opaque, but the title seems to refer to the staircase one must climb to reach the Man's apartment. By bargain and trickery, the biblical Jacob got the birthright and the blessing that was intended for his twin Esau. On his journey to take a wife among the daughters of Laban, he saw a ladder ascending to heaven in a dream. Later in life he wrestled with an Angel on the banks of the Jabbok. The biblical scenario is incorporated into the events of Hermosillo's play by means of the pervasive presence of the Man's Subconscious and the dream act. The Man wrestles with this presence that is constantly urging him to engage in trickery and deceit. Like Jacob, the Man wins his battle since his love for his wife remains unshaken when he awakes, but the future before him is bleaker than that before the newly named Israel. Where Israel becomes the father of twelve tribes, the Man in Hermosillo's play is the sterile one, and his happy days come, ironically, only when the woman whom he wanted to make happy dies. The ladder he must climb in order to find a better life for himself is endless. Hermosillo gives us a vision of the poor in which, regardless of their abilities or creativity, their own internalized fears, jealousies, and doubts cause them to fail. They blame themselves for the societal conditions that create their penury and, consequently, each rung on the ladder leads only to the next rung, never to a sense of accomplishment.

Perhaps the best-known mid-twentieth-century Mexican playwright is Rodolfo Usigli (1905–1979). A great friend of George Bernard Shaw, Usigli was a strong force for the development and professionalization of the Mexican theatre. In addition to writing a prodigious number of plays, he dedicated himself to teaching and writing theatre history. While Usigli pushed for innovation, Nomland is correct in his assessment of Usigli's works themselves:

Usigli isn't a theatrical experimenter, but a playwright who more or less continues the middle class tradition of the Comedia Mexicana. His contribution to the Mexican theatre lies more in his dialogue and the temperate ingenuousness of his commentaries, than in innovative themes or situations. His principal preoccupation is to demonstrate what he considered to be a weakness in the national character, the defects of the middle class brought on by apathy and despair, on the stage.[49]

In plays such as *El gesticulador* (The gesturer; 1947) or *Corona de sombra* (Shadow crown, 1947), Usigli employs events from Mexican history to create a picture of a hypocritical society that, lacking a firm sense of its own identity, manipulates and distorts even the most crucial events of its own national history such as the Revolution or the destruction of Maximilian and Carlota's ill-fated empire. While the landscape Usigli presents is Latin American, the formal aesthetic he uses is European and does little to advance a Latin American theatrical identity.

There are two playwrights from this period who do advance the course of the Mexican theatre and, additionally, serve as precursors to the kind of socially engaged theatre dealing with religious themes and structures that surfaces in Latin America in the 1960s. They are the Guatemalan resident in Mexico, Carlos Solórzano (1922–), and the Mexican national Emilio Carballido (1925–). Like Usigli, Solórzano not only wrote plays, but taught and engaged in writing theatre history. His *Teatro latinoamericano del siglo XX* is one of the pioneering works in the field of Latin American theatre history and criticism. His plays, however, go far beyond those of Usigli in presenting innovative themes and structures. Three of Solórzano's plays are particularly noteworthy. They are *Las manos de dios, Mea culpa*, and *El sueño del ángel*.

Las manos de dios (The hands of God; 1956) draws upon a number of sources: Calderón's *auto sacramental*, Unamuno's metaphysics, and a variety of expressionistic techniques, to achieve a type of theatre designed to provoke and agitate the spectator. It concerns the story of a young woman named Beatriz, whom the Devil convinces to steal the jewels from the hands of God's statue in the village church. She uses the jewels to bribe the jailkeeper to free her brother, who has been imprisoned for questioning the Master's right to take their land. When the jailkeeper demands more money she returns to the church, where the Priest catches her repeating her crime. After a debate between the Priest and the Devil, the appearance of "the wind from the North" convinces the townspeople to sacrifice Beatriz.

Solórzano uses the *auto*'s figural characterization to present characters who are symbolic representations of specific ideas: Beatriz = Rebellion, the Devil = Reason, the Prostitute = Free Will, the Townspeople = Submission, the Priest = Dogmatism, and the Jailer = Oppression.[50] There is an ascending order of treatment of these characters marked by an increase in the subtlety of characterization. Thus, the townspeople move as a block, never speaking until the climactic scene of debate between Reason (the Devil) and Faith (the Priest). In that scene they physically swing back and forth like a pendulum between the Priest and the Devil. The Prostitute, who demands more jewels for her services, is next, followed by the Jailer, who is convinced by the Prostitute's demand to extort more from Beatriz. Although both of them, as well as the Priest, remain emblematic representations, they are slightly more elaborated than the Townspeople. Beatriz and the Devil are the most fully developed, representing Reason and Individual Liberty that throws off the shackles of dogma in the tradition of Prometheus and Galileo.

Unamuno's metaphysics are evident in the play's aesthetic basis: to agitate. As Unamuno wanted to bring his neighbors to a transcendent state by disquieting them, thereby forcing them to consider their position clearly, so does Solórzano want his spectator to think. Solórzano, like Brecht, is interested in "diverting" his audience not in the sense of pure entertainment, but in the sense of discovering new paths. For Unamuno, according to Solórzano, liberty is only worthwhile when it is total. Total liberty can only be achieved by a recognition of all dependencies in all relationships and generations.[51]

The play is also pervaded by expressionistic qualities. The scenery Solórzano calls for is of an expressionistic perspective that depicts a richly decorated, baroque church – "it should have a fabulous aspect to it. Like a palace in a legend" – amidst the town's arid streets and miserable huts. Each character's entrance is marked by the introduction of a new musical theme. These themes appear within the body of the action as well, marking the moment when a character is influenced in one direction or another. There is also a very effective use of crowd scenes and an acknowledgment of the theatre space. When, at the end of Act I, Beatriz screams to the townspeople to kill the Devil:

(The townspeople look around them and move as if looking for the Devil without being able to see him. The Devil moves toward Beatriz shouting.)
THE DEVIL: Here I am.
BEATRIZ: Don't you see him?
THE DEVIL: But how are they going to kill me when they can't even see me? For them it's as if I were behind a curtain; the curtain of fear. (Shouts) Open the curtain, open it for once and for all. (The curtain begins to close, while the townspeople look for the Devil uncomprehendingly.) Open it, I said! Open it! (The Devil keeps up his clamor until the curtain closes.)[52]

What finally convinces the townspeople to side with the Priest/Faith is not any of the arguments advanced in the debate but the coming of "the wind from the North" that has always ruined their crops. The Priest seizes upon its presence as evidence of divine wrath and the townspeople flagellate themselves in the town square before entering the church to pray for forgiveness.

While Pedro Bravo-Elizondo is certainly correct in his analysis of the play when he associates the Master with God (neither ever appears in the action of the play but both are continually present; the jewels Beatriz steals and bribes the Jailer with are sold by the Prostitute to one of the Master's many female friends, thus figuratively returning to divine hands), I think he goes too far in associating "the wind from the North" with the Spanish Conquest and the history of imperialism in Latin America.[53] Solórzano seems to be suggesting something much more elemental, namely that the omnipresence of superstition is the evil that Reason must always battle against.

DEVIL: (Sobbing) I've lost this battle of rebellion so many times and each time pain rises in my breast as if it were the first. The wind from the North will move your body, poor Beatriz, and it will beat against the window of the cell of Man, who will continue a prisoner. (Pathetic) I won't fight anymore. Never again.

BEATRIZ: Yes, you'll fight again. Promise me that you'll do it for me. Some day they'll tire of believing in the wind and they'll know that the only thing that's impossible is what they don't want to accomplish. Their own will is the wind, with which one must completely envelop the surface of this earth. (She dies. The wind beats furiously, whipping Beatriz' hair and clothing.)[54]

The play ends with an element of hope as the Devil promises to continue fighting for them both.

While lacking the active dramatic tension of *Las manos de dios*, *Mea culpa* (1958) deals with virtually the same themes. In it a dying man enters a church seeking absolution for one sentence he passed in his life as a judge. His confessor, a mad Bishop, refuses to absolve him and forces him to hear his own confession instead. At the end of the play the Bishop is dragged off screaming for pardon by two novices while the Man takes his place in the confessional.

The Man asks for absolution for having condemned a religious fanatic to death, perhaps unjustly. The Bishop begs forgiveness "for having spent so many years indoctrinating the people with a religion of fear and torment, rather than the true religion of happiness and beauty."[55] The Man is a parallel to Pilate and the religious fanatic to Jesus. The Bishop is the representation of Church dogma which he has spent centuries "poisoning" people with by indoctrinating them with fear. While the play lacks the expressionistic, dance-like movement of *Las manos de dios*, the interior dramatic tension in both the Man and the Bishop's monologs is immense. Solórzano's position regarding man *vis-à-vis* religion is evident in the fact that the Bishop turns to the Man as his only possible confessor. Everyone within the Church has refused to judge him, claiming his doubts exist only within his own mind. With the final image of the Man sitting in the confessional and pulling the curtain closed, Solórzano seems to be implying a radical renovation of Church structure. By assuming the role of confessor the Man also takes on the mantle of Christ – the first confessor and the carrier of all sins. This is, however, a Christ freed from dogma who will evaluate confessions based upon his human reactions in the short space before he dies.

El sueño del ángel (Dream of the angel; 1960) is a dialog between a woman and her guardian angel in which the angel insists that the woman reveal what she did the one time he dropped his vigilance. At first she resists him, then she confesses that she made love to her brother-in-law, and begins to flagellate herself to expiate her sin. Theatrically, *El sueño del ángel* displays an expressionistic tendency similar to that of *Las manos de dios*. The guardian angel always stands behind and upstage of the woman. His movements and commands cause her to move as if they were connected by invisible strings. The angel himself is a "baroque Saint Michael" whose appearance "recalls, in short, that of an archangel of any church, rubicund and athletic with an air of insolent authority."[56] The angel is a figural representation of a dogma that insists upon the presence of guilt and repentance as a means of maintaining order. The woman, predisposed to this order, allows him to become her conscience and, finally, her executioner. The play ends with a bitter denunciation of passive acceptance of dogma in a parody of the reading and response in the Mass itself. As in *Mea culpa* and *Las manos de dios*, Solórzano, though violently anti-clerical, posits his plays in Christian terms. There seems to be a vital connection to the idea of crucifixion as liberation vs. the repressive teachings of Catholic dogma in his plays.

Emilio Carballido's first play, *La zona intermedia* (The intermediate zone; 1950) also utilizes a combination of religious and Mexican icons to develop its theme. Carballido subtitles the play an *auto sacramental*, but the purpose of this *auto* is not one of religious but of secular witness. It seeks not to reinforce the primacy of a particular hierarchy but to give birth to a new, essentially Mexican order. The order is based upon the figure of the Nahual, a mythological Aztec figure whose major characteristic is his ability to assume various forms. He is the one element in the world that is completely fluid, the trickster who maintains his freedom by rebelling against definition, who can say to the Devil:

You are your own slave. You can't do good even if you want to. *I* can. In other days, there were gods in my land. They were neither good nor *bad*. They had their principles, of course... I don't want to be a devil *or* a man. I live well the way I am, free, running like lightning, like the ancient gods, free from any standards but my own.[57]

Refusing to be defined, the Nahual embraces all definitions and becomes the consummate allegorical figure. A precursor to Octavio Paz' theory of Mexicans as a people trapped in an endless series of masks, the Nahual combines in one form the features of all the other main characters in the play. He is as libidinous as the Woman, and as indifferent to human suffering as the Virgin. Before he undergoes his transformation he ingests the Little Man, who subordinates his own desire to a superior order, and the Critic, the rational censor of the creative act.[58] It is, in fact, the fusion of all four that makes the Nahual's transformation possible. Each of the nonhumans present in *La zona intermedia* represents a single aspect of the *potential* characteristics of the New Man the Nahual becomes. Unlike Paz' Mexican, the Nahual, after his resurrection as the New Man, has been given a chance to utilize his Aztec origins. He is not only a representation of lost innocence caused by the imposition of Christian morality on indigenous forms,[59] but also the potential extension of those indigenous forms into contemporary reality. Even this early work of Carballido's displays, albeit submerged beneath the *auto* style, the social critique present in later plays such as *El día que soltaron los leones* (The Day they freed the lions; 1963) or *Silencio, pollos pelones, ya les van a echar su maíz!* (Quiet, you mangy mutts, you'll get your bone!; 1963). Carballido writes plays that run the gamut from provincial realism to what has been called a kind of "Artuadian Gothic," but the plays always present a critique that insists upon the potentiality of humankind for achieving ultimate self-realization. The New Man is sent back to earth to suffer, but, as the Angel tells him, he still possesses the Nahual's ability to create new forms. Where the Nahual changed his outer appearance as if he were replacing one mask with another, the New Man will create "with words, with sounds, by action alone,"[60] thereby formulating his own consistent identity. The Nahual, who was incapable of distinguishing the relative value of one course of action over another, was relegated to a position outside space and time. When he is reborn as the New Man he has entered the temporal state given to human beings that will lead to the Day of Judgment, but his indigenous heritage gives him the tools he needs to control his own destiny.

As we have seen, twentieth-century Mexican theatre through the 1950s begins by following two divergent paths: one that presents theatre that is dedicated to the principles and ideology of the Revolution, the other that gets its primary impetus from middle-class forms and the rural drama. By the end of the 1950s these two paths were beginning to merge in a way that recaptured the religious basis of the Aztec and missionary theatre, but recast in a new form, one that lays the basis for the liberation theatre of the 1960s and 1970s. Twentieth-century Chilean theatre followed a similar trajectory when, between 1900 and 1930, theatre became an important organizing tool of Luis Emilio Recabarren's Socialist Workers' Party.

THE MEXICAN MODEL IN OTHER REGIONS

We have seen the influence of socialist and anarchist thought on early-twentieth-century playwrights in the Río de la Plata region, and the propensity of nineteenth-century writers such as Camilo Henríquez to adapt neoclassical ideals of the education value of the stage to calls for independence from Spain. Early-twentieth-century Chile saw the combination of all these strands in theatre created for and by the working class. Eugenia W. Herbert has observed that "Of all the facets of art, one held a supreme fascination for socialists in all countries. This was the theatre. Socialists and anarchists alike were aware of the power of the drama and anxious to exploit its possibilities in spreading their gospel."[61] The Chilean adeptness in using theatre for proselytization has been well documented in Pedro Bravo-Elizondo's valuable study on workers' theatre and culture in the Chilean nitrate fields, *Cultura y teatro obrera en Chile 1900–1930*. Nitrate, with its uses in manufacturing gunpowder and fertilizer, was a kind of "white gold" that filled the coffers of the Chilean treasury and the pockets of the primarily English companies who mined it between 1880 and 1930. As they did in Argentina, the British attempted to shore up their declining empire by economic exploitation in Chile as well. As a contemporary historian observed: "Centuries ago this Chilean territory was conquered by the most powerful country in Europe at the time. It was conquered with harquebus, lance, and culverin. Today it is being conquered by the countries that have succeeded Spain in power. No longer with harquebus and culverin, the arms of that time, but with work and capital, the arms of today."[62] Exploitation of the nitrate fields brought roads and railways into the northern desert provinces of Tarapacá and Antofagasta, turning the provincial city of Iquique into the second most important commercial and industrial port after Valparaíso. Chilean and foreign workers flocked to the nitrate fields in search of work, leading to a two-tiered system of existence that paralleled some of the worst abuses of North American coalfields. The English administrator and his assistants lived in well-constructed and well-maintained homes with electricity and all the comforts of Britain. As a North American traveler to the region at the time, Theodore Child, wrote:

In the drawing-room the ladies exercise the same refining influence that they would at home, in the dining-room the table is served with English correctness, in the bedrooms a stock of novels with the familiar stiff board covers and sensational pictures of passionate heroines offers a soporific to the uneasy sleeper; other illustrated papers and magazines and the ubiquitous *Punch* are seen lying in handy places; indeed, if Mr. Du Maurier happened to be banished to the *pampa* of Tamarugal he could still continue to find types and incidents for his drawings; athletic Englishmen wearing clothes that fit them, and young ladies who play lawn-tennis in provokingly coquettish costumes, and ride like Amazons across the dusty plains to pay visits in the neighboring establishments.[63]

In contrast to the lifestyle of the resident English administrators, the mine workers lived in quite different conditions: "a few rows of corrugated iron sheds, at the back of which the tenants build out huts of poles and old bags, where they prefer to spend their time rather than in the iron rooms heated by the unclouded sunshine of the rainless desert."[64] The workers were also obliged to purchase anything other than fruit and vegetables through the company *pulpería*, a kind of general store. As Child observes,

These stores are carried on with a view to making a profit out of the sales, and not merely for the accommodation of the workmen. We may say, further, that through the *pulpería* the company calculates to make a profit of ten dollars on an average from each workman. From another point of view we may say that sixty percent of the earnings of the men are spent in the company's store, and the other forty percent wasted on drinking and gambling, either inside the camp or in neighboring villages.[65]

To confront these conditions a number of workers' self-help and educational organizations, newspapers, magazines, unions, theatres and other cultural organizations began to appear. Frequently inspired by poor translations of Europeans such as Bakunin, Proudhon, Ruskin, Tolstoy, Saint-Simon, Iglesias, Malatesta, and Eliseo Reclus, these organizations provided a medium for opposing the workers' abusive and miserable existence.[66] In 1928–1929 the cultural activity of workers' organizations was particularly intense, with forty-six artistic groups, twenty-two cultural and sports centers, two musical groups, thirty-nine societies with diverse ends, both mutualist and cultural at the same time, and seventeen unions with cultural programs.[67] By 1931 there were fifteen amateur theatre groups made up of working-class participants in Iquique alone. This kind of workers' theatre was not unique to northern Chile; it existed throughout the country. In each case it reflected an attempt by working people themselves to present their own vision of their world, and to utilize any means at their disposal of bettering the conditions under which they lived.[68]

The cultural activity by workers' organizations in northern Chile seems to have passed through various stages. The first was the utilization of the press as a consciousness-raising force. In 1910 Luis Emilio Recabarren (1876–1924) wrote an article called "El balance del siglo: ricos y pobres a través de un siglo de vida republicana" (Balance of the century: rich and poor during a century of republican life). His main thesis was that 100 years of independence from Spain had improved the lot of the Chilean bourgeoisie, but done nothing to better the economic and social position of the vast majority of the working class. Shortly thereafter Recabarren gave a speech in which he called for the "founding of publications, the printing of pamphlets, the creation of schools, and the realization of educational lectures."[69] Recabarren took his own advice when he began to write for the workers' newspaper, *El Trabajo* (Work). *El Trabajo* hoisted the working-class banner, carrying it with apostolic fervor across its pages. The newspaper was prone to mix Christian symbolism with socialist sentiment, presenting the Savior as a "man of flesh and blood who rebelled against an unjust order, and punished the temple merchants."[70]

While the separation of Church and state was achieved in Chile without the occurrence of civil war that we saw in Mexico, the kind of material published by *El Trabajo* in the context of the economic depression, labor unrest, and military coups of the late 1920s and early 1930s led the Church to fear a leftist regime and unbridled anti-clerical sentiment.[71] In northern Chile, where the mining industry had led to unrest even earlier than the 1920s, the Church, under the leadership of Monseñor José María Caro, bishop of Tarapacá from 1912 to 1926, went to battle with the socialist and anarchist forces. The spectacle of socialists and priests debating each other in Iquique's main square became a common sight. Monseñor Caro proposed the nationalization of the nitrate fields in such a manner that they would be worked and managed by workers' cooperatives under proper spiritual guidance.[72]

In 1912, Monseñor Caro's first year of ecclesiastical leadership, Recabarren founded his own newspaper, *El Despertar de los Trabajadores* (The workers' awakening), and was highly instrumental in the foundation of the Partido Obrero Socialista (Socialist Workers' Party), of which he became the leader and presidential candidate. These two institutions were to work together for many years, members of each frequently coming together in the workers' theatre, Arte y Revolución, founded by Recabarren and Elís Lafertte, which used the offices of *El Despertar* for its activities.

Arte y Revolución, and the workers' theatre movement in general, lasted from approximately 1912 to approximately 1933, when, starting in 1931, a wave of repression swept through Chile, bringing with it political persecution, assassination, and exile. The theatre, easily identifiable by the regime for its popular political activity, suffered more than any other cultural form, and the Chilean popular theatre disappeared until the work of the Teatro Experimental in the 1940s. While the Teatro Experimental and theatre groups in other parts of Latin America such as La Candelaria and Teatro Experimental de Cali in Colombia, or Teatro Escambray in Cuba, would evolve their own brands of popular theatrical expression, the Chilean movement of the early twentieth century is notable for its creation and performance by the workers themselves.

In a specific social and historical space they gave their class a sense of cohesion and brotherhood, that implicitly confronted a society that didn't allow them to participate in its culture or its riches. The historical judgment that some authors displayed in their works accomplished not only a political objective, but also the educational objective of forming new generations. They saw society's transformation effected not only by means of art, but also by the accompanying action of combatative theoretical knowledge, by the vision of the new world they wanted to forge.[73]

Like their neighbors to the north in Mexico, however, the Chileans also had a middle-class and rural tradition. Where Mexican commercial theatre was transformed by the Teatro de Orientación and the Teatro de Ulises and the Group of Seven, Chilean theatre was transformed by the appearance of the so-called "generation of 1927."

The "generation of 1927" includes those writers born between 1890 and 1904 and whose mature work begins to be seen between 1935 and 1949. As Rojo has pointed out, these writers began to search not only for the "national soul" displayed in the *costumbrista* drama, but for a way to interpret that soul's place in the immediate present. What this meant was a radical reinterpretation of tradition as a collectively held consciousness, actual as well as general, a possession held by all for the use of all. These playwrights turned to an "approximation of the problem that naturally ended by channeling its yearnings for a new nationalism in the direction of an active, semi-Jungian imagination of the past with its burden of atavistic voices, symbols or allegories, [a past] that concluded by imposing its existence upon life in the present."[74] The search for a "national soul" was by no means confined to the theatre. Perhaps the best example is Violeta Parra's radio recitals that rescued popular forms of expression in poetry and music from becoming merely artifacts for touristic consumption.

In Chile this movement towards a new dramatic conception of the national soul received its strongest impetus with the 1956 revival of Germán Luco Cruchaga's (1894–1936) play, *La viuda de Apablaza*. *La viuda de Apablaza* (Apablaza's widow; 1928) is a *costumbrista* drama in which a rich widow cares for and educates her dead husband's illegitimate peasant son, Ñico. Ñico so resembles his father that the Widow falls in love with him and denies him permission to marry her niece Flora, revealing her love for him and offering to turn her entire estate over to him if he forgets about her niece. Ñico accepts her offer and two years later is the boss and becoming rich in his own right. He is so completely in control that he now brings Flora, whom he truly loves, to live with them. When Flora arrives the Widow shoots herself. The play ends with Ñico keening over the Widow's body, lamenting that he had always loved her as the mother he never had. The play presents us with the common stereotypical *costumbrista* characterizations such as the peasants and the Spanish shopkeeper, but most of all, Cruchaga gives us the domineering figure of the Widow that proves so influential in subsequent Chilean theatre.

The revival of *La viuda de Apablaza* provided a whole generation of Chilean playwrights with a basic model of the "national soul" to build upon in their quest for the creation of a new socially engaged theatre. Directed by Pedro de la Barra, and performed by the university-affiliated Teatro Experimental, the production of *La viuda de Apablaza* can also be seen as the beginnings of a professional, socially engaged theatre that became prevalent throughout Chile in the 1970s. It is only with Egon Wolff's (1926–) first two widely acclaimed plays, *Discípulos del miedo* and *Mansión de lechuzas*, however, that the kind of drama described by Rojo comes into its own.

Mansión de lechuzas (Owl mansion; 1957) demonstrates Wolff's ability to construct plot and to create character. It is psychological realism of good quality but undistinguished. Wolff has yet to find the personal style that is so strong in his later plays. That style is hinted at here with the final image, the theatrical appearance of the "invader" (the outsider who is so prevalent a figure in Wolff's work) disguised as the Easter Bunny, at the time for the family's new life and the time of the Resurrection.

More fully realized than *Mansión de lechuzas* is Wolff's play written and published in the following year, *Discípulos del miedro* (Disciples of fear; 1958) about a middle-class family. The father was a school teacher happy with his lot, but the mother, having come from a poverty-stricken background, was not. She wanted more for her family and pushed him to leave his profession and go into business. At the beginning of the play they have earned enough money from their store to consider buying a factory. Their three children are all adults, and the mother has mistreated each of them in some way in the name of helping them. She has urged her daughter to break off an engagement with the man she loved because he was not good enough for her and has forced one son to leave school at an early age to help in the store, and then deprecated every job he has ever had because it would not get him anywhere. He is now a mechanic and enjoys his work, although she cannot see any future in it. Her other son, her favorite, has followed in his mother's footsteps and is an unhappy businessman, unable to treat either his colleagues or himself honestly. When the father, driven by his wife's obsession with buying the factory, goes to a loanshark for the money they need to tide them over and they cannot pay on time, they lose everything. The father dies, and the last scene of the play shows the mother living above the garage with her son the mechanic and his wife. She still tries to rule everyone else's lives, refusing to believe that they could be happy with what they have. The final moments of the play are:

RICARDO: You will have to live with me until the day you understand. The day may come when you will sit at this table and take a pleasure in the things I bring you: in this onion, in these potatoes, in this wine. I hope it will be so. (He leaves.)
MATILDE: Where are you going? Ricardo...! Where are you going? Don't leave me alone...I'm afraid, I'm afraid![75]

Although Matilde's fear is a psychological one, it is one that has been created by social forces. Wolff writes about the bourgeoisie and the various "invasions" it suffers. His is a realistically based drama that has sociological and political consequences.[76]

It is the combination of the psychological, sociological, and political elements that make Wolff's drama live and breathe. While he would probably object to the analysis, it is quite possible to see the sort of domineering consciousness that Matilde (as a direct descendant of the Widow of Apablaza) represents, the consciousness that maintains the status quo and forces all to conform to it, as the sector of Chilean society that was outraged by Allende's ascension to power, and that has, until recently, enthusiastically supported Pinochet. Wolff shows us that class perceptively and unsentimentally here, and it is a terrain that he explores even more fully in his later plays of the 1960s and 1970s such as *Flores de Papel* (1970) and *Los invasores* (1963).

The scenario of independent and university-affiliated theatre groups such as the Grupo de los Siete, Teatro de Orientación, Teatro de Ulises, and Teatro de Ahora, in Mexico or the Teatro Experimental in Chile, that served to restore vigor to the Latin American theatre by combining a reinterpretation of the past with a universalization of theatrical technique is repeated throughout the region in the twentieth century. In Argentina the Teatro del Pueblo and Teatro Juan B. Justo were the precursors of the independent theatres of the 1960s and 1970s. In Cuba Teatro Adad united the disparate artists attempting to reinvigorate the Cuban stage. In Puerto Rico, university-affiliated theatre groups gave broad impetus to the renovation of the Caribbean island's theatre. Representative of these companies are the Argentinians Eichelbaum, Cuzzani, and Dragún, the Cuban Piñera, and the Puerto Rican Marqués.

EICHELBAUM, CUZZANI, AND DRAGÚN

After Mexico, the most theatrically active Latin American nation at the turn of the century was Argentina. The works of Florencio Sánchez, Armando Discépolo, and Francisco Delfillipis Novoa have been examined in an earlier chapter. The Argentinian playwright who epitomizes the sort of combination of *costumbrista* dramaturgy with a deeper understanding of character and the exploration of social themes that we have been examining is Samuel Eichelbaum (1894–1967). His play, *Un guapo del 900* (1940), describes the unraveling of an entire way of life. In it Ecuménico, a *guapo* or species of gangster-like bodyguard, tough, and utterly loyal to his *caudillo* or boss, Alejo, discovers that Alejo's wife is having an affair with one of his political rivals, Clemente Ordoñez. Ecuménico feels as if he himself has been betrayed and bursts in on the two lovers, intending to put an end to the affair by intimidating Clemente. Clemente calls Ecuménico a coward and pulls his gun on him, forcing Ecuménico to kill him. Rather than rewarding him for having disposed of a political rival, Alejo is furious with Ecuménico. Clemente was an incorruptible politician, respected by all, the harbinger of a new order, and suspicion for his death will inevitably fall on Alejo. To ward it off and safeguard his political standing, Alejo turns Ecuménico in. For months he languishes in prison, until his mother, Natividad, calls upon the loyalty her family has shown the caudillo for generations, and convinces Alejo to use his influence to set Ecuménico free. Ecuménico returns home convinced of the absurdity of his act. His mother, who has strongly defended him and who has represented the vigor of the old ways throughout the play is devastated and confused by his attitude. In the play's final scene both of them realize that they no longer recognize the other, something has changed. As Natividad says at the end of the play: "I feel like I'm someone else. And you seem to be someone else as well. You're like a spirited, but tired horse. I look at your mane, your neck, your ears, and your snout, and it's like I'm seeing you for the first time. I need to see you standing in order to recognize you, to look at your footprint so I can know you are my son. Suddenly, you seem to have been raised on someone's else's milk."[77]

The play is a dramatic and theatrical manifestation of the transition into the twentieth century. This is no longer the *costumbrista*/naturalistic world where everything is cut and dry, people are who and what they are, and each act has meaning. Ecuménico kills the representative of change, the new type of politician, but the assassination will not stop that change from occurring. In fact, he is denounced by the very person who, according to the conventions of the old world, should protect him. Ecuménico's difference and distance is symbolized by his weapon of choice, the knife. Both Alejo and Clemente carry guns and, as Ecuménico says, "I prefer the knife as a weapon. It's more of a man's weapon. It forces you to fight close." The problem is that the world no longer functions on the basis of that kind of *hombría*, the *honor y honra* convention that values face-to-face confrontation in an expression of virility, and self-sufficient individuality.[78] Everything here is in flux and, for that reason the play can offer no definitive answers and is open-ended. As with the Chilean theatre of this century, Eichelbaum and other playwrights signal the beginnings of a new, vital dramaturgy in Argentina, but it is not until the 1950s that the vitality becomes widespread. Two playwrights representative of the new dramaturgy are Osvaldo Dragún and Augustín Cuzzani.

Osvaldo Dragún's (1929–) work is well known throughout Latin America and has received a fair amount of attention in the United States, largely as a result of his plays *Historias para ser contadas* (Stories to be told; 1957), *Historia de mi esquina* (My corner's story; 1957), and *Historias con cárcel* (Jail tales; published 1973). Dragún's "story" plays were innovative in both form and content. In form they present brief scenes which utilize a mixture of song, dialog, and pantomime in an epic format. In content they bring to life a socially committed theatre which uses the indigenous Argentinian milieu as its material, thus wedding the traditional *costumbrismo* form of local color to a new aesthetic impetus. Dragún's work has frequently been cited as a Latin American version of Brechtian theatre, and his political and social concerns are evident from his first full-length play, *La peste viene de Melos*. *La peste viene de Melos* (The plague comes from Melos; 1956) was inspired by the CIA-engineered coup against Guatemala's President Jacobo Arbenz in 1954. In the play a large and powerful empire attacks a small country, accusing it of exporting the plague. Infuriated by Melos' stance of independence towards the Athenian empire, Alcibiades, Athens' governor, hatches a plan to invade Melos. The pretext is that the island is the source of a mysterious plague killing off Athenian citizens. When the Athenian fleet reaches Melos, Melesian merchants appoint a well-to-do peasant, Pitias, as their negotiator. They believe he will sue for peace to protect his land. Instead, he refuses to bow to the Athenian yoke and causes a war that lasts two years. At the end of that time the Athenians are winning but Melos has been destroyed by the Melesians and, following Melos' example, many other Athenian client-states are rebelling against the empire. In Dragún's schema Athens is clearly equated with the United States and the plague with communism. *La peste*, however, is far from merely a didactic work. The materialistic greed that motivates the Athenian merchants to goad the war on, and the Melesian merchants to turn against Pitias, is in sharp contrast to the pride and dignity of Pitias and his peasant army. Dragún returns to Aeschylean aesthetics by associating Pitias and company with the telluric and maternal vs. the nontelluric, nonmaternal aspects of the invaders and the Melesian merchants.[79] Pitias destroys the creative fecundity of the land rather than see it fall into Athenian hands, and his is the only complete family unit presented in the play. Alcibiades, on the other hand, hates women, Tisia – commander of the Athenian forces – yearns for a woman, and Acanto, a Melesian merchant, tries to negotiate with the Athenians by offering his daughter's virgin body in exchange for peace. Melos' very defeat is a creative, fertile act, for it inspires other rebellions. Dragún also suggests in *La peste* that an imperialistic venture produces exactly the sort of resistance and revolutionary change it was designed to prevent when he depicts the starving peasant–warriors attacking the Melesian merchants' warehouses.

Agustín Cuzzani (b. 1924) died in 1987 after a long and distinguished career in Argentinian arts that included plays such as *El centroforward murió all amanecer*, *Los indios estaban cabreros*, and *Para que se cumplan las escrituras* (1965), as well as work in film, television, and radio and adaptations of foreign plays such as *Hair* and *Marat/Sade*.

It is the earliest period of Cuzzani's work that concerns us here and his first four plays: *Una libra de carne* (1954), *El centroforward murió all amanecer* (1955), *Los indios estaban cabreros* (1957), and *Sempronio* (1957) all fall under the rubric of what he called his "farce–satires." They mix highly farcical elements with biting satire relating to humanity's condition. The result is a dramaturgy that relies upon the humor created when spectacle is presented out of its proper context.

Los indios estaban cabreros (The Indians were angry) is the most sophisticated of Cuzzani's "farce–satires." The play depicts the Indian Prince Tupa, who, after seven unsuccessful rebellions against the Aztec dictator of twelfth-century Mexico, decides to journey to the horizon in order to make the Sun god aware of his people's misery. Along with two other Indians he is shipwrecked and caught in the nets of a Spanish fisherman. When the fisherman's daughter falls in love with one of his "fish," the fisherman denounces the Indians to the Inquisition. Condemned to prison for thirty days to see whether they rot or not, they are sent to Granada, where the fisherman's daughter succeeds in getting them an audience with Queen Isabella at the same time as Christopher Columbus. Prince Tupa sends one of his companions back to Mexico as Columbus' guide and all of the men of art and science he has met in prison as the crew. Realizing the Spaniards will bring his people medicine and learning at the cost of many lives and a large part of their culture, Prince Tupa decides to wait in prison until the thirty days have passed and he will be burned at the stake.

As in the other "farce–satires," *Los indios* presents us with a series of farcical choruses, adding to them the hilarious scenes in Spain as the fisherman insists the three Indians are fish because he caught them in the sea. By placing his story in an historical framework, however, Cuzzani increases his ability to put across his thematic material. Like Brecht in *Mother Courage*, the historical setting allows Cuzzani to criticize contemporary society at a distance, questioning the assumptions beneath surface loyalties. In addition, *Los indios* presents the spectator with the constant use of anachronism – for example, a policeman dressed in contemporary uniform appears in both Mexico and Spain – that serves to remind the spectator of his or her place as a critical viewer of the twentieth century.[80] The prison scene contains satirical references to the past and present of both Spain and America, reminding us of the cyclical nature of history. As one of the imprisoned sages, Abnib Ben Benib, remarks; "They are called Americans from the Italian *amare i cani*, because legend has it that these people are obliged to love the tyrannical dogs and despots who seem to appear throughout the region."[81]

Tupa's disillusionment, when he realizes that he cannot alleviate his people's suffering without bringing death and destruction upon them as well, is mirrored in various ways throughout the play. When it is announced that all Aztec beggars will have to pay a monthly tax of a bag of fleas, one of them says, "The flea is an instrument of human reciprocity, a form of exchange, an agent of social progress."[82] When Tupa hears that Columbus really wanted ships to look for God, he says:

TUPA: I reached this land looking for god in the East.
COLUMBUS: And you can see what you found. In the West, on the other hand...
TONATIO: You'll see what you'll find there.[83]

Tupa's decision to stay in Spain and be burned at the stake returns him to prison as we hear the Indian Chorus that began the play chanting once more the Aztec word for "aurora," *Tlausicalpán*.

VIRGILIO PIÑERA

The mid-twentieth-century Cuban independent theatre is best represented by the works of Virgilio Piñera (1912–1979) with his plays, *Electra Garrigó* (1948) and *Jesús* (1950). Each of these plays turn to mythical sources, investing them with resonance for the Cuban society of the period. *Electra Garrigó* is a very interesting play that uses the Greek myth in a humorous and grotesque manner. In both style and content the play is similar to Dragún's *La peste viene de Melos* and, especially, to José Triana's (1933–) later play, *La noche de los asesinos* (1964).

In Piñera's equally interesting play, *Jesús*, a 33-year-old barber named Jesús García, son of José and María, becomes the object of neighborhood rumors that he can perform miracles. Although he insists that he is incapable of doing so, people keep bringing him their sick children and pets, demanding that he cure them. The logic is that if everyone says he can perform miracles, he must be able to do so. This logic extends to the police as well, who believe that if everyone believes he can perform miracles he must have given them some reason to think so. Jesús continues to insist that he is Not-Jesus, collecting a small band of disciples who believe him.

Gradually, his barbering business becomes impossible due to the demands of Church, state, and civic groups upon his time. The Church wants him to neither deny nor affirm that he is Christ, thereby maintaining the validity of its doctrinal power. The government wants him to claim that he is Christ, thereby putting an end to their crowd-control problems, and the public follows him, insisting that he is Christ regardless of what he claims. When Jesús refuses to bring a little boy's dead dog back to life, he is stoned by a crowd and has to be rescued by the police. They give him the option of making a public declaration that he is Christ or going to jail. He chooses jail and, when they try to transfer him from the station, the crowd sets upon the police, allowing Jesús to escape.

He reunites with his disciples for a Last Supper in which he performs several magic trick "miracles" and then returns home to his barber shop. In the shop he finds a completely bald assassin from the country's interior who insists upon getting a haircut. The assassin has been hired by the government to kill Jesús and remove the public menace he represents.

When Jesús sees the knife in the mirror he turns, spreads his arms and receives the fatal blow in his chest. As the assassin leaves, one of Jesús' disciples enters and discovers the body. He came to warn Jesús that people were coming for him and says:

I'll wait for them here; now they'll finally know that he isn't Jesus nor can he perform miracles. (Shouts and whistles are heard, a stone breaks the glass in the door to the street. The people enter asking for Jesús' head.)
CLIENTE: Here it is. Are you convinced? (The people fall to their knees shouting: Jesus, forgive us! Slow curtain...)[84]

Piñera himself provides a very interesting analysis of the play, in which he dubs his Jesús the anti-Fidel. That is:

My Jesus poses the paradox in which we lived [in 1948]: this barber, and his proselytes as well, are honest people. They do not accept playing the government's game, and are therefore ready to sacrifice their lives. But they have the great defect of not knowing how to act. I would define them by means of the title of a well-known film: I'd call them "Rebels without a Cause"... That is their mistake: they are rebels but they do not know what to do with their rebellion. They are gratuitous rebels, and the only solution that occurs to them is to sacrifice their lives, a perfectly useless sacrifice that does not bear any fruit whatsoever.[85]

What Jesús and his disciples fail to understand is that this populace is desperately in need of salvation and that they will find that salvation in his claims not to be Christ as much as if he did claim to be Christ. By calling for his head, by stoning him, they place upon him the burden of acting for them. He is refusing to perform their "miracles" for them and therefore deserves to die. What Jesús keeps insisting upon is that each person is as capable as he is of taking responsibility for their own actions. If they were to follow his preaching they would find themselves empowered. This is a critique of human activity similar in its content and the conclusions drawn to that of contemporary liberation theology. Jesús tries to make people see that temporal and spiritual power comes not from above, but from below. The Church and the government hold power over them only because of the willingness of those who form the social base, the "base communities," to cede their own power to those institutions. As it is, his death simply erects another martyr to whom they can pray, from whom they can ask for pity. Nothing has changed.

RENE MARQUÉS

The Puerto Rican playwright Rene Marqués' (1919–) work *La muerte no entrará en palacio* (published 1956) is another play that, like Piñera's *Electra Garrigó* and Dragún's *La peste viene de Melos*, employs a radical restructuring of Greek mythology to treat Latin American political and sociological themes. Best known in the United States for his realistic *La carreta* (The oxcart; 1950), Marqués' work has spanned a variety of styles and genres. *La muerte no entrará en palacio* (Death won't enter the palace) epitomizes one of the concerns that runs throughout Marqués' work: a passionate rejection of US intervention in Puerto Rico's economy, culture, and politics.

Don José, governor of a small Caribbean island for the last twenty years, strives to maintain and consolidate his power by imprisoning his former mentor, Don Rodrigo, and making the island a protectorate of a superpower to the north. Alberto, son of one of the men who brought Don José to power and who is to be his son-in-law, resolves to assassinate Don José. He pays one last visit to Casandra, his fiancée, and is accidently killed when Casandra tries to take his gun from him. As Don José signs the papers making the island a protectorate, Casandra, using Alberto's gun, shoots her father and then kills herself.

Marqués is relating actual historical events in dramatic terms. Don José is patently equivalent to Puerto Rico's governor between 1948 and 1964, Luis Muñoz Marín. Don Rodrigo is Marqués' name for Albizu Campos, a Nationalist leader convicted for his part in a 1950 revolt, and Casandra is Lolita Lebrón, who was arrested for firing some pistol shots in the US Congress when the commonwealth agreement was signed.[86] Although the play is based on historical fact, Marqués does not develop it in an entirely realistic manner. The frame of the play is the prologue and epilogue, in which Tiresias, friend to the governor and one of the triumvirate of poet, philosopher (Alberto's father), and politician that liberated Puerto Rico from colonial rule, tells us about the statue of Casandra that, hand raised like the Statue of Liberty, stands in the ruined palace garden. Casandra embodies liberty, an unswerving force that moves inexorably to completion.[87] Marqués manifests this theatrically by lighting and music that he characterizes as "unreal." The epilogue contains a Female Chorus that chants "Love, pain, love!" as the lights dim on the statue's uplifted arm, the arm Casandra lifted to shoot down her father.

Marqués further attempts to give the play a classical structure and symbolism. Doña Isabel, Don José's wife, is intimately connected with the land. Don José is associated with power, Tiresias has a seer's vision, and Alberto is the Antigone-like idealist. The play's major flaw is that Casandra has no true understanding of the value of her act of assassination. She acts out of rage and blind faith in the validity of Alberto's ideals. The choral chant of "Love, pain, love!" is appropriate to her but not for the reasons Marqués wishes it to be. He intends the chant to refer to Puerto Rico itself, but Casandra's all too abrupt conversion does not allow that interpretation. She is, throughout the play, fighting first and foremost for her own and Alberto's liberation, not for the liberation of the island.[88]

Structurally, Marqués mixes a number of different formal techniques in *La muerte*. The majority of the story's action is told in an extremely realistic manner which yet contains numerous symbolic elements. The most blatant is a valueless rock that a young peasant brings Don José for analysis saying, "Our reality can be as hard as a rock ... I mean ... we need to know how to sacrifice ourselves. Sacrifice ourselves in order to be ... ourselves."[89] Marqués also combines amplified offstage voices with lighting and music for all the scenes of revolt, the first assassination attempt and Don Rodrigo's speeches. Don Rodrigo's speeches themselves contain close parallels to the Sermon on the Mount, and are intended by Marqués to give the entire play a feeling of the symbolic and eternal nature of the struggle for liberation.[90] Unfortunately, the realistic elements undercut the symbolic ones. Rather than giving the play the expanse of Greek tragedy or the intellectual range of Symbolism, we are painfully aware of the thinness of the symbolic elements. They lack the three-dimensional quality of the realistic scenes that exist alongside them. If, as has been claimed, Marqués' work may be measured by his intent to be provocative, the play, which has been banned from performance in Puerto Rico, succeeds. As a fully integrated work of theatre, however, *La muerte* is often at war with itself.

MIGUEL ANGEL ASTURIAS

Curiously enough, perhaps the best example of the return to historical and mythological elements that we have identified as the prime characteristic of mid-twentieth-century Latin American theatre, can be found in the Guatemalan author Miguel Angel Asturias' plays. While Asturias (1899–1974) is widely known for novels such as *El señor presidente* and *Hombres de maiz*, Guatemala has historically lacked a strong theatrical tradition. Asturias wrote four plays: *Soluna* (1955), *La audiencia de los confines* (1957), *Chantaje* (1964), and *Dique seco* (1964). As Carlos Solórzano has written:

Miguel Angel Asturias' dramatic work...shows the writer in a double dimension; that of the polemicist who makes use of dramatic dialogue to purify his ideas about the political and social order, and that of the poet who tries to capture some of the magical suggestions of prehispanic cultures in vivid, corporeal images...Asturias turned towards the theatre in a purposeful manner. He was disposed to give a structure to some of the "personal experiences" that had been expressed in a dialogic form in the *Legends of Guatemala*. [They appear there] in reiterated forms, more appropriate to mythic evocation than to communicating a limited conflict, one that, like the theatre demands, finds its course within its own problematic.[91]

While Solórzano's assessments of the two strongest elements of Asturias' theatre is accurate, he appears to want to limit the theatre's possibilities to a classical understanding of conflict. As has been proven time and time again, conflict is not the only measure of theatrical power, and Asturias' play *Soluna* succeeds precisely because it utilizes the same sort of combination of popular characters, folklore, and mysticism that make his novels so powerful. In *Soluna* Mauro, the *patrón* (owner) of a country estate, has married Ninica, a city woman. They love each other a great deal but, due to Ninica's fear that she will not be able to live in the country, they make a pact that she will be able to return to the city whenever she wants to. Before we are aware of any of this information we see the two of them arguing, Mauro desperately trying to dissuade Ninica from leaving on the next train as he runs after her in the pouring rain.

While they are at the station a band of Gypsies enters the house, singing and dancing. One of them predicts that the mistress will return to the house that night during the lunar eclipse. Mauro comes home and, also convinced that Ninica will return, has another place laid for her at the table. He then takes up a mask of the god/sorcerer Chamá Soluna, a mythic combination of the Sun and the Moon, and falls asleep with it in his arms. The Nahual of his servant Porfirión appears and tries to take the mask away from Mauro, but fails. The stage is then filled with hordes of peasants, divided into allies of the Sun and allies of the Moon, singing, dancing, and beating tambourines. The two groups drive each other back and forth across the stage until Porfirión appears, bringing the news that horses have gone wild and jumped over cliffs, proving the advent of the Day of Judgment.

The peasants are crazed with fear, first begging God's forgiveness, and then turning to Chamá Soluna, yelling that they will kill non-Christians and drink their blood. Ninica then appears, proving that it is not Judgment Day, and everyone drinks to Mauro and Ninica's health. Suddenly the stage becomes black and the lights come up, revealing Mauro, asleep with the mask at his feet. The Nahual enters, seen by the terrified servant Tomasa, and takes the mask. Tomasa's screams wake Mauro, who grabs a rifle and shoots the fleeing Nahual. At this point friends and neighbors arrive, carrying the wounded Ninica on a bower. It seems that as the peasants beat their drums and pots and pans to help the Moon ward off the Sun, they heard a terrible crash. The train to the city had left its rails. Porfirión returns, his left arm wounded by a gunshot, carrying the blood-soaked mask. As Tomasa goes off to clean the mask Ninica says, "Your little animal has returned... The person who left was less yours, a city person, the one who has returned to stay with you always is a little country animal."[92]

The play is a marvelous combination of psychological and fantastical elements, woven into the fabric of peasant life and beliefs. It is the land that reclaims Ninica in the end; she discovers the "little animal," the natural forces, within her that make her want to stay in the country with Mauro. The pact they have made has figuratively been signed with their hearts' blood and the peasant superstition that it is a pact with the devil adds mystery and force to the events. The fight over the mask, the two groups of dancers, the Gypsies at the beginning of the play, and the Nahual are all highly theatrical elements introduced in a gradual development that builds to a climax no less powerful for its logical conclusion. Asturias skillfully interweaves the mystical and the realistic. The mystical is introduced by the Gypsies, brought to a peak by Mauro's dream and concluded by Porfirión's return carrying the mask. In its highly ritualistic midsection the play is reminiscent of the *Rabinal Achí*, and the raw power that stems from its folk traditions and beliefs reminds one of Lorca.

The Chamá Soluna mask brings this all together in its presentation of a physical object that has profound symbolic importance. The mask is present in the play's most effective scenes, such as the first time Mauro tries it on. As he dons the mask the stage lights and the house lights bump up full. The scene rapidly builds, the lights alternately blazing and going dark as he puts on and removes the mask, until the stage is left bathed in the yellow light of the eclipse as the two groups of dancers erupt on to the stage. Other elements, such as the Nahual's burning eyes, have great potential for theatrical effect. It would be necessary to guard carefully against exaggeration and poverty of expression here, since it would be very easy for all of this to look ridiculous in performance if it were not approached with the proper respect for the traditions it explores. Asturias has written the piece with complete respect for those sensibilities. By doing so he reaches back in history not only in terms of the subject matter he employs but also in his manner of presentation. When Mauro dons Chamá Soluna's mask he is, in a sense, reenacting the Aztec ritual donning of the Quetzalcoátl actor's skin. Where the Aztec spectators "got into the god's skin," donning the Chamá Soluna mask seems to endow the wearer with divine powers. Spilling the actor-as-Quetzalcoátl's blood served to maintain the movement of the Sun. Spilling the heart's blood of Mauro and Ninica's pact serves to maintain the vigor of their marriage. That marriage's having been sanctified by the Church brings us once more to a situation in which indigenous ritual and Christian doctrine converge in the theatre. The melding of traditions creates new methods of proceeding that show themselves in the forms created by theological and theatrical circles in the latter half of the twentieth century.

CHAPTER 5

Liberation theology and liberation theatre: the convergence of parallel lines

As any traveler in Latin America has observed, at the center of any village or city will be found a plaza or central square. On one side of the plaza stands the church or cathedral, on the other side the municipal or national government building. Religious and temporal powers face each other across the space where the community's daily life, its markets, its festivals, its strolls, take place. Funeral corteges, wedding processions, children in white on their way to first communion, all cross this space. It provides a stage for the daily life and death of the community, as well as frequently becoming an actual stage for festive celebrations and theatre performances. While Church and state face one another from opposite sides of the plaza, the two institutions have by no means been constantly in opposition. Latin American history, in fact, is, to a large extent, a history of mutual support between the two institutions. From the days of the Conquest to the twentieth century the Latin American Church has frequently turned to the ruling elite for both monetary and legal support for its spiritual mission. By the same token rulers from Cortés to the "national security" government of Augusto Pinochet in Chile have appropriated and consolidated power in the name of expanding or protecting Western "Christian" civilization. The moral justification for the decimation of indigenous populations or the "disappearances" and torture of those perceived to be political foes, was found in Church doctrine.

LIBERATION THEOLOGY: ORIGINS, THEORY, AND PRAXIS

It is precisely the conditions created by such a historical symbiotic relationship between Church and state, namely the immense disparity between rich and poor, that have given birth to a new theological approach that attempts to comprehend Latin American reality with compassion for all, not just a handful, of Latin Americans. These new theologians are attempting to find a way to redress centuries of grievous injury visited upon large masses of the population. Theological contemplation is seen as a means of liberation from oppressive conditions. This "theology of liberation" is a theology directly concerned with both spiritual *and* temporal life. It is a theo-logy, a discussion of God, that finds no separation between God's word and the daily world of the poor and the oppressed. Such a stance puts the liberation theologians in direct opposition to the institutional church which formed them but, in their constant stress upon the necessity of conversion, liberation theologians can be seen to be continuing the evangelical mission that has formed the basis for the Latin American church since Cortés greeted the twelve Franciscans at Tenochtitlán.

Liberation theology, with its stated mission of giving "the voiceless" a means of expression and upon restoring dignity to the poor and powerless, through elaborating a method by which they can transform their situation, is all too easily seen in simplistic and stereotypical terms. On the one hand, it is seen as a peculiar mixture of Marxism and Christianity, on the other, as a movement of militant priests hell-bent upon challenging Church authority. They are recalcitrant adolescents who need to be silenced (Leonardo Boff) or censured (the Nicaraguan priests holding office in the Nicaraguan government) by the parental church. Given this reductive image of what constitutes liberation theology, it is necessary to explore the movement's roots.

Liberation theology is a concept first articulated in, and disseminated by, Gustavo Gutiérrez' book, *A Theology of Liberation*. In that book Gutiérrez explicitly states:

Our purpose is not to elaborate an ideology to justify postures already taken, nor to undertaken a feverish search for security in the face of the radical challenges which confront the faith, nor to fashion a theology from which political action is "deduced." It is rather to let ourselves be judged by the Word of the Lord, to think through our faith, to strengthen our love, and to give reason for our hope from within a commitment which seeks to become more radical, too, and efficacious.[1]

This kind of approach to spirituality is by no means new. As Gutiérrez points out, the early years of the Church looked to a reclusive, monastic lifestyle in which one withdrew from worldly cares as the only appropriate forum for such contemplation.

Gradually, in approximately the twelfth century, the concept of sharing contemplation appeared, leading to the establishment of the various mendicant orders, whose lifestyle mixed contemplative life with active preaching and apostolic activity by which they attempted to "transmit to others the fruits of contemplation." The mendicant orders laid the groundwork for the Jesuit spirituality which sought to synthesize contemplation and action as expressed in the Ignatian motto: *in actione contemplativus* ("contemplative in action").[2]

What this progression has led to over the years is an attempt to find a spirituality of the laity, a means by which the nonreligious could actively share in the Word of God while maintaining and, indeed, strengthening, their position in social and political life. The modern era of such theology in the Catholic Church can be seen to have begun in 1891 with the publication of Pope Leo XII's encyclical *Rerum Novarum*. In that encyclical Pope Leo spoke forcefully in defense of the rights of labor and against the exploitation of the working class. As has been pointed out, however, the audience addressed, the one called upon to pursue justice and aid the poor, is the wealthy, politically and socially powerful elite. Since the encyclical emphasizes stability and public order, its message to the majority population of poor and powerless is to pray for better treatment from those who exploit them, while meekly accepting their position in emulation of the crucified Lord.[3]

The ideas formulated in *Rerum Novarum* led, early in this century, to the Catholic Action movement founded in Europe by the Belgian priest Joseph Cardign. Cardign began by contacting young people, primarily factory workers, outside the traditional parish structures. He would then hold meetings in which a particular problem, such as an abusive foreman, was discussed. The discussion concentrated not on doctrine, but action, the motto being "observe–judge–act." Those gathered would observe the relevant information, judge whether or not the situation was in accordance with the gospel, and then resolve to take some sort of action, however minor. The next meeting would evaluate the action's effect and decide whether further action was warranted. Cardign himself did not lead these discussions. He trained the leaders and served as their advisor and chaplain.[4]

In addition to the Catholic Action movement, there was also the Cursillos de Cristianidad movement, which began among professional and business people in Spain. In weekend retreats, participants would undergo an experience carefully designed to lead to an emotional conversion experience. The *cursillos* tended to focus upon such issues as marital infidelity, drinking, or treatment of others. Little concerned with the social impact of their activities, the *cursillistas* promoted their new-found sense of spirituality among their own class. Poor people might initially be attracted to the atmosphere of brotherhood, but would soon leave, questioning its sincerity since the notion of "brotherhood" espoused was, in reality, an exclusive club. As Phillip Berryman has pointed out, both the Catholic Action and the *Cursillo* movement were important precursors to the Christian base communities evolved by practitioners of liberation theology.[5]

Although both movements were brought to Latin America in the 1950s, they remained European in origin and orientation. While the focus upon experience and action in the Catholic Action movement is similar to the focus utilized in the base communities, the practitioners of Catholic Action saw it as a means of reintroducing an element of Christian spirituality into the de-Christianized European milieu. Such activity carried with it tinges of a modern Christian mysticism. In contrast to the Europeans, the great majority of Latin Americans were not alienated from their religion, and certainly did not possess the wealth of the *cursillistas*. It would take the impetus provided by the Vatican II Council to inspire a specifically Latin American approach to an active spirituality for the laity and, especially, for the poor.

Latin American bishops and theologians did not play a leading role in the formulation of the sweeping reforms of Vatican II. But the liberalizing atmosphere the council engendered was extremely important in terms of encouraging Latin Americans to take a critical look at their own institutions and society. To begin to ask, in effect, specifically Latin American questions. Vatican II called upon Church people to enter into a dialog with "the world." The world seen through European eyes was one of progress and technological advance. The world seen through Latin American eyes was one of institutionalized stagnation, tremendous disparity between rich and poor, and, on a national level, a dependency that seemed to pawn national resources and prosperity for the dubious benefits of the presence of foreign companies in their economies. In short, their world was one of poverty and oppression, seemingly ripe for revolution.

In 1968 the Latin American Bishops conference met for its second plenary meeting in Medellín, Colombia. In Medellín the bishops formulated ways in which the teachings of Vatican II could be applied to the Latin American situation. The bishops exhorted their followers to become involved in the transformation of society and called for the formation of "revolutionaries" throughout Latin America. These revolutionaries were defined as people who sought radical change based upon the people's ability to formulate their own means of action, rather than those who adopted violent means. Frequently employing terms such as "liberation," the bishops called for "consciousness-raising evangelization" and committed themselves to sharing the poor's condition out of solidarity.[6] Medellín's clear commitment to the poor in 1968 was reaffirmed by the bishops' next plenary session in Puebla, Mexico in 1979, where they stated: "We affirm the need for a conversion on the part of the whole Church to a preferential option for the poor, an option aimed at their integral liberation."[7]

What is the meaning of the term "liberation" in liberation theology? Gustavo Gutiérrez has written:

"For freedom Christ has set us free" (Gal. 5: 1), St. Paul tells us. He refers here to liberation from sin insofar as it represents a selfish turning in upon oneself. To sin is to refuse to love one's neighbors and, therefore, the Lord himself. Sin – a breach of friendship with God and others – is according to the Bible the ultimate cause of poverty, injustice, and the oppression in which men live. In describing sin as the ultimate cause we do not in any way negate the structural reasons and the objective determinants leading to these situations. It does, however, emphasize the fact that things do not happen by chance and that behind an unjust structure there is a personal or collective will responsible – a willingness to reject God and neighbor. It suggests, likewise, that a social transformation, no matter how radical it may be, does not automatically achieve the suppression of all evils.[8]

This being the case, it becomes incumbent upon the Christian to find a means of proceeding, a praxis,[9] that enables one to find a means that brings the liberation from sin that Christ the Saviour presents in the Bible, "sin being the ultimate root of any disruption in friendship and of all injustice and repression."[10] How is this achieved in practical terms? One of the primary bases for the methods used in liberation theology can be found in the techniques developed by the great Brazilian educator, Paulo Freire, in the 1950s and 1960s.

FREIRE: LIBERATION PEDAGOGY

Freire's techniques, as articulated in his books, *Education as Liberation Practice* and *The Pedagogy of the Oppressed*, take the general name of *conscientización* (roughly, "consciousness-raising"), and came directly out of his dissatisfaction with traditional, top–down methods of literacy training. Such methods, by adopting the Brazilian equivalent of "Dick and Jane" reading materials, treated adults like children. Freire and his associates set out to develop techniques that were based upon the assumption that the people they were working with were intelligent adults who needed to be respected and engaged, not patronized. Rather than use traditional forms of instruction that treat students as receptacles or containers to be filled by the teacher, what Freire derisively calls the "banking" method of teaching in which "deposits" are made for the purpose of short-term reward, Freire promoted the idea that his literacy students merely lacked the proper linguistic tools for reading and writing, and what was needed was a form of instruction that would enable the students to manipulate those tools over the entire course of their lives. For that reason teaching would begin with a period of investigation in which the literacy trainers would observe and enter into a dialog with the people themselves about life in their village. From this period of investigation certain "code" words would be selected and images formulated, such as crops, tools, and customs, that dealt directly with the peasants' lives.

A session would begin with a poster or slide projection of peasants harvesting a crop. The participants would be asked "What do you see here?" and then the discussion would move from the picture itself to the larger issue of the value of the work, and how to survive on the return it brought. The session leader would always try to get people to respond to the picture of their lives itself. In this way they were dissecting or "decoding" their own existence. Only after this sort of discussion would they move on to reading skills, using words such as "hoe," "land," "corn," "mother," "father" that had come directly out of the previous discussion. In this way it was the peasants themselves, not the teacher, who were directing the course taken by the instruction while, at the same time, developing a critical awareness of the conditions of their own lives. By using a method that moves from the effects of a situation (their own poverty) to its causes (social and power structures), Freire brought people to a critical consciousness while affirming the value of the peasant culture he was working in, rather than seeking to impose an alien culture upon it.[11]

The "preferential option for the poor" formulated by the Latin American bishops at Medellín and Puebla implies within it a decision upon the part of the Church and society as a whole to bring the poor, marginalized communities into the spiritual and social fold. It is only the nonpoor who can "opt" for the poor. The poor themselves have no choice. Over the past two decades pastoral workers have "opted" for the poor, have actively gone to them to share their lives, and attempt an understanding of the condition of poverty through the eyes of the poor. In an extension of Freirean methods priests, nuns, and other religious workers have gone to live in rural villages and urban shantytowns. By doing so they have radically altered the people's relationship to their clerics. A priest is no longer someone you encounter only in the formal, forbidding Sunday Mass, but your neighbor or co-worker with whom you confront the hardships of daily existence. While these pastoral workers by no means became poor themselves, they were usually highly educated before arriving in the *barrio* and they could always exercise their option to leave; their presence changed the way in which the Church was conceived. The institutional edifices of cathedral and municipal building were removed; religion joined the people, mingling with them on the plaza.

Jesus said, "Where two or three are gathered in my name, there am I in their midst" (Matt. 18: 20). The "preferential option for the poor" has led to a situation in which rural peasants and urban slum-dwellers have come to see themselves as contemporary incarnations of the "house-churches" spoken of in the New Testament. In small groups the Bible is read for its relationship to their own lives. These are the *communidades de base* (basic or base communities). Relatively small in number, there are many more active Protestants and evangelicals than members of Catholic base communities, their importance must be evaluated in qualitative not quantitative fashion. As Phillip Berryman has written, "The social and political impact of base communities may be viewed in terms of (1) initial conscious-ness-raising, (2) the vision of life and motivation for involvement, (3) the sense of community and mutual aid they generate, (4) the experience of grass-roots democracy, (5) the direct actions they engage in, and (6) directly political action."[12]

The members of these communities come to conceive of the word "base" here as describing their position within both the social and the religious structure. They are at the bottom in terms of recognized power, but as the foundation, the base upon which the social and religious structures have been built, their potential power is immense. The primary difference between Freirean literacy training and the type of *concientización* that occurs in the base communities, is the use of the Bible as the catalyst for action. Perhaps the most important result of both techniques, beyond a particular issue, or even learning to read, is the way in which participants learn to ask questions, to develop a critical awareness of their surroundings. Through biblical images of a life of sharing, friendship, and equality, members of the base communities discover models of ways in which life could be lived that are diametrically opposed to the actual condition in which they find themselves. Since a base community has often been the driving force behind a particular project of benefit to the local community, its participants come to see that they can pressure public officials to undertake social projects of a larger scale. They can no longer be told that it cannot be accomplished. Their new consciousness, their new critical awareness, has created a new societal dynamic.[13] While the initial impetus was scriptural, the eventual impact is social and political. It is a true lay spirituality that puts the Ignation motto "contemplative in action" into practice.

LIBERATION THEATRE: FREIRE, BOAL, BUENAVENTURA, AND BOLT

Freirean-inspired methods are by no means limited to the religious sphere in Latin America. Freire's ideas have had as great an impact upon theatrical, as upon theological practice. Numerous theatre practitioners have looked to Freire for a means by which they can form a way of doing theatre that communicates with the Latin American audience. Such a method is one that enables the audience to speak *for* itself through theatrical forms rather than using theatre as a means of speaking *to* the people in the audience in a patronizing way that mirrors centuries of colonial oppression. The theatre, in other words, should become as much a vehicle for *concientización* as the Christian base communities. The theatre should become another force for liberation from certain inherited structures, whether societal, political, or aesthetic, that have been externally imposed. Perhaps the best known of these new Latin American approaches is that developed by the Brazilian Augusto Boal in Peru in the early 1970s.

As Boal describes in his book *Theater of the Oppressed*, he was hired by the Peruvian revolutionary government to participate in a literacy campaign called the Integral Literacy Operation (known by its Spanish acronym ALFIN) that was charged with the task of eradicating illiteracy within four years. Faced with the presence of at least forty-one dialects of Quechua and Aymara, the two principal languages besides Spanish, and up to forty-five other languages in some areas of the country, ALFIN's stated objective was a monumental undertaking. The immensity of the project led its participants to the conclusion that

All idioms are "languages," but there is an infinite number of languages that are not idiomatic. There are many languages besides those that are written or spoken. By learning a new language, a person acquires a new way of knowing reality and of passing that knowledge on to others. Each language is absolutely irreplaceable. All languages complement each other in achieving the widest, most complete knowledge of what is real.

Assuming this to be true, the ALFIN project formulated two principal aims:
(1) to teach literacy in both the first language and in Spanish without forcing the abandonment of the former in favor of the latter;
(2) to teach literacy in all possible languages, especially the artistic ones, such as theatre, photography, puppetry, films, journalism, etc.[14]

The Freirean impetus behind such a program is readily apparent, but ALFIN, and Boal in his role as head of the theatre arm of the campaign, further elaborated Freire's methods. Where Freire and his associates had collected images of the people's lives, choosing, in conjunction with someone from the village, the most evocative images for use in instruction, ALFIN put the means of producing those images into the hands of those being taught themselves. Thus the participants would be given a camera, shown how to use it and told: "We are going to ask you some questions. For this purpose we will speak in Spanish. And you must answer us. But you cannot speak in Spanish: you must speak in 'photography.' We ask you things in Spanish, which is a language. You answer us in photography, which is also a language."[15] Questions such as "Where do you live?" or "What is exploitation?" would be asked, the participants would bring in their photographic images and the Freirean system of general discussion leading to specific literacy instruction would be employed.

Boal utilized similar approaches to literacy with the theatre wing and those approaches lead to the techniques described and elaborated upon in *Theatre of the Oppressed*. What Boal calls for is the creation of a *theatrical language*. This language has two main components: everyone can and should be an actor; and the concerns addressed should be those which cut across class barriers to affect everyone within a given social, cultural, or economic milieu. The literacy work in Peru led to such techniques as the "joker system," the "forum theatre," and the "invisible theatre," among others. In the joker system all actors take all the parts in a given scenario utilizing collectively created "masks" or personas to do so. From this type of rehearsal technique comes a performance in which any actor has the possibility of acting as the "wild card" or "joker" at a given point in the piece that requires an imaginative leap, and each actor sees the piece not from a single, but from multiple perspectives. In the "forum theatre" the spectators are invited to suggest alternative solutions to a given problem and then to enact those alternatives themselves. In the "invisible theatre" a group of actors enters into a given situation in order to raise social questions. For instance, an actor orders an expensive meal in a fancy restaurant, eats it, and then reveals he has no money, comparing the price of the meal to the salaries of the waiters, the kitchen help, the garbage men, etc. In the meantime other actors take up a collection to pay for the meal. All of these techniques are designed to create a theatre which actively engages not only the performer but the spectator as well. Since the theatrical representation is "invisible," or unacknowledged, the spectator cannot become passive.

While the initial impetus for these sorts of techniques was Boal's experience with a Freirean-inspired literacy campaign, the result being that both actors and audience are called upon to appraise critically the theatrical exchange, Boal has also formulated a dialectical theory of acting itself which says that an action is the result of a Will in conflict with a Counter-will which creates a Dominant Will. The actor must ask not "Who am I" but "What do I want?" and investigate each aspect of that need, always keeping it at arm's length. For Boal, emotion itself is worthless. It must be rationalized, examined clinically, before it can be of any effect. While there is an obvious connection with Brechtian aesthetics here, Boal finds Brecht's approach wanting. He feels that, while superior to the repressive nature of Aristotelian catharsis which purges the audience of any revolutionary impulses, Brecht does not go far enough. Brecht avoids the cathartic trap and raises the possibility of revolutionary action outside the theatre, but that action depends upon the subsequent activity of each individual audience member. The theatrical language formed by the theatre of the oppressed becomes truly revolutionary theatre because there is no possibility of division between actor and spectator and the spectator is not given the opportunity to be passive.[16]

Since 1976 Boal has been based primarily in Europe, only beginning to work in Brazil once more in 1984. His Center for Investigation and Popularization of the Boal Method of Active Techniques of Expression in Paris has been the point of departure for the dissemination of the Theater of the Oppressed throughout Europe and, indeed, the United States. Curiously, this theatrical language developed in order to address the needs of the marginalized in the so-called First World. Boal's books have been translated into more than twenty-two languages and he has given workshops throughout Europe, at his center in Paris, and in the United States.

By his own admission his work in these contexts has altered the emphasis of the Theater of the Oppressed from strictly social and economic oppression to embrace aspects of human consciousness more often associated with psychotherapy. The new populations with which he was working had the ability to meet their essential material needs but found themselves faced with problems stemming from solitude, an inability to communicate, and emptiness. To counteract these problems, Boal has developed within the larger framework of the Theater of the Oppressed, the technique of "the cop in the head." "The cop in head" addresses the internalized oppressions of those who feel themselves cut off from, and unable to participate in, social and political action. The participant in this exercise becomes an active spectator by presenting images of his or her own oppression. Formulating those images causes the participant to recognize "the cop in the head," performing the image causes the spectator to "play with the reality of those images." By objectifying the image of oppression, by making it "theatre," the participant has moved from social reality into fiction. "The cop in the head" exercise, then, encourages the participant to alter the image of oppression in order to mitigate its oppressive structure. By altering the aesthetic image the participant creates the tools by which he or she can change his or her own social reality.[17]

Freire and Brecht have been the twin pillars upon which the work of other Latin American theatre practitioners such as the Colombian Enrique Buenaventura and the Nicaraguan Alan Bolt have rested as well. While each man has worked within his own country, both Buenaventura and Bolt share with Boal (and many others who go unmentioned here), a central perception that the Latin American theatre is historically an art form that solely reflects the concerns of the region's colonial and neocolonial oppressors. Each man approaches the task of liberating the theatre from those inherited structures in a different way, but the wishes for result is the same: to put the means of producing theatre into the hands of the Latin American people themselves.

Buenaventura (1925–) finds an historical antecedent for what he calls the "new theatre" in Lope de Vega's famous 1609 polemic *El arte nuevo de hacer comedias* (The new art of writing plays). He sees a parallel between the *comedia nuevo* and the new theatre in:

(1) The character of a theatrical movement that both share.
(2) A conception of dramaturgy that, if not a presupposition in either movement, does appear as a result in both movements (and, of course, in other movements as well).
(3) A break with certain aspects of tradition, theoretical as well as practical, especially with old and new perceptions that weigh upon the artistic production process.
(4) A new relationship with a new audience under new spatial and performance conditions, one that determines the types of production and dramaturgy that both movements engender.
(5) The formulation of a new poetics and, even, of a new perspective, with the characteristics of each historical–social context.[18]

The most important of these conjunctions between the two movements for Buenaventura is the idea of the theatrical space. Saying that an understanding of Shakespeare, *Noh*, *Commedia*, or Molière would be impossible without an understanding of the theatrical space from which their texts arose, all of Buenaventura's work has sought to create texts which arise directly from the theatrical space created between actor and audience. Similar to Boal's call for an active spectator, or to Brecht's analysis of the commercial theatre as one in which the text is created and then presented in dramatic form as a consumable commodity for the unthinking spectator, Buenaventura's theatre is Freirean in its emphasis upon raising the critical awareness of both the audience and the actors. Perhaps the best example of this kind of theatrical *concientización* is the Teatro Experimental de Cali's (TEC; Buenaventura's company) production of the adaptation of *Soldados* (The soldiers; 1966) by Carlos Reyes (1941–), a novel about the protracted strike on Colombian banana plantations in 1928. The TEC took this production to a variety of different audiences: workers, universities, peasants, children, traditional theatre audiences, and elicited their responses. What they quickly discovered was that all these audiences were more interested in the causes behind the strike and the strikers themselves than in the soldiers who were called in to quell the strike. As a result of these discussions the play went through five different drafts, each one tested with the various audiences. The final text was one collectively created by both actor and spectator. The final spectacle, in other words, is created by the space shared by both actor and audience.

This dramaturgical method that seeks to avoid imposing a particular point of view upon an audience, especially one that displays no relationship to that audience's experience, has also led to new form of theatrical process in the TEC and, indeed, throughout a great deal of the Colombian theatre. That process views the international repertory as the artistic equivalent of a colonial governmental structure that oppresses the indigenous population. Consequently, in order to liberate oneself from the colonial master, it is necessary to find a specifically Latin American dramaturgy. The result of such a stance has been that the TEC (and many other Colombian theatre groups, such as Santiago García's La Candelaria) have frequently utilized Latin American short stories, poetry, popular myths, and songs as the basis for their productions. It is the actor's improvisational responses to the material provided that shape the course of the finished piece.[19] This is similar in practice to Freire's use of the villagers' responses to images from their own lives to shape the course of literacy instruction. In the new theatre the actor is theoretically freed from the tyranny of the playwright, in the same way that Freire attempts to free his students from a method of literacy instruction that subjugates them to a particular world view in which they themselves are seen as inferior. In the final analysis, however, there is always a text being worked from; whether that text is a play or a short story, poem, or song, does not seem to be a particularly significant change in theatrical creation. What is new is the insistence upon texts that come out of, or reflect, the Latin American situation, and the testing of theatrical performances against the perceptions of a critically awakened audience that responds out of its own experience. It is interesting to note, in fact, that the majority of changes in different versions of TEC productions tend to be gestural or the way in which the material is expressed, rather than in the written text itself.[20]

While Buenaventura's stature in contemporary Latin American theatre cannot be denied, his latest work has lacked the dynamism of the TEC's earlier productions. The TEC formally disbanded as a company in 1990, leaving Santiago García's (1929–) La Candelaria as Colombia's preeminent "New Theatre" company. Recent productions of high artistic quality with a pronounced social and political thrust by La Candelaria, such as *El paso* (1990), which deals with the drug violence of the 1980s in Colombia, demonstrate that the type of dramaturgy forged by Buenaventura and García is very much alive.[21]

Perhaps the most radical example of Latin American liberation theatre is the work of Alan Bolt, and his group Nixtayolero (Nahuatl for "new dawn"), in the Nicaraguan Communitarian Theater Movement. Bolt's work in Nicaraguan arises directly out of recent Nicaraguan history. As a Sandinista militant in the 1970s Bolt attempted to use theatre to spur social change. He and his theatre group at the time went and lived with the poorest of the poor, sharing their lifestyle and analyzing the reasons for their oppression. What they discovered was a high incidence of domestic violence. Out of frustration with their situation, parents would turn upon their own children. Bolt's theatre group organized a school in which children were encouraged to analyze why they were hit, why their parents got drunk. Bolt and his associates "began to realize that for theatre to make a social change, theatre had to change."[22] Sent underground in the heavily Indian-populated region of Masaya by the Sandinista front, Bolt, who grew up in an Indian village, discovered how fully he had internalized the lessons he had learned in school that taught him that the Indian was no better than an animal, lessons that taught that to be European (or at least North American) was far superior to being Indian or Nicaraguan. As a result of this discovery, Bolt began to help the Indians in Masaya to recapture their own indigenous traditions and to see such traditions as vital and valuable. These experiences of what theatre was capable of in terms of social change, and of how deeply colonial attitudes had been internalized, led to the extensive use of theatre in the National Literacy Campaign after the Nicaraguan Revolution in 1979.

Bolt's method, and the method employed by other collectives within the Communitarian Theater Movement, is derived from his pre-revolution experiences. His group will go out into a given community, live there, and research the community's problems in order to create theatrical pieces which directly address the community's needs. In addition to such investigation is added the component of rescuing the indigenous artistic forms from the perception of inferiority created by hundreds of years of colonial rule. Whether such indigenous art is in the shape of dance, music, or ritualistic story-telling, its use, and pride in its continued existence after so many years of oppression, is encouraged. The third component of Bolt's work is directly related to the second. Centuries of inculcation in the colonial mentality have led Nicaraguans to perceive of themselves as colonized. What Bolt helps people to see is that by internalizing that perception they become colonizers as well. In order to break through the barriers created by such a colonial mentality Bolt attempts to tap a sort of Jungian "collective memory." The research done looks for archetypes and symbols which can be brought to the community in theatrical form where they are analyzed and discussed. The questions asked of the audience are always "What did you *see*?" not "What was the story, what happened?" and "What forms of oppression were present?" This type of investigation is designed to create not a product of theatrical activity – the production – but a process of investigation.

This emphasis upon process is even more prevalent in the workshops given at the group's home base La Praga, a farm in Matagalpa province. Nixtayolero and other groups in the Communitarian Theater Movement see themselves as agrarian collectives above all. As Bolt himself has said, "Our motto should be: each theater person is a technician. When we go to communities knowing how to graft, how to cultivate plants we can coordinate with existing institutions in order to achieve something economic and practical, as well as artistic and practical."[23] When groups from a given community go to the farm in Matagalpa for a residency they are constantly encouraged to investigate what is important to *them*, whether that be indigenous dance or veterinary techniques for artificial insemination. The villagers leave the farm with their own process of investigation which they can take back to their homes and implement by themselves. This method of working has created over 300 groups throughout Nicaragua who utilize theatre as a means of coping with and transforming their social reality. In a number of instances the creation of a theatre piece dealing with a particular problem of importance to a given community, its performance, and subsequent discussion of that performance, has led to the removal of both union and government officials. In these cases the theatre was the means by which the officials' incompetence or corruption came to be recognized by the community. Its consciousness was raised. More common, however, is the kind of theatrical investigation encouraged at the farm in Matagalpa where the participants employ theatrical expression as a method to bring forth possible solutions to a problem upon which they themselves can then act. In a sense the theatre is being used in a way designed to eliminate theatre. The point is never the final production but always the process undertaken. That process is worthless unless it demonstrably contributes to building a better life.

TEATRO ESCAMBRAY

In common with Bolt's company, the Cuban Teatro Escambray has also evolved a theatrical method that employs theatre as a means of formulating solutions to communal problems. In contrast to the Nicaraguan company, however, Teatro Escambray has always taken a specific political stance, as Escambray director Sergio Corrieri (1938–) has put it – "Theater, an effective weapon in service of the Revolution."[24] From Teatro Escambray's formation in 1968 by a group of theatre professionals dissatisfied with the type of work they were doing in Havana that seemed disconnected from the profound changes that the Revolution has brought to Cuba until the present, the company's orientation has been perhaps the most expressly political of those working in the contemporary Latin American theatre.

Moving to the remote Escambray region in 1968, the new Teatro Escambray set out to create theatre that would address the particular reality of the people living in the region. The Escambray had been largely ignored by the government prior to the Revolution, had subsequently become the staging ground for various counter-revolutionary activities, and was now the setting for an ambitious development project. With food and lodging provided by the regional

Communist Party, the actors proceeded to spend their first few months in Escambray fanning out in pairs to study the economic, social, and cultural aspects of the region. They interviewed, worked with, shared meals with, and befriended people throughout the region and by doing so familiarized themselves with the rural population's concerns and problems. The material gathered was then evaluated as to its importance to the progress of the Revolution. From that evaluation two subjects were chosen for Teatro Escambray's initial theatrical investigation: the first was the Plan Lechero; and the second the strong presence of the Jehovah's Witnesses in the region.

The *Plan Lechero* (Milk Plan) was a development project begun by the Cuban government in 1970. It proposed to turn what it saw as the inefficient and unproductive region of small landowners into a collective dairy-farming region that would cover approximately 10,000 *caballerías* (around 130,000 hectares), and move the small farmers into four strategically placed towns where they would be provided with modern apartments and appliances. Such a plan with its attendant road construction and introduction of new technologies obviously meant the total disruption of life as the population living in Escambray had known it. The government elaborated a three-step method of procedure in order to convince the population to participate. That plan stated that each farmer would receive a monthly rent for his parcel of land, a plot for raising food whose size would depend upon the size of the farmer's family, and that no one would be forcibly moved from the land. Each person had the right to remain where he was until he voluntarily agreed to move to one of the newly constructed villages. The fledging theatre company was enlisted to help bring the Plan Lechero to completion.[25]

After conducting hundreds of interviews with farmers in Escambray, the company created a play called *La vitrina* that painted a picture of life in the region and demonstrated various reactions to the implementation of the Plan Lechero. As Sergio Corrieri put it:

The basic aim of the production is the following: to show the peasant a contradictory image of himself (one which we can judge critically). This image is shown with regards to his social conduct within the Revolutionary framework. Conduct that, with the arrival of the Plan, places new and continuous demands upon his ideological growth.

The production does not offer any solutions, it presents an analysis that should lead to argument and polemical discussion. Such is the feeling that it proposes to incite in the spectator in order to make him rethink his own reality.[26]

La vitrina was performed throughout Escambray from 1970 until 1978. Every performance was followed by an open-ended debate with the audience that often led to revisions in the play itself. The final version of the play was performed in 1978 for the inhabitants of La Yaya, one of the new towns that had been constructed as part of the Plan Lechero. In keeping with Teatro Escambray's commitment to speaking to its audience, the new version presents a theatre group who, as a means of narrating the town's history, perform a play called *La vitrina* on the occasion of the town's anniversary. The final portion of this last version of the play presents a series of characters who die and are resurrected with ease, a symbolic rendering of the death of old ideas and the birth of a new life that the townspeople themselves had experienced.

The second subject Teatro Escambray chose to work upon was the presence and influence of the Jehovah's Witnesses in the region. Unlike other countries in Latin America, the Cuban rural population historically has lacked a strong religious orientation. The Catholic Church concentrated its efforts in the main urban centers, with the rural ecclesiastical effort largely restricted to ceremonies such as baptism. During the 1950s the Batista dictatorship, in the midst of the suspension of constitutional guarantees of assembly, sanctioned the Jehovah's Witnesses' national congresses and proselytizing work. The Jehovah's Witnesses' doctrinal beliefs against political action and against military activity were used by the Batista regime as a brake upon the growing guerrilla activity in rural areas. After the Revolution the Castro government claimed that the CIA supported the Jehovah's Witnesses' missionary work that counseled non-violence, refusal to salute the flag as a graven image, and non-compliance with governmental development plans since one's efforts should be directed towards salvation hereafter not life on earth. Such religious beliefs were seen as anti-social and counter-revolutionary and Teatro Escambray set out to confront the Jehovah's Witnesses' influence through the theatre.

The company created a number of productions dealing with the Jehovah's Witnesses, including *Y si fuera así...* (1968) by Sergio Corrieri, three different versions of *El paraíso recobrado* (1978) by Albio Paz, and *Las provisiones* by Sergio González. *Y si fuera así...* (If it were so ...) is an adaptation of Brecht's *The Guns of Carrar* in which the Spanish Civil War setting is adapted to Cuba in the early 1970s. Instead of refusing to let her children fight for the Second Republic, Teresa, the Carrar character of *Y si fuera así* ..., refuses to allow her children to join the militia fighting a US-sponsored invasion of Cuba. Teresa justifies her position with the teachings of nonviolence she has learned from the Jehovah's Witnesses since she became a convert after her husband died in the militia.

As in Brecht's *The Guns of Carrar*, the larger part of the play is taken up with a debate between Teresa and her brother Pedro over the true nature of her neutrality. In the debate Pedro maintains that not to defend the Revolution is to aid its enemies, while Teresa counters that the invaders will not hurt noncombatants and that to fight is to risk eternal damnation. When her eldest son is summarily killed by invading paratroopers as he peacefully tills the family field, Teresa joins the militia herself, breaking out the guns her dead husband has left behind. The play has vitality and the characters are well drawn but, by suggesting that Teresa has joined the Jehovah's Witnesses solely as a means of protecting her children, rather than as a result of a conversion of belief after her husband's death, it fails to address seriously the doctrine of nonviolence, thereby negating its lengthy historical roots and dismissing those who preach it as a counter-revolutionary evil.

Teatro Escambray's second piece dealing with the Jehovah's Witnesses is a play by Albio Paz (1937–) entitled *El paraíso recobrado* (Paradise regained). As a result of open forums with the audience following each performance, *El paraíso recobrado* exists in three different versions. Each version deals with a Kingdom Hall meeting in which the various members of the congregation relate conversion stories to all those assembled as teaching tools. The play is structured dramatically and scenically in such a fashion that the audience is considered part of the congregation and is often addressed directly by the actors. The conversion stories are all told by means of short sketches that show new converts brought into the fold by means of playing upon their grief at the death of a loved one or by trickery. The play makes plain the counter-revolutionary nature of the Jehovah's Witnesses who cause people to forsake the collective work of the community for the general social good in order to work individually, and encourage them to refuse to participate in the construction and the protection of the Revolution.

By far the most dramaturgically sophisticated of Teatro Escambray's plays concerning the activity of the Jehovah's Witnesses in Escambray is *Las provisiones* (The provisions; 1975), by Sergio González (1924–). *Las provisiones* expands the basic situation of *Y si fuera así*…taking into account the various comments made by audience members and actors regarding the original adaptation. What emerges is a much more fully realized play that produces an effective portrait of a family in crisis whose grief causes it to turn to the Jehovah's Witnesses for solace. Structurally, the scenes are all introduced and commented upon by a traditional peasant band singing *décimas*, or Cuban country ballads. The *décimas*, as well as an assembly that is built into the play's structure, are used to underscore and analyze the contradictions the character's actions present.

The plot is as follows: Juan, the son of Damasia and Pedro, has accidently drowned and they are grief-stricken. The Jehovah's Witnesses comfort them by assuring them that Juan will return to them one day if they only believe. Damasia desperately clutches at the possibility and converts. Pedro and their daughter Clara accompany her to the meetings out of concern and love for her without believing in the doctrine. As Damasia becomes more fiercely devoted to her new religion the family, once well liked and respected, becomes increasingly isolated from the community. To placate his wife, Pedro stops engaging in communal work and Clara cuts off all ties with her nonbelieving friends. It is only when Pablo, the son of their former best friends Chole and Cleto, returns from military service and proposes to Clara that a confrontation occurs. Damasia forbids Clara to marry Satan and forbids Pedro to lease his land to the Plan Lechero.

It is after the scene in which Pedro refuses to lease his land that the assembly takes place. The scene ends with Cleto yelling: "No sir, we can't permit this. We can't permit this here!" From there we move directly into the assembly – a discussion with the audience over the events that have taken place in the play so far. Beneath a banner that reads "Peasants to the Vanguard" and pictures of Fidel and Che, the actor who plays Cleto leads the discussion in such a way as to touch upon five different points: (1) powerlessness before the Witnesses; (2) the use of violence; (3) defense of religious freedom; (4) complicity motivated by old relationships; (5) ignorance of collective responsibility. In order for the play to conclude the assembly must come to the conclusion that Pedro's land should be plowed by the community without his consent.

Plowing the land is the catalyst that causes Clara to leave her family for Pablo and Damasia, half-crazed, to believe that a lunar eclipse is the sign that Juan is returning. Refusing to eat or drink, she sits in the road for three days praying and reading her Bible. At that point a young man coming to work on the Plan Lechero appears on horseback. Disoriented with hunger, thirst, and grief, she thinks he is Juan, and only realizes her profound mistake when she hears her husband explain to the perplexed young man how their son drowned. Pedro directs the young man to Chole and Cleto's house where he is to tell Clara to prepare a strong broth for her mother. The play ends with the peasant band singing:

> One has to say things as they are
> It's time to react
> We can't allow them
> to campaign for respect.
> All Escambray
> must cut their wings.[27]

In its structure *Las provisiones* is similar to that of another Escambray piece called *El juicio* (The trial; published 1978). In *El juicio* the judges for the trial are chosen by the audience from its own ranks before the play begins. The play itself presents the history of a *campesino* named Leandro Pérez González, who joined the counter-revolutionary bands operating in the Escambray, was captured and tried by a revolutionary court, and subsequently underwent re-habilitation. Throughout the play the elected judges, as well as any member of the audience, can stop the action at will to question the eight actor–witnesses who relate González' past and present actions. The witnesses appear in rapid succession and the events they relate do not follow any chronological sequence. This structural device, coupled with the interjections of questions by judges and audience members alike, gives the play a structural and narrative complexity that forces the active engagement of the spectator, who must remain attentive and constantly evaluate and analyze González' attitude and actions. At the end of the play the audience is asked to determine why this man whom the witnesses have presented as neither good nor bad became a class enemy. "Why did Leandro always make the wrong choice? Was it out of ambition, ignorance, or pride? You must decide."[28]

Teatro Escambray's working methods certainly create an engaged audience that is encouraged to analyze and evaluate the theatrical images presented. These images, however, are as openly didactic as those created by the evangelical mendicants in the sixteenth century. Both the assembly in *Las provisiones* and the end of *El juicio* make clear that debate is only encouraged within circumscribed boundaries. The dramaturgical and rhetorical form in which questions are posed to Escambray's audience negates the possibility of questioning the basic tenets of the Revolution itself.

Curiously, Escambray's theatrical procedure is not that distant from the methods employed by the Jehovah's Witnesses that their plays criticize. Both groups seek to indoctrinate the people of Escambray with a specific doctrinal approach to life in the region. While the Jehovah's Witnesses are certainly more obvious in their paternalistic approach to guiding their converts down the path to salvation, the various ways in which Teatro Escambray's plays seek to orient their audiences towards a specific plan of action shares that paternalistic attitude. An attitude that departs from an *a priori* stance that the Revolution is correct in all of its actions. Interestingly, Fidel Castro himself has shown a much more flexible approach to the position of religious activity within and alongside the Revolution in the past few years.[29] At the same time Teatro Escambray's work has been suspended and the company members have moved on to a variety of different cultural and political pursuits. Among the most notable former Escambray members active in the theatre today are Flora Lauten with her young theatre company, Grupo Buendía, and Herminia Sánchez, who has engaged in collective creation with dock workers in Havana's port.

CHILE

Nowhere in Latin America have the ideas and practices of liberation theology and liberation theatre met with such success at such great cost as in Chile. The aims of Freirean educational theory, "the preferential option for the poor" as articulated by the Catholic Church in Medellín, and the implications for artistic practice and cultural position of a theatre that adopts a desire for social change as its fundamental aesthetic and political position were all realized to a great extent in Chile in the 1960s and early 1970s. Eduardo Frei's

Christian Democratic government from 1964 to 1970, and Salvador Allende's Popular Unity government from 1970 to 1973 set out to create a country in which both the urban and rural poor would become fully integrated into the social fabric. Agrarian reform, the expansion of social programs for industrialized sectors, and a commitment to the promotion of popular culture, revolutionized the country through democratic means. This social transformation was directly reflected in the theatre between 1968 and 1972.

In contrast to the *costumbrista* and psychologically oriented theatre of previous years, the late 1960s and early 1970s saw the creation of a directly political theatre that, if it did not necessarily point the way towards a particular solution, had as its explicit aim the fomentation of a consciousness of class struggle. This orientation directly affected theatrical practice, with both independent and university companies such as Teatro Aleph, Teatro ICTUS, the Taller de Creación Teatral at the Universidad Católica, and El Túnel among others turning to collective creation in order to create works that spoke to the contemporary Chilean and Latin American reality. Governmental support for this kind of work included not only subsidies to universities but also inclusion of these companies in the mass media. Film and, particularly, television opened its doors to, and actively promoted, socially conscious theatre, television series, even sketches, on its screens. ICTUS, for example, had its own highly successful television program, *La manivela* (The crank or handle) from 1970 to 1972. María de la Luz Hurtado, Carlos Ochsenius, and Hernán Vidal have delineated three distinct periods in Chilean theatre history from 1973 to the present – 1973–1976, 1977–1980, and from 1980 on – that provide a useful means of viewing recent contemporary Chilean theatre and society.[30]

With the CIA-backed coup against Salvador Allende and the installation of the brutal Pinochet regime in 1973, the national cultural and political orientation previously described came to an abrupt end. The years 1973–1976 saw a profound social transformation, actively promoted by the state, that presented a new social model economically based upon the free-market ideology of the Chicago School, and highly authoritarian in the judicial and political spheres. The very marginalized populations towards whom the previous Christian Democratic and Popular Unity governments had directed their efforts now found themselves fighting with one another for survival. In terms of the theatre during this period the subsidized theatres either closed or changed their repertoire in order to maintain funding, and a program of self-sufficiency for all governmental agencies took a heavy toll on the theatre, television, and cinema. The Universidad de Chile's theatre program, so instrumental in renovating the Chilean theatre in earlier years, was effectively shut down, while the other influential theatre program at the Universidad Católica turned inward. Political blacklisting and censorship caused many theatre professionals to seek work in other professions, and about 25 percent of those professionals went into exile either willingly or, like Teatro Aleph, whose 1974 production *Al principio existía la vida* (In the beginning there was life; 1974) resulted in the company's imprisonment for a long period of time, as a result of political repression.

Theatre during this period was largely forced out of the public eye, becoming even more of a space for reflection upon the prevailing social and political situation. Performed largely by nonprofessionals in poor neighborhoods, political concentration camps, and isolated university settings throughout the country, this kind of theatre provided a means by which victims of state-sponsored repression could confront their situation and give each other hope. An excellent example of this is a play called *San Pablo dirigente* (Saint Paul, the leader; 1976), which was collectively created by political detainees in the Puchuncaví concentration camp for Holy Week in 1976.

Performed in the camp's dining hall on April 19, 1976, the play consists of five scenes in one act and takes place in Nero's Rome, thirty-three years after the death of Christ. The play presents a stark contrast between the rich, orgiastic nature of Nero's court, where Nero appears dressed as a grotesque Venus – since all the gods are his relatives they are embodied in him – and forces his court to do obeisance and pay tribute to him in that form. All who refuse are assassinated. From the first scene we are introduced to the growing threat to Nero's power from the spread of Christianity by a captured Christian who, when questioned, tells Nero that Paul, a former Roman citizen, showed him the path to conversion. The prisoner is tortured until he tells them where Paul might be.

All of this is contrasted with a scene depicting the humble, fraternal gathering of the Christians in the catacombs, and Paul's recounting of his conversion on the road to Damascus. As they are performing Mass, the Romans burst in and carry off Paul. In his final interview with Nero, Paul warns Nero that he too will be afraid when his time comes, a time when the fruit that the seed of Christ and Paul's blood has fertilized will blossom and Rome shall fall. The last two scenes of the play show the Christians reorganizing themselves after Paul's death and Nero, in his increasing madness, hearing their sung Psalms. Listening to the music, he drops to all fours in abject terror as the dead Christians fill the stage.

The play's use of the spread of Christianity and Rome's gradual conversion, with its incorporation of the scriptures and its performance during Holy Week, obviously has significance beyond a dramatization of religious history. Given its context and the nature of the actors, all political prisoners themselves, the allegory for Pinochet's Chile is unavoidable. While Paul could certainly be seen as Allende (his first name, Salvador, making an interesting parallel here) it is not necessary to take the play quite so literally. What is much more important is the message that, like the seeds of Christianity fertilized by every martyr's blood, so are the seeds of Chile's lost democracy kept alive by the prisoners and the disappeared. The parallels seem especially clear in the edict read at Paul's condemnation, where his execution is justified upon the following grounds: his refusal to practice the official religion and to give tribute to Caesar; his preaching among slaves and commoners of ideas that run counter to governmental institutions and doctrine; and his persistence in practicing foreign religious rites in secret. Each of these charges could be translated to Pinochet's justifications for imprisoning the political prisoners that are performing and watching the play.

While relatively simple in terms of execution, the play is by no means facile in terms of conception. By utilizing the religious theme the prisoners are able both to avoid the wrath of their jailers and to reaffirm their own commitment to their ideals. The final scene, in which all the dead Christians enter the stage carrying lighted candles as the psalm is sung, is both an excellent theatrical image and a highly charged statement of hope – the flame of Allende's Chile is still alive. Perhaps even more importantly, the collectively created nature of the piece, and the sheer number of prisoners whose involvement is suggested here, must have provided a means of combating the degradation and horror of the concentration camp itself. Paul tells Nero that love is the most powerful weapon of all. The creation, conception, and performance of the play under these conditions is a demonstration of that doctrine.[31]

The second period delineated by de la Luz Hurtado and Ochsenius is that of 1977–1980. This period was characterized by the strengthening of Pinochet's economic policies and authoritarian rule, as well as the slow reemergence of political and cultural alternatives to the Pinochet regime. In the professional theatre this meant that the only space left for a modicum of free expression was in the independent theatres. Groups such as ICTUS, La Feria, the Taller de Investigación Teatral, and Imagen began to produce plays, such as *Pedro, Juan y Diego* (1977), *Cúantos años tiene un día?* (1979), *Tres Marías y una Rosa* (1979), *El último tren* (1978), and *Testimonios sobre las muertes de Sabina* (1980), that present the possibility of a future which, having confronted the current situation, will return to a society that resembles that in existence before Pinochet; or they examine the possibility of the regime's continued existence given the great disparity in the amount of power held by the masses and the government. Other plays, such as *Lo crudo, lo cocido, lo podrido* (1978) by Marco Antonio de la Parra (1952–), directly confront the regime's legitimacy through the use of theatrical metaphor, or present historical figures as an oblique way to criticize the current regime. Another tactic was to use elements of popular culture – songs and legends, for instance – as a means of exposing the contradictory nature of the current society.[32]

As was the case in the earlier part of the decade, however, there was only limited space for such societal critiques in the professional theatre. While outright governmental censorship was curtailed, effective censorship was carried out by other means. For example, in 1977 Teatro de La Feria produced a piece called *Hojas de Parra*, based upon the work of the Chilean poet. Performed in a large circus tent in an upper-middle-class neighborhood of Santiago, *Hojas de Parra* depicts a poor circus company that rents its ring to a funeral director in order to obtain the funds necessary to survive. Throughout the course of the play the circus ring gradually fills with crosses, converting the circus tent into a cemetery for all those who have died in Chile since Pinochet came to power. The piece attracted a diverse audience from all social strata and played to more than 6,000 people in nine days. When the authorities failed to find legal means to shut down the tent theatre, persons unknown torched the tent during the nightly curfew, effectively ending the production on the tenth day. In addition to such terroristic acts of censorship, the regime created an extremely precarious financial climate for Chilean theatre by

repealing the 1935 law that exempted works by Chilean authors from
taxation and imposing a 22 percent tax on the gross box-office
receipts of any production that a governmental commission had not
certified as possessing a high cultural level.

Given the strictures placed upon the professional theatre by the
government in the 1970s, a great deal of theatre was to be found
outside traditional venues. Beginning around 1975 demonstrations in
favor of human rights became the occasion for short sketches that
made use of poetry, biblical stories, and fables to perform metaphoric
representations of the repressive reality. In 1977 more formalized
theatre groups began to appear in urban neighborhoods, growing out
of church social-action committees, or neighborhood mutual-aid
societies. Initially performing works from the 1940s and 1950s, by
1979 these groups were performing pieces that denounced the regime
and agitated for such fundamental rights as individual liberty,
freedom of expression, jobs, education, and a living wage. Like the
Christian base communities' use of the scriptures to analyze their
social situation, these base theatre groups are interested in the theatre
as a means of confronting their social reality.

One such performance by a group called Refugio in Santiago
presented four testimonials drawn from dozens of interviews with
people in the community. As described by Carlos Ochsenius the
dramatized interviews tell the stories of the following: the wife of a
man who was detained and disappeared; an adolescent only
interested in soccer who, as the result of an angry discussion, kills his
father; a homosexual who prostitutes himself in the *barrio alto* or rich
district of the city; and of several students who had abortions.

The actors narrate the testimonials directly to the audience respecting the
original syntax and vocabulary. What could be a monotonous spectacle is
mitigated by a brilliant production. On the one hand, a folkloric band opens
the show and ties each testimonial to the next with songs and original
instrumental music, on the other the actors themselves roam throughout the
performance space, stopping every once in a while so that one of them can
narrate one of the stories. In this fashion the production assumes a strong
ritual character reminiscent of that effected during Holy Week (Via
Crucis).

At the same time the work's focus, transmitted through song and
recitation, recaptures the Catholic view of people's lives as a pilgrimage
through this earthly vale of pain and suffering. The production, however,
does not counsel resignation to this state of affairs. On the contrary, it fosters
a sense of comprehension of and solidarity for human beings we ignore on a

daily basis and invites us to revise our conceptions and attitudes regarding the causes of their suffering. All considered, such a stance is taboo within the dominant cultural and social order.

This production has been performed on numerous occasions, including masses and liturgies.[33]

This *teatro de base* movement parallels the religious base communities in that it is theatre made by the marginalized population for itself, not by university students or professionals who bring "culture" from outside of the community. Here, as Ochsenius has noted, the actor is the author and the performance deals directly with the actor's daily life. Unlike previous Chilean socially engaged theatre that tended to treat the popular masses as a homogeneous group whose problems would be solved through socialism, the *teatro de base* provides these communities with a means of celebrating their own special qualities, of communicating with each other, and of educating themselves in order to develop the community at a local level in an autonomous fashion.

One of the most effective forms of this kind of theatre is a return to, and an updating of, the Chilean *chingana* we first encountered in the nineteenth century. Varied in content, the contemporary *chinganas* may contain music, song, dance, theatre, poetry, games, audiovisual presentations, and even quasi-sporting events. Interspersed throughout these elements one finds readings of letters or testimonials, lessons, stories, legends, anecdotes, jokes, guessing games, and conversational exchanges, all revolving around a central theme such as working, special skills, or the organization of life in the neighborhood. The *chingana* may also contain brief training sessions in which lessons or techniques are put into practice. The end of the *chingana* and any intermissions are moments celebrated with food and drink. Differing in structure depending upon the occasion, the *chingana* is performed by from three to five people and follows more or less the following outline:

In whatever space is available, lacking a stage or special lighting, two people serve as animators–guides. They are the ones who connect the different activities, whether that means announcing them verbally, by means of brief humorous dialogs, through songs and popular poetry...The rest of the performers join in from time to time, surprisingly from amidst the audience. Their participation is as characters in a dramatic sketch, a musical orchestra, ushers, etc. All of their interventions are carried out with the intention of causing active participation by the audience. In this sense there exists a permanent feedback between animators and audience. Some activities are rejected or postponed, others are proposed and carried out by the audience itself.

The actual theatrical interventions are varied. Some follow a method-ology similar to "invisible theatre," others create diverse characteriz-ations (realistic or "magical", drawn from the popular tradition) by means of a few very expressive resources (masks, costumes), who interact among themselves, with the song and music, or with the audience. Puppet theatre pieces or a complete play of a "traditional" type might also be performed. Finally, audience members are encouraged to create their own brief theatrical pieces: sketches, "image theatre," collective improvisation, which can, in turn, be modified by other audience members.[34]

As Ochsenius puts it, the *chingana* is "a complete experience: recreational–educational–artistic, where the audience is the principal actor." Believing themselves to lack skills or knowledge, the audience members leave the *chingana* apprised of their own power to effect change. This new-found knowledge is one to be employed not only within the performance space of the *chingana* itself but, more importantly, at home and at work as well.

While the kind of work described in the *chinganas* and the *teatro de base* movement continued into the 1980s, the new decade marked a shift in emphasis for Chilean theatre as a whole. The openly political theatre of the 1960s and 1970s, frequently a result of collective creation, declined markedly and a new focus upon the individual emerged. Partially, this shift can be attributed to the 1980s plebiscite that, to the shock of many in the artistic community, confirmed General Pinochet's absolute power until 1988, when a new con-stitution that would put into place a system of "protective democ-racy" and constitutionally approve the authoritarian regime's economic, social, and cultural policies would take effect.

As Hurtado and Ochsenius have pointed out, the productions of the early 1980s, such as *Cuestión de urbicación* by Juan Radrigán (1937–), and the "La linea blanca" episode from ICTUS' *Lindo país con visto al mar*, all satirize the consumer society promoted by the government. In *Cuestión de ubicación* a poor family uses all its resources to buy a color television that it then has trouble finding the proper spot for in its furnitureless and floorless home while a malnourished daughter starves. In "La linea blanca" a secretary sells her soul to the devil in exchange for a complete line of household items. As the decade progresses there is a continuation of this move towards a more interior and subjective theatre, along with a move away from excessive realism. New groups appear, such as Teatro de la Memoria, directed by Alfredo Castro, Grupo Ay!, led by José Andrés Peña, Grupo de los que no Estaban Muertos, directed by Juan Carlos Zagal, Grupo del Teniente Bello, led by Gregory Cohen, and Teatro de la Pasión Inextingible, led by Marco Antonio de la Parra. Comprised primarily of young people and working unlikely spaces, these groups begin to forge a new theatrical language for Chile, one that concentrates itself upon the visual, sensations, mystery, and disjunction rather than linearity.[35]

Incorporated into the productions of more established groups as well, these elements can be seen in ICTUS' excellent adaptation of *Este domingo* by José Donoso, with its investigation of the social and psychological pitfalls encountered by an employer and her servant when the employer attempts to move beyond the traditional class boundaries; in *Cartas de Jenny* (Grupo Imagen), which tells the story of a domineering widowed mother ruled by her passion for her son who wishes to cut his apron strings; in the highly successful *La negra Ester* adapted and directed by Andrés Pérez from Roberto Parra's autobiographical poem about his love for a prostitute; or in *La manzana de Adán*, adapted by Alfredo Castro from Claudia Donoso's work on transvestite prostitutes in the outskirts of Santiago. Although these pieces have all achieved varying artistic and popular success, and the technical and thematic means employed bears a resemblance to international theatrical investigation of the same period, like the work of the 1960s and 1970s, that of the 1980s responds to a particular historical, social, and political context. The focus has shifted but it is still Chilean.

ARGENTINA

Two factors separate Argentina's experience during the 1960s and 1970s from much of the rest of Latin America: the existence of a highly professional theatre from at least the mid-nineteenth century; and the political climate formed by a series of military regimes. Those regimes include the so-called "Liberating Revolution" that deposed Juan Domingo Perón's first presidency in 1955, and the "years of lead" that began with the activities of the right-wing paramilitary group Triple-A (Argentinian Anti-communist Alliance) in the last years of Perón's widow, Isabel's presidency, and continued from 1976 through 1983 with the brutal military dictatorship that deposed her in which countless Argentinians were tortured, "disappeared," or forced into exile. In such a context, Argentinian political theatre was necessarily of a different order. Rather than state its political positions in a didactic or even straightforward manner, the Argentinian theatre of this period had recourse to metaphor, allusion, and historical allegory. In primarily dramaturgical terms, this meant the creation of some of the most complex and disturbing pieces of dramatic literature and theatrical performance to be found in the region. The work of playwrights such as Griselda Gambaro (1928–) (*El campo* [1968], *El desatino* [1965], *Las paredes* [1966], *Viejo matrimonio* [1965], *Los siameses* [1965]) and Eduardo Pavlovsky (1933–) (*Somos* [1962], *La espera trágica* [1962], *Acto rápido, Robot* [1966], *La cacería* [1969]) with the Instituto Di Tella in the 1960s, and Roberto Cossa (1934–) (*Nuestro fin de semana* [1964], *Los días de Julián Bisbal* [1966], *La ñata contra el libro* [1967]) laid the groundwork for an outpouring of political theatre in the 1970s of which perhaps the best example is the work of Ricardo Monti.

The experimentation of the late 1960s created a climate where, as Julia Elena Sagaceta has pointed out, playwrights presented their ideological and political positions through the medium of characters who delve into their own interior selves, but do so by means of a highly allegorical, metaphorical, expressionistic, even carnivalistic theatrical language.[36] This can be seen in Gambaro's plays from the early *El campo* to her plays of the early 1980s, such as *Decir sí* (1981), *La malasangre* (1982), and *Del sol naciente* (1984), with their intricately woven psychological patterns and characters who, as heirs to those found in Discépolo's *grotesco criollo*, find themselves deformed by a physical context that delimits and destroys their dreams and aspirations. It can also be seen in Pavlovsky's *La mueca* (1971) and *El señor Galíndez* (1963), where an almost Pinteresque use of confined domestic settings (a living room, a basement) into which enters a menacing force from outside, devolves into a violent struggle between victim and victimizer in which both parties are intimately engaged in acts of torture. In Pavlovsky's latest work, such as *Paso de dos* (1990), which takes place in a small ring whose floor has been covered with mud, even the realistic trappings of the earlier plays have been torn away to expose fully the struggle for power between torturer and tortured. A play like Roberto Cossa's *La nonna* (1977) employs characteristics of the *sainete* and the *grotesco criollo* in its depiction of a grandmother whose rapacious appetite literally eats her family out of house and home. Other playwrights turned, as in Chile, to treatments of historical figures as allegorical representations of the contemporary reality such as in *Lisandro* (1972) and *Túpac Amaru* (1973) by David Viñas (1929–). For their coherence and peculiar power two plays by Ricardo Monti (1944–), *Una noche con el Sr. Magnus e hijos* (published 1970) and *Historia tendenciosa de la clase media argentina* (published 1971), are particularly noteworthy. While *Historia tendenciosa de la clase media argentina* (A tendentious history of the Argentinian middle class) is more overtly political in its references to historical events from the turn of the century to the 1970s, both plays present a forceful critique of the contemporary society.

Historia tendenciosa is quite Brechtian in structure – a series of scenes in two acts that theatrically examines certain key historical events. The play is narrated by *Teatro* (Theatre), who both presents and comments upon the action, and there are numerous "interruptive gestures" including songs and what Monti calls "implosions" in which actors step out of character to describe personal experiences related to the historical events being treated. Argentina itself is portrayed as an aging prostitute caked in make-up named Pola, who showers her affections first upon the land-owning Argentinian oligarchy, then upon British (Mr. Hawk), followed by US (Mr. Peagg) imperialism. Throughout the play a silent *Obrero* (Worker) observes the proceedings from various points of the stage, in front during Perón's rule, caged at the far reaches of the stage during the subsequent governments. The entire play is permeated by grotesque and carnivalistic elements, creating a circus atmosphere throughout. Characters are murdered only to spring back to life. Mr. Hawk is literally eaten by Mr. Peagg in a cannibalistic frenzy, ineffectual clowns portray industrialists and generals, while the Development Dames parade presidential candidates like the latest fashions before Mr. Peagg for his approval.

Una noche con el Sr. Magnus e hijos (An evening with Magnus and sons) takes place in Magnus' house. Although the door is never locked, Magnus' three sons, Gato, Wolfi, and Santiago, live in dire fear of leaving the world that Magnus has created for them while simultaneously hating the control that he exercises over them. The world outside the house has the dual character of threat and of liberation and its existence is skillfully manipulated by Magnus to maintain his power. Monti clearly intends us to see the play as a reflection of an Argentinian society in which his audience members are manipulated by the powers-that-be as effectively as Magnus rules over his sons. The play offers a potential solution to this situation with the arrival of a young woman named Julia from outside the house. She joins the sons in their final act of rebellion against their father in which, to the rhythmic noise of a factory outside the house, Magnus is stabbed to death and revealed to be nothing more than a mass of putrefied flesh. While Magnus has given his sons an identity, only his destruction will allow them to exercise their own wills, only his elimination will allow the creation of a new world.

Both plays place great weight upon performance, with the presentational circus atmosphere in *Una historia tendenciosa*, and the series of games, rituals, and fantasies enacted by Julia, Magnus, and his sons in *Una noche*. This stress upon performance is more than a structural device. It shares with contemporary performance art and the modern drama in general since Pirandello, a consciousness of the referential character of performance itself thereby forcing our recognition of the nature of the theatrical exchange. Within Monti's aesthetic universe the audience members in the theatre inhabit the same space as his performers, the theatre is a mirror of the deformed social reality and only as long as performance (in all its senses) continues both within the theatre and without can death and the putrefaction of the flesh be staved off.[37]

MEXICO

This study began with Cortés' arrival in Mexico in the sixteenth century and it is only fitting that the final instance of liberation theatre presented here should come from Mexico as well. As described in the previous chapter, the kind of evangelical theatre developed by the mendicants in the sixteenth century still exists today in rural Mexico in the form of the Passion plays, biblical stories, and religious processions performed at Easter and on Catholic holidays in the indigenous languages of Nahuatl, Maya, Zapotec, Mixtec, and Tarasca, among others. While the Cultural Mission Program had largely discarded the use of theatre by 1950, the 1960s and 1970s saw the creation of a *teatro campesino* (peasant's theatre) that links education and theatre through a Freirean approach.

Originally begun by students from the national drama school, the Instituto Nacional de Bellas Artes (INBA), a theatre program called Arte Escénico Popular toured plays into rural areas where the students would work in the fields and perform plays in exchange for a small wage. Due to the twin factors of a repertory that seemed irrelevant to the audience's lives and the difficulty in maintaining a stable company with students who frequently left after short stints, INBA ultimately revised the program. Now the plays are performed by the rural people themselves. In a similar fashion to the cultural animation work done by the Cultural Mission Program, amateur artists or school teachers receive four months of theatrical training from INBA and then are sent back to their own communities to form theatre groups. These groups are often composed of the indigenous population and perform plays in both Spanish and indigenous languages that focus upon the necessity of communal organization in order to solve common problems. In addition, INBA also supports several puppet-theatre groups whose performance style blends pre-Columbian puppetry techniques with those introduced by the Spaniards, and performs a repertory including folklore pieces for children and dramatized *corridos* (Mexican ballads) for adults.

In the late 1960s students from the Prestaciones Culturales division of the Bureau of Mexican Social Security formed a theatre group called Transhumante, after the Transhumante Indians – a nomadic tribe from central Mexico that disappeared after the Conquest. Transhumante took performances into the sprawling *barrios* of Mexico City and taught drama classes in factories and church halls. In 1972 Transhumante obtained a trailer truck that they converted into a traveling theatre. With the truck came the expansion of the group's work from solely theatrical performances into more wide-ranging educational programs. A small library of elementary geography and history texts on the truck was made available to the group's audiences before and after each performance. Slide-shows on basic hygiene and sanitation were developed and, since many of the *barrio* dwellers regularly returned to family plots in the countryside, educational films revolving around such topics as soil conservation and greater crop yields were shown.

In addition to Transhumante, the Proyecto de Animación Desarrollo (PRADE; Cultural Animation Project), which centers its work around the Mexican indigenous population, also uses theatre as a means of empowering its audience. PRADE has created a company called Nimayana in the village of San Miguel Tzinacapan that creates plays through improvisations that focus upon the loss of indigenous identity as people leave the village for the city and the remaining population finds itself exploited by nonvillagers through commercialization, the health-care system, and alcoholism. The conclusions of these plays generally deal with the need for collective action to address the problems confronting the community.

As well as Transhumante's work in Mexico City, the Mexican Institute for Community Development (IMDEC) has also used theatre as a tool for social change in urban areas. In Guadalajara, another prominent Mexican urban center, IMDEC started the Experimental Workshop on Popular Expression (TEEP). While the primary concern of IMDEC rests with improving health care, housing, and cooperatives, theatre is employed as a means of raising the community's consciousness regarding such issues. A theatre company was created out of the urban migrant youth population of the Santa Cecilia *barrio*. Its first collectively created piece was a play called *Thrown Out There and Kept Down Here* (1979), which treated the story of a rural migrant family that had left the countryside to move to the city and the problems that they confronted in an urban environment. The play was based upon the company members' personal experiences and gave both the company and their audience a sense of historical awareness and a means of dealing with their present. The play demonstrated that there was no reason to be ashamed of the rural past, and provided a stimulus for confronting the problems that both the performers and their audience members faced in common.

The work of another group of youngsters sponsored by IMDEC even more forcefully presents the interconnections of religion, politics, and theatre traced here. Asked to perform the Stations of the Cross during Holy Week, the group chose to perform the Seventh Station and its depiction of Christ's second fall on his journey to Calvary. Rather than presenting the typical image common to such religious processions, the group adapted the image of the Seventh Station to contemporary reality by creating a performance that showed industrial workers repeatedly beaten down by injustice and oppression. This performance was so positively received that the group decided to concentrate their efforts upon theatre as a means of *concientización*. The themes they chose were simple yet powerfully resonant for their community. For example, two of their subsequent plays were entitled *The Trial of a Mother* (1979) and *The Trial of a Father* (1979) and dealt with, respectively, Mother's Day and Father's Day. In the first play the family's propensity to neglect and abuse the mother except for one day a year is treated, and the second characterizes the father as a member of the working class, thereby introducing aspects of the class struggle. Much like Teatro Escambray's *El juicio, The Trial of a Father* makes use of a public tribunal composed of audience members which evaluates and passes judgment upon the character's actions. As with all of the liberation theatre groups discussed, the IMDEC groups pay particular attention to audience response in open forums after each performance, revising and refining the productions based upon that response. In each case the aim is to create theatre that truthfully depicts the audience's own experience with injustice and oppression, and, more importantly, to provide a catalyst towards action that will solve the various problems faced by the community.[38]

LIBERATION THEOLOGY/LIBERATION THEATRE: CRITICISM AND CONVERSION

The most forceful critique of liberation theology's "preferential option for the poor" is that advanced by neoconservatives such as Michael Novak who see in the practice of Christian base communities the potential for collective dictatorship. While reading the Bible and critiquing the world through the eyes of the poor, so the theory goes, may enable one to discover previously unknown forms of injustice and oppression, it also runs the risk of following the road towards a Hitlerite state in which only the poor possess theological truth and are capable of dispensing secular justice. Such a situation is one in which collective will is superior to individual will, and the individual is subjugated to the hegemonic force of the poor masses. A similar critique has been advanced towards the practices of the liberation theatre. This critique sees a great danger in allowing an audience to dictate the content of a piece of theatre through the constant revisions based upon audience reaction. In this case it is the individual artist or theatre group's artistry that is being subjugated to the collective will of the audience, rather than the art presenting a particular, personal point of view by means of theatrical presentation. Such a critique holds that collective creation is simply another term for tyranny by the masses.

As the previous discussion should have made clear, such a critique of either liberation theology or liberation theatre is fundamentally flawed. The Freirean basis upon which both the activities of the

Christian base communities and the theatre of Boal, Buenaventura, Bolt and others is based seeks not to inculcate participants with a specific party line, but to awaken their critical awareness of the conditions that surround them.[39] What is sought by both liberation theology and liberation theatre is a means by which the marginalized masses of Latin America can free themselves from centuries of neglect and inherited colonial attitudes that make them think of themselves as worthless. The fundamental basis for the practice of liberation theology or liberation theatre is not the willing submission of the individual that the conservative critique implies, but an active, aware, critical questioning of society by the individual that moves by degrees towards a collective consensus. The kind of group dominance warned against, in fact, is much more characteristic of the practices of the North American religious right in its utilization of Bible study groups for specifically political purposes; Bible study groups in which dissent from a particular line of scriptural interpretation is not tolerated. Similarly, the Pentecostal "shepherding" movement utilizes "cell groups" in which Christian doctrine and proper lifestyle is taught to members through direct obedience to a "shepherd."[40] In all of these cases what seems to be at issue is the semantic distinction between "the individual" and the collective mass of the poor. The plain fact is that what the conservative critique fears is that the "right" of the elite and powerful individual to behave as he or she pleases without regard to such behavior's impact upon others will be curtailed. Liberation theology and liberation theatre, in contrast, both demand a respect for the rights of the oppressed and marginalized in the social, political, and artistic spheres.[41]

That demand is one that leads to a further area of convergence between liberation theology and liberation theatre, a convergence that takes us back, in fact, to the confluence of religion, theatre, and politics with which these pages began. That convergence is the concept of *conversion*. Gustavo Gutiérrez has written:

A spirituality of liberation will center on a *conversion* to the neighbor, the oppressed person, the exploited social class, the despised race, the dominated country. Our conversion to the Lord implies this conversion to the neighbor. Evangelical conversion is indeed the touchstone of all spirituality. Conversion means a radical transformation of ourselves; it means thinking, feeling, and living as Christ – present in exploited and alienated man. To be converted is to commit oneself not only generously, but also with an analysis of the situation and a strategy of action. To be converted is to know and experience the fact that, contrary to the laws of physics, we can stand straight, according to the Gospel, only when our center of gravity is outside ourselves.[42]

This idea of "conversion to the neighbor" that is developed by liberation theology through the "preferential option for the poor" and the formation of Christian base communities is expressed in liberation theatre by the way in which such theatre strives to transform itself and its audience by *converting* the passive individual spectator into an actively engaged component of the theatrical exchange. Scholars such as Patricia González have seen a fundamental difference between the Latin American "new theatre" and the evangelical theatre that accompanied the Conquest in that the former does not seek "immediate ideological conversion" while the latter "had an immediate ideological end and was impelled by the priests' interest in converting the Indians."[43] Such an interpretation of mendicant evangelical theatre, however, incorporates only a portion of its theological basis. For while Franciscans such as Gustavo de Mendieta saw the Indians as taking no part in their own liberation, such a liberation was to be effected by their acceptance of the Messiah. The Messiah was to be the agent by which the Indians' economic exploitation was to be removed so that they might experience "the most perfect and healthy Christianity that the world had ever known." A distinction must be made, in other words, between the secular use of evangelical theatre by the *conquistadores* (as symbolized by Cortés), and the purpose of evangelical theatre as conceived by the Franciscans and other mendicant orders. As Phelan has commented:

In Mendieta's terrestrial paradise man's temporal necessities were to be satisfied. He seemed to imply that an adequate supply of food, clothing, and shelter were the indispensable prerequisites for leading the good life. The exploitation of native labor by the Spanish laymen was preventing the Indians from becoming good Christians. Mendieta's implication that a man cannot be economically enslaved and spiritually free is an idea with a modern ring.[44]

It has the ring of liberation theology which, through the *concientización* of the base communities, helps participants to form an effective critique of their own economic situation, and of the type of liberation theatre practiced by Alan Bolt that strives to put the means of self-sustaining agricultural production into the hands of its audience. Bolt's theatre is one that consciously tries to rescue Nicaragua's indigenous heritage. Buenaventura's theatre serves a similar function through the use of popular songs and dances to inform its audience of its national history. For the liberation theatre Latin American history, unadulterated by colonial or neocolonial interpretations, becomes an important means of *concientización*. Cortés' performance when he greeted the twelve Franciscans on the outskirts of Tenochtitlán was a religious, political, and theatrical construction carefully calculated to cement his newly won power over the Aztecs and to link the Church, morally and politically, to his secular ends. Liberation theology and liberation theatre return religious, political, and theatrical power to the participants' indigenous roots. In the twentieth century, however, that indigenous presence is no longer isolated as it was at the time of the Conquest, when the conqueror was a being from an incomprehensible culture. The conqueror's culture, and the Christian ideology it brought with it, is now fully known. By resuscitating the indigenous heritage liberation theology and liberation theatre give participants the possibility of controlling their own destiny. Where the colonial Church and state saw theatre as a means by which the indigenous populations could be manipulated unconsciously, liberation theatre gives contemporary Latin Americans a means by which they can begin consciously to manipulate their own lives.

Whether consciously or not, these theatre practitioners are reincarnating the Aztec conception of themselves as "a people with a mission." That conception came directly out of their knowledge of their own history: "Their history told of their remotest origins and even attempted to reveal their future, thus enabling the Nahuas to feel themselves an integral part of their world. They were no longer strangers but creators of, and heirs to, a culture symbolized by the word *Toltecáyotl* – 'the summing up of ancient wisdom and art.' "[45] Coupled with this historical consciousness was the religious conception of opening "one's window" to the universe in order to discover the essence of one's being. By the same token the word "door" was frequently used, during the Middle Ages, as a mystical symbol of Christian salvation. Thus Franciscan millenarianism held that "Cortés was elected by Divine Providence to conquer the Aztecs so that 'the door might be opened and a path made' for the ministers of the gospel."[46] Alan Bolt, trained as a Nahuatl wizard or shaman, has described his method of working as "opening a window in his heart" to those he meets who are in need.[47] The Aztec sensibility reemerges from the colonial Christian ideology. When it does so, it finds itself confronted by a vastly altered universe. One in which the Aztec, medieval, and contemporary openings will, of necessity, lead to a new order. Gustavo Gutiérrez has written: "It is important to keep in mind that beyond – or rather, through – the struggle against misery, injustice, and exploitation the goal is the *creation of a new man*."[48] Through the opening of these apertures comes the possibility of conversion for the participants in liberation theology and liberation theatre; that conversion is one capable of leading to creation of a new Latin American reality or, as in the Nahuatl name of Alan Bolt's theatre group Nixtayolero, a "new dawn."

Conclusion

One of the recurring images throughout this historical survey of Latin American theatre has been the battle between the city and the country, or, to put it another way, between the forces of "civilization" and indigenous forms. The tensions reflected here have been articulated by Latin Americans themselves in the ideological underpinnings of the regional perspectives proposed by the Argentinian Domingo Faustino Sarmiento and the Cuban José Martí. Sarmiento, in his classic work, *Facundo*, posits an opposition between "civilization" and "barbarity" with the only means by which to rise above the "barbarity" of the region that of implementing the "civilized" models of Europe and the United States. In contrast, Martí, in all of his writings and actions, rejected all types of colonialism and called for the establishment of *Nuestra América* (Our America), one that will be free, proud, and conscious of mutual dependency among countries in order to progress.[1] City vs. country, civilization vs. indigenous forms, Sarmiento vs. Martí, the battle lines have been drawn in Latin American politics, society, literature, art, and the theatre, the nineteenth-century theatre for liberation from colonial rule, the conflict between city and country in the Río de la Plata region as evidenced in the drama of the early years of this century, or the attempt to revitalize Latin American theatre incorporated indigenous ritual forms and skillfully used them to its advantage as it undertook the task of Christianizing the New World, thereby undercutting and replacing the existing Aztec authority. The eighteenth-century Jesuit education that was so common to the participants in the wars of independence from colonial rule championed the value of indigenous Latin American culture, actively cultivating a sense of nationalism as an adjunct to political theory that the king's authority was not divinely rendered but the result of the people's will. The nineteenth century turns to the figure of the *gaucho* and the indigenous characters who represent the social politic of the *sainete*, as well as the tutelary power of the *chingana* and the neoclassically oriented drama of the coliseums as a forum for class struggle. The twentieth century demonstrates this principle in a virtual explosion of theatrical forms. Those forms present a direct attack upon a social order that reduces human dignity and manifest themselves in the *grotesco criollo*, with its biblical imagery, the workers' theatre of Recabarren's Chile, with its use of Christian symbolism, the *teatro de masas*, with its reorientation of the methods of the evangelical theatre to revolutionary principles, the Cultural Mission Program, with its missionary zeal, the *carpas*, with their direct popular appeal, and the independent and university-affiliated companies of the mid-century, with their mixture of theatre, politics, and religion. With the 1960s and 1970s that dynamic increasingly parallels the techniques and tactics of liberation theology as theatre practitioners search for a socially engaged, politically vital liberation theatre. Frequently the content of the plays performed in the liberation theatre employs biblical imagery cast, through the use of masks, song, and dance, in an indigenous form.

The 1960s and 1970s also saw the proliferation of theatre festivals throughout the region and abroad. Initially, festivals such as those in Manizales, Caracas, Cordoba, Bogotá, Londrina, Havana, New York, and Cadiz were of immense importance in establishing links between theatre practitioners and breaking down the historic barriers to communication between countries. These venues provided a space for interchange of ideas and techniques as well as a stage for the presentation of theatre created upon an aesthetic foundation directly linked to specific communities and reflecting those communities' problems, preoccupations, and means of expression. By the 1980s, however, many of these festivals began to take on a different character, with work created specifically for the festivals. Often displaying spectacular technical ability, these pieces were rootless and soulless, speaking only to those momentarily gathered together for the festival itself and responding to the needs of no community.

This phenomenon of "festival theatre" is only one aspect of the directions in which Latin American theatre as a whole has moved in the 1980s. The end, in varying degrees and at a variety of speeds, to the majority of the authoritarian and totalitarian regimes throughout the region has meant that the politically and socially engaged theatre of the 1960s and 1970s has also had to shift its focus. In the early part of the decade the theatre was, in several instances, extremely important as a democratizing force. In Argentina the Teatro Abierto appeared in 1981. Within the social context of a continuing breakdown in the social order, an extension of the reign of terror that had plagued the country since the late 1970s, and an apparent weakening of the dictatorship, Osvaldo Dragún organized the presentation of new short works by twenty-one playwrights, directed by twenty-one directors, and utilizing a great number of actors, designers, and technicians. All of the artists donated their work and admission was free, the stated purpose being to bring people into the theatre and demonstrate the vitality of the Argentinian theatre after so many years of oppression.

The festival opened on July 28 in the Teatro del Picadero in Buenos Aires. On the morning of August 5 repressive forces set the theatre aflame and from that point on Teatro Abierto '81 became a *cause célèbre* for the intellectual and artistic community as well as attracting a substantial audience from the general population. Virtually all of the plays presented in Teatro Abierto '81, whether openly or metaphorically, attacked the totalitarian regime and provided an effective theatrical means of confronting the government and calling for social change. While Teatro Abierto became an annual event repeated from 1982 to 1986, it began to decline in 1983 with the disappearance of the dictatorship that had been its primary target.

In 1983 as well Teatro de la Libertad began work on a new production of the Argentinian classic *Juan Moreira* in Buenos Aires. Adapted and directed by Enrique Dacal, the text was fundamentally the same as the original Gutiérrez/Podestá version with the addition of several scenes designed to connect the oppression and death suffered by Moreira to the contemporary actions of the dictatorship. For instance, when Moreira, having rebelled and become an outlaw in response to the abuses heaped upon him by the authorities, asks about the fate of his wife and son, a torture scene is interposed in which parallels are drawn between Moreira's situation and that of all those who oppose dictatorial power. Another scene added to the original presents the erection of a statue to Moreira after his death while someone in the crowd publicly laments the death of a man who has been the "victim of our excesses and errors." "Excesses and errors" being the euphemistic language used by the dictatorship to refer to the 30,000 people who "disappeared" between 1976 and

1984. Teatro de la Libertad's production of *Juan Moreira* was performed in the streets of Buenos Aires, throughout the country, and at the First Latin American Theatre Festival in Cordoba in 1984. At the end of seven long years of dictatorship, Teatro de la Libertad used this production to recapture the concepts of honor and justice, so often invoked by the repressive regime, for the populace at large and to affirm the vibrancy of life over the horror of death that Argentina had experienced.[2]

Similar instances of theatre used to further the process of democratization in the 1980s can be seen in the activities of the Mexican group CLETA to promote freedom of speech in Mexico in 1984,[3] and in the early 1990s, with the work done by Teatro ICTUS in Chile in favor of the "No" vote against a constitutional continuation of the Pinochet dictatorship. For the most part, however, as the 1980s continued, strictly politically oriented theatre in Latin America waned as a force. Together with the decline of the widespread use of collective creation, this meant that the decade was one of initial confusion for theatre practitioners. The decade was a period for questioning aesthetic orientation and theatrical practice, and searching for new forms. While the liberation theatre of the 1960s and 1970s was by no means abandoned, it became decidedly less doctrinaire. The liberation theatre of the 1980s is one that admits the possibility of magic, of sacrament, and of a sense of diversion in the theatre. Having firmly established a sense of Latin American identity, it borrows from European and North American forms in order to enhance its own practice in a veritable profusion of forms. While it is still too early to predict which trends of Latin American theatre in the 1980s and 1990s will endure, one direction that seems to be emerging with particular force, and that is directly related to the development of the Latin American theatre that has been traced in this study, is an increasing incorporation of an anthropological awareness of indigenous culture with twentieth-century theatrical practice. Various experiments have been carried out in this arena, some more successfully than others, but it seems to me to be a particular promising path to follow for the elaboration of a specifically Latin American theatre. In general terms, then, the last decade in Latin America has been one in which theatre practitioners have continued to search for, and to create, their own theatre. That theatre is one that emerges organically out of the historical context of Latin America itself and that carries with it the artistic force to hold its own with any theatrical tradition in the world: a theatre, in short, that reflects José Martí's call for *Nuestra América*.

The forms of theatre I have described throughout this book do not by any means represent the only theatre that existed during these time periods. Latin America has always had its share of commercial and imported theatre. What I have attempted to isolate here, however, is a kind of theatre that can be seen as peculiarly Latin American. The Aztecs believed in the cyclical nature of the universe, as evidenced most strongly by the recurring appearance of the Sun. Latin American theatre presents us with a cyclical universe as well, one that continually underscores the dynamic between what is perceived as a repressive authority and a populace striving for its independence. These pages demonstrate that such a theatre has a wide-ranging historical foundation. When Cortés greeted the twelve Franciscans by kneeling and kissing their hands and attempting to kiss their robes, in a nearly identical repetition of the Aztecs' dirt-eating gesture of humility and honor, he began a theatrical tradition that has persisted to the present day. That tradition consciously combines politics, religion, and theatre in a way that is unique to the Latin American region.

Appendix: Latin American playwrights

Cossa, Roberto (1934–)
Cuzzani, Agustín (1924–1987)
Defillipis Novoa, Francisco (1889–1930)
Discépolo, Armando (1887–1971)
Dragún, Osvaldo (1929–)
Eichelbaum, Samuel (1894–1967)
Fuentes del Arco, Antonio (?–1733)
Gambaro, Griselda (1928–)
Gutiérrez, Eduardo (1853–1890)
Leguizamón, Martiniano (1858–1935)
Monti, Ricardo (1944–)
Morante, Luis Ambrosio (1775–1837)
Pavlovsky, Eduardo (1933–)
Podestá, José J. ("Pepino 88") (1858–1936)
Sánchez, Florencio (1875–1910)
Viñas, David (1929–)

CHILE

Cruchaga, Germán Luco (1894–1936)
Henríquez, Camilo (1769–1825)
Parra, Marco Antonio de la (1952–)
Radrigan, Juan (1937–)
Recabarren, Luis Emilio (1876–1924)
Wolff, Egon (1926–)

COLUMBIA

Buenaventura, Enrique (1925–)
Fernandez Madrid, José (1788–1830)

García, Santiago (1929–)
Reyes, Carlos (1941–)
Vargas Tejada, Luis (1802–1829)

CUBA

Corrieri, Sergio (1938–)
González, Sergio (1924–)
Heredía, José Marí (1803–1839)
Martí, José (1853–1895)
Paz, Albio (1937–)
Piñera, Virgilio (1912–1979)
Triana, José (1933–)

GUATEMALA

Asturias, Miguel Angel (1899–1974)
Solórzano, Carlos (1922–)

MEXICO

Alvarez, Elena (dates unknown)
Aycrado, José Soledad (dates unknown)
Becerra de Celis, M. Concepción (1906–1973)
Bustillo Oro, Juan (1904–)
Cantinflas (1911–1993)
Carballido, Emilio (1925–)
Cruz, Sor Juana de la (1648?–1695?)
Fernández de Lizardi, José Joaquín (El Pensador Mexicano) (1776–1827)
Flores Magón, Ricardo (1873–1928)
Gamboa, Fedrico (1894–1939)
González Franco, Francisco (dates unknown)
Gutiérrez Hermosillo, Alfonso (1905–1935)
Isla, Ezquiel de la (dates unknown)
List Arzubide, Armando (dates unknown)
List Arzubide, Germán (1898–)
Magdaleno, Mauricio (1906–1986)
Oneto Barenque, Rodolfo (dates unknown)
Orozco Rosales, Efrén (1903–1973)
Solórzano, Carlos (1922–)
Usigli, Rodolfo (1905–1979)

PERU

Espinoso Medrano, Juan (El Lunarejo) (1632–1688)

PUERTO RICO

Marqués, René (1919–)

URUGUAY

Martinez, Juan Francisco (dates unknown)
Morante, Luis Ambrosio (1775–1837)
Podestá, José J. ("Pepino 88") (1858–1936)
Sánchez, Florencio (1875–1910)

Notes

(Unless indicated otherwise, all translations are my own.)

I RELIGION, POLITICS AND THEATRE: CORTÉS GREETS THE
TWELVE FRANCISCANS

1 Willis Knapp Jones, *Behind Spanish American Footlights* (Austin: University of Texas Press, 1966), 460.
2 *Chrónica seraphica*, ed. J. Torrubia (Madrid: 1725–1756), vol. IX, 291–295, cited in George Kubler, *Mexican Architecture of the Sixteenth Century* (Westport, Conn.: Greenwood Press, 1972), 7.
3 John Leddy Phelan, *The Millenial Kingdom of the Franciscans in the New World: a Study of the Writings of Gerónimo Mendieta (1525–1604)* (Berkeley: University of California Press, 1956), 33–34.
4 Ibid., 17–18.
5 Ibid., 9.
6 Esther Pasztory, *Aztec Art* (New York: Harry N. Abrams, 1983), 12–13.
7 Ibid., 12–13.
8 José Cid Perez, *Teatro indio precolombiano* (Avila: Aguilar, SA, 1964), 15.
9 James Robert Moriarty, "Ritual combat: a comparison of the Aztec 'War of Flowers' and the Medieval 'Mêlée,'" in Museum of Anthropology, *Miscellaneous Series, No. 9.* (Greeley, Colo.: November, 1969).
10 Bernardino de Sahagún, *Historia general de las cosas de Nueva España*, ed. A. M. Garibay, 4 vols. (Mexico: UNAM, 1950–1969), Bk. 12.
11 Sahagún, *Historia general*, (trans. Arthur J. O. Anderson and Charles E. Dibble, *General History of the Things of New Spain* [Santa Fé, N.Mex.: the School of American Research and the University of Utah, 1978]), Bk. 12, 42.
12 Miguel León-Portilla, *Aztec Thought and Culture: a Study of the Ancient Nahautl Mind*, trans. Jack Emory Davis (Norman: University of Oklahoma Press, 1963), 56.
13 Sahagún, *Historia general*, trans. Anderson and Dibble, bk. 3, 1–5.
14 Victor Turner, *From Ritual to Theatre: the Human Seriousness of Play* (New York: PAJ, 1982), 79.
15 Fray Diego Durán, *Historia de las Indias de Nueva España e Islas de la Tierra Firme*, ed. A. M. Garibay, 2 vols. (Mexico: Porrúa, 1967), I, 193.

16 Fernando Horcasitas, *El teatro náhautl: épocas novohispano y moderna* (Mexico: Universidad Nacional Autónoma de México, Instituto de Investigaciones Históricas, 1974), 42.
17 Durán, *Historia de las Indias*, I, 63.
18 Ibid.
19 Turner, *From Ritual to Theatre*, 80.
20 Códice Florentino, bk. VI, fol. 43v.
21 León-Portilla, *Aztec Thought and Culture*, 122.
22 Cid Perez, *Teatro indio precolombiano*, 89.
23 Ibid., 91.
24 Clements Markham, *The Incas of Peru* (London: Smith, Elder, 1910), 105.
25 Cid Perez, *Teatro indio precolombiano*, 93–94.
26 Pedro Sarmiento de Gamboa, *Histórica índica*, reproduced in Roberto Levillier, *Don Francisco de Toledo, supremo organizador de Perú* (Buenos Aires, 1942), 80, 83, cited in José Juan Arrom, *El teatro de Hispanoamérica en la época colonial* (Havana: Anuario Bibliográfico Cubano, 1956), 31.
27 Sarmiento de Gamboa, *Histórica índica*, 80–83.
28 Ibid., 105.
29 Ibid., 212.
30 Francisco Monterde, *Teatro indígena prehispánico: Rabinal Achí* (Mexico: Ediciones de la Universidad Nacional Autónoma, 1955), ix.
31 Ibid., xxvi.
32 Ibid., 129.
33 Classroom discussion in a graduate art history seminar entitled "The Aesthetic Response to the Discovery of the New World" at Yale University in the spring of 1987.
34 Charles S. Braden, *Religious Aspects of the Conquest of Mexico* (New York: Ames Press, 1966), 62.
35 Ibid., 63–69.
36 Robert Ricard, *The Spiritual Conquest of Mexico* (Berkeley: University of California Press, 1966), 32–33.
37 Cited in Braden, *Religious Aspects*, 71–72.
38 Cited in Braden, 73–74.
39 Bernardino de Sahagún, *Informantes de Sahagún*, trans. from Nahautl to Spanish by Angel María Garibay and included in *Revista Tlalocan*, 2, no. 3 (1947), 236–237, English trans. by Marilyn Ekdahl Ravicz in *Early Colonial Religious Drama in Mexico: from Tzompantli to Golgotha* (Washington, D.C.: The Catholic University of America Press, 1970), 20–21.
40 Durán, *Historia de las Indias*, I, 194, in Horcasitas, *El teatro náhuatl*, 38.
41 This design may have been borrowed from the Indians, whose pyramids' steps opened onto plazas and were known for their acoustic properties.
42 Horcasitas, *El teatro náhuatl*, 120.
43 Joaquín García Icazalceta, *Nueva colección de documentos para la historia de México. Códice Franciscano Siglo XVI* (Mexico: Editorial Salvador Chavez Hayhoe, 1941), 214.

44 Ibid.
45 Ravicz, *Religious Drama in Mexico*, 41–42.
46 Horcasitas, *El teatro náhuatl*, 145.
47 Thomas Gage, *A New Survey of the West Indies: or The English American his Travail by Sea and Land* (London: E. Cotes, 1655), 54.
48 Fray Torbio de Venavente Motolinía, *Historia de los indios de la Nueva España* (Mexico: Editorial Chavez Hayhoe, 1941), 92.
49 Gullermo Lohmann Villena, *El arte dramático en Lima durante el Virreinato* (Madrid: Escuela de Estudios Hispanoamericanos de la Universidad de Sevilla, 1945), 73–74.
50 Horcasitas, *El teatro náhuatl*, 81.
51 See Horcasitas, *El teatro náhuatl*, and Ravicz, *Religious Drama in Mexico*.
52 Fray Bartolomé de Las Casas, *Apologética historia summaria* (Mexico: Instituto de Investigaciones Históricas, UNAM, 1967), I, 334.
53 Othón Arróniz, *Teatro de evangelización en nueva españa* (Mexico: Universidad Nacional Autónoma de México, 1979), 40.
54 Ravicz, *Religious Drama in Mexico*, 157.
55 See Robert Potter, "Abraham and human sacrifice: the exfoliation of medieval drama in Aztec Mexico," *New Theatre Quarterly*, 2, no. 8 (Nov. 1986).
56 Ravicz, *Religious Drama in Mexico*, 97.
57 Horcasitas, *El teatro náhuatl*, 254–255.
58 Ibid., 516.
59 Durán, *Historia de las Indias*, II, 486 in Horcasitas, *El teatro náhuatl*, 39.
60 Cited in Motolinía, *Historia de los indios*, 87.
61 Bartolomé de Las Casas, *Apologética historia de las Indias* (Madrid: Biblioteca de Autores Españoles, 105, 1958), 214.
62 Motolinía, *Historia de los indios*, treatise I, ch. 15, in *Colección de documentos para la Historia de México* (Mexico: Joaquín García Icazbalceta, edición facsimilar, 1971).
63 Ibid.
64 Ibid.
65 An interesting footnote to *La conquista de Jerusalén* is the performance in 1794 by the Mechanical Theatre of New Orleans in Havana of a puppet play concerning the destruction of Jerusalem. In a spectacle that involved 35,000 figures that were moved about on a 2 meters long stage, the Habaneros were treated to a performance that showed them "corpses rising up out of their tombs, the Final Judgment, and life in Hell." "Papel Periódico de La Habana," nos. 25–40, March 27 – May 18, 1794. Cited in Mayra Navarro, *Escenarios de dos mundos: inventario teatral de Iberoamérica* (Madrid: Centro de Documentación Teatral, 1988), II, 53.

2 CHURCH, COLONIALISM, AND THEATRE IN LATIN AMERICA

1 Robert Ricard, *The Spiritual Conquest of Mexico: an Essay on the Apostolate and the Evangelizing Methods of the Mendicant Orders in New Spain: 1523–1572*,

trans. Lesley Byrd Simpson (Berkeley: University of California Press, 1966), 239–263.

2 Fernando Horcasitas. *El teatro náhuatl: épocas novohispana y moderna* (Mexico: Universidad Nacional Autónoma de México, Instituto de Investigaciones Históricas, 1974), 161–163.

3 Ibid.

4 Carlos Miguel Suárez Radillo, *El teatro barroco hispanoamericano*, 3 vols. (Madrid: Ediciones José Porrúa Turanzas, SA, 1981), III, 639–640.

5 José Juan Arrom, *El teatro de Hispanoamérica en la época colonial* (Havana: Anuario Bibliográfico Cubano, 1956), 115.

6 Suárez Radillo, *El teatro barroco*, I, 224.

7 While a new cultural amalgam of Spaniard and Indian was the end product of the colonization of Latin America, this by no means implies that such was the Spanish intention. Cortés' attitude towards the indigenous population was clearly that it should be subjugated to his will, and even the missionaries who strove to protect the Indians from ill-treatment in effect worked to destroy Indian culture. This is true of Las Casas' efforts on the Indians' behalf, and can also be seen in the history of Jesuit "reductions" in Brazil and Paraguay. A direct parallel can be drawn between such activity and that of the Jesuits during the colonization of Canada. See James S. Saeger, "Eighteenth-century Guaycuruan missions in Paraguay," in Susan E. Ramírez (ed.), *Indian–Religious Relations in Colonial Spanish America* (Foreign and Comparative Studies/Latin American Series, 9), (Syracuse, N.Y.: Maxwell School of Citizenship and Public Affairs, 1989), and Urs Bitterli, *Cultures in Conflict: Encounters between European and Non-European Cultures, 1492–1800* (Oxford: Polity Press, 1989).

8 The first theatrical indication of this upheaval is the performance in 1684 in Mexico City of Francisco de Acevedo's curious play about St. Francis de Asisi called *El pregonero de dios y Patriarca de los pobres* (God's proclaimer and the poor's Patriarch). The Holy Inquisition took umbrage at the play, claiming that it presented the saint's life "obscured by clouds of amours, jealousies, fights, rivalries, wooing, and licentiousness, without any basis in history, nor verisimilitude in fiction, even if one only pays attention to the saint's secular life." The play was banned, Acevedo was ordered to destroy all his copies, and to pay a 100 ducat fine. See *El pregonero de dios y Patriarca de los pobres* (Mexico: Imprenta Universitaria, Edición de Jiménez Rueda, 1945), Introduction.

9 Arrom, *El teatro de Hispanoamérica*, 123.

10 Gabriel Méndez Plancarte, *Humanistas del siglo XVIII* (Mexico: Ediciones de la Universidad Nacional Autónoma, 1941), XI.

11 Julio Jiménez Rueda, *Herejías y supersticiones en la Nueva España (Los heterodoxos en México)* (Mexico: UNAM, 1946), 245–246.

12 Arrom, *El teatro de Hispanoamérica*, 177–179.

13 From his *Epístola II*, reprinted by Harvey L. Johnson in *Revista Iberoamericana*, 10, no. 20 (March 1946), pp. 206–226, cited in Arrom, *El teatro de Hispanoamérica*, 187.

14 "Memoria del virrey Vértiz", *Revista del Archivo General de Buenos Aires*, 3 (1871), 288–289, cited in Arrom, *El teatro de Hispanoamérica*, 188.

15 Carlos Miguel Suárez Radillo, *El teatro neoclásico y costumbrista hispano-americano*, 4 vols. (Madrid: Ediciones Cultura Hispánica, Instituto de Cooperación Iberoamericana, 1984), III, 306.

16 Willis Knapp Jones, *Behind Spanish American Footlights* (Austin: University of Texas Press, 1966), 65–66.

17 Suárez Radillo, *El teatro neoclásico*, 364; Eugenio Pereira Salas, *Historia del teatro en Chile* (Santiago de Chile: Ediciones de la Universidad de Chile, 1974), 84; Knapp Jones, *Spanish American Footlights*, 183–184.

18 Knapp Jones, *Spanish American Footlights*, 416–417.

19 Ibid., 394.

20 Ibid., 436–437.

21 Jefferson Rea Spell, *Rousseau in the Spanish World Before 1833: a Study in Franco-Spanish Literary Relations* (Austin: University of Texas Press, 1938), 22.

22 Ibid., 36–73.

23 Ibid., 133–134.

24 José Joaquín Fernández de Lizardi, *Don Catrin de La Fachenda y fragmentos de otras obras*, ed. Jefferson Rea Spell (Mexico: Editorial Cultura, 1944), xxix–xxx.

25 Rine Leal, *La selva oscura* (Havana: Editorial Arte y Literatura, 1975), I, 119.

26 Julio Durán Cerda, "El teatro en las tareas revolucionarios de la independencia de Chile," *Anales de la Universidad de Chile*, 119 (1960), 230.

27 *Memorial* in the *Colección Eyzaguirre*, II, Archivo Nacional, reprinted in Eugenio Pereira Salas, *El teatro en Santiago del Nuevo Extremo* (Santiago: Imprenta Universitaria, 1941), 14–18.

28 Camilo Henríquez, "Del entusiasmo revolucionario," *La Aurora de Chile*, 31 (Santiago, September 10, 1812), 139–142.

29 Suárez Radillo, *El teatro neoclásico*, II, 398–400.

30 Miguel Luis Amunátegui, *Camilo Henríquez* (Santiago de Chile: Imprenta Nacional, 1889), 306.

31 John A. Cook, *Neo-classical Drama in Spain: Theory and Practice* (Dallas: Southern Methodist University Press, 1959), 76–77.

32 Suárez Radillo, *El teatro neoclásico*, IV, 379–386.

33 Suárez Radillo, *El teatro neoclásico*, II, 369.

34 Pereira Salas, *Historia del teatro en Chile*, 112.

35 José Fernández Madrid, *Atala y Guatimoc* (Selección Samper Ortega de Literatura Colombiana, Teatro No. 92) (Bogotá: Editorial Minerva, SS, 1936).

36 Suárez Radillo, *El teatro neoclásico*, I, 48.

37 Leal, *La selva oscura*, 15–69.

38 *Breve historia del teatro Argentino*, I: *De la revolución a Caseros*, ed. Luis Ordaz (Buenos Aires: Editorial Universitaria de Buenos Aires, 1962).

39 Bartolomé Hidalgo, *Obras completas*, Preface and notes by Walter Rela (Montevideo: Editorial Ciencias, 1979), 3–5.
40 Pereira Salas, *Historia del teatro en Chile*, 53–54.
41 Ibid., 82.
42 Ibid., 83–84.
43 Samuel Haigh, *Sketches of Buenos Ayres and Chile* (London: James Carpenter, 1829), 267–269.
44 Pereira Salas, *Historia del teatro en Chile*, 153.
45 Ibid.

3 HOMEGROWN EMPIRE: THE CONTRADICTIONS OF AN EMERGING
REGION

1 For an analysis of this feudal social and economic structure see Jean Franco, *La cultura moderna en América Latina* (Mexico: Joaquín Mortiz, 1971), and Manuel Lopez Gallo, *Economía y política en la historia de México* (Mexico: Editorial el Caballito, SA, 1972).
2 Alejo Carpentier, *América Latina en las confluencias de coordenadas históricas y su repercusión en la música en América Latina* in *América Latina en su música* (Mexico: UNESCO – Siglo Veintiuno Editores, 1977), 15.
3 George Black, *The Good Neighbor: How the United States Wrote the History of Central America and the Caribbean* (New York: Pantheon Books, 1988), 12.
4 Cited in Black, *The Good Neighbor*, xvii.
5 Armando de María y Campos, *Los payasos, poetas del pueblo: el circo en México* (Mexico: Ediciones Botas, 1939), 11.
6 Enrique García Velloso, *Memorias de un hombre de teatro* (Buenos Aires: Editorial Guillermo Kraft, 1942), 139–140.
7 María y Campos, *Los payasos*, 146.
8 García Velloso, *Memorias*, 164.
9 Rine Leal, *Breve historia del teatro cubano* (Havana: Editorial Letras Cubanas, 1980), 67, and *La selva oscura: de los bufos a la neocolonia* (*Historia del teatro cubano de 1868 a 1902*) (Havana: Editorial Arte y Literatura, 1975), II, 347.
10 Leal, *La selva oscura*, 31–32.
11 James J. O'Kelley, *La tierra del Mambí* (Havana: Instituto del Libro, 1968), 254–255.
12 Leal, *La selva oscura*.
13 Luis Ordaz, "El teatro: desde Caseros hasta el zarzuelismo criollo," in his *Historia del teatro argentino* (Buenos Aires: Centro Editor de América Latina, SA, 1982), 174–175.
14 Eduardo Gutiérrez, *Juan Moreira* (Buenos Aires: Centro Editor de América Latina, SA, 1980), I–V.
15 José Hernández, *Martín Fierro*, dramatization by José Gonzalez Castillo (Buenos Aires: Instituto Nacional de Estudios de Teatro, 1952), 25–26.

16 See introduction to *Teatro gauchesco primitivo*, ed. by Juan Carlos Ghiano (Buenos Aires: Ediciones Losange, 1957), and *Los clásicos del teatro hispanoamericano*, ed. by Gerardo Luzuriagia and Richard Reeve (Mexico: Fondo de Cultura Económica, 1975).

17 García Velloso, *Memorias*, 159.

18 José J. Podestá, *Medio siglo de farándula* (Río de la Plata:Argentina de Cordoba; 1930), 56.

19 Ibid.

20 Raymond Williams, *The Country and the City* (New York: Oxford University Press, 1973), 17, 47–48, 72, 82–85.

21 Jorge Lafforgue, "Panorama del teatro," in Ordaz, *Historia del teatro argentino*, 331; Ordaz, "Desde Caseros," 357.

22 Luis Ordaz, *El drama rural* (Buenos Aires: Librería Hachette, SA, 1959), 11.

23 *Teatro gauchesco primitivo*, 14–15; Walter Rela, *Teatro uruguayo 1807–1979* (Montevideo: Alianza Cultural, 1980), 26–27.

24 Julio Durán Cerda, "Civilización y Barbarie en el Desarrollo del Teatro Nacional Rioplatense," *Revista Iberoamericana*, 24, no. 55 (1963), 114–116.

25 See Florencio Sánchez, *Obras completas* (Buenos Aires: Editorial Schapire, SRL, 1968), 1.

26 Ordaz, *Historia del teatro argentino*, 412.

27 Sebastián Covarrubias y Orozco, *Tesoro de la lengua castellana o española* (Madrid: Luis Sánchez, NS, 1911), 920, cited in Claudia Kaiser-Lenoir, *El grotesco criollo: estilo teatral de una época* (Havana: Casa de las Américas, 1977), 37.

28 Kaiser-Lenoir, *El grotesco criollo*, 39–40.

29 Ordaz, *Historia del teatro argentino*, 149–158.

30 Kaiser-Lenoir, *El grotesco criollo*, 7–12.

31 Ordaz, *Historia del teatro argentino*, 420.

32 Kaiser-Lenoir, *El grotesco criollo*, 31–33, 35–36, 61–62.

33 Ordaz, *Historia del teatro argentino*, 386–392.

34 Williams, *The Country and the City*, 156.

4 RELIGION, POLITICS, AND THEATRE: THE TWENTIETH CENTURY AND THE RETURN OF RITUAL

1 Frances Toor, *A Treasury of Mexican Folkways* (New York: Crown, 1947), 175–176.

2 *The Shepherds' Play of the Prodigal Son* (*Coloquio de pastores del hijo pródigo*), ed. George C. Barker (Berkeley: University of California Press, 1953), 3–4.

3 Ibid. The name Bato has passed into general Spanish usage to denote "a stupid man, a rustic without much sense" and, by extension, took on the value of "man" in Mexican slang. From there it has entered Chicano speech as "vato" with the colloquial meaning of "guy" or "homeboy".

4 *Drama de la Pasión que se representa en Ixtapalapa, D.F. llamado "Los tres caídos de Jesucristo"* (Mexico: Imprenta Universitario, 1947), 7.
5 See Ch. 1, 9–11.
6 Adalberto Fuentes Cruz, *Drama de la pasión como se representa en Milpa Alta, D.F.* (Mexico, 1949).
7 John B. Nomland, *Teatro mexicano contemporáneo (1900–1950)* (México: Instituto Nacional de Bellas Artes, Departamento de Literatura, 1967), 16–18.
8 Antonio Magaña Esquivel, *Imagen del teatro* (Mexico: Ediciones Letras de México, 1940), 48.
9 Nomland, *Teatro mexicano*, 89.
10 Rodolfo Usigli, *México en el teatro* (Mexico: Imprenta Mundial, 1932), 125.
11 Magaña Esquivel, *Imagen del teatro*, 48.
12 Nomland, *Teatro mexicano*, 90.
13 Efrén Orozco Rosales, *Liberación* (Mexico: Departamento del Distrito Federal, Dirección General de Acción Cívica, 1935), 2.
14 Nomland, *Teatro mexicano*, 91–92.
15 Efrén Orozco Rosales, *El mensajero de sol* (Mexico, D.F., 1941), 40; English section translated and edited by A. J. Brooks.
16 Robert E. Quirk, *The Mexican Revolution and the Catholic Church (1910–1929)* (Bloomington: Indiana University Press, 1973), 116.
17 Ibid., 117.
18 Ibid., 117–118.
19 Lloyd H. Hughes, *The Mexican Cultural Mission Programme* (Paris: UNESCO, 1950), 10–11.
20 Ibid., 12.
21 Katherine M. Cook, *La casa del pueblo: un relato de las escuelas nuevas de acción en México*, trans. Rafael Ramírez (Mexico, 1936).
22 See Ch. 1, 22–23.
23 Cook, *La casa del pueblo*, 146.
24 Concha Becerra Cellis, *Teatro y poemas infantiles* (Mexico: Ediciones Encuardernables, 1938), 73–74.
25 See *NACLA*, 14, no. 6 (November–December 1980), 41–43; 15, no. 3 (May–June 1981), 25–30; and *Cultural Survival Quarterly*, 4, no. 4, 8–9; 6, no. 1 (winter 1982), 20–26.
26 Hughes, *Cultural Mission Programme*, 67–68.
27 Toor, *Mexican Folkways*, 98–99.
28 Quirk, *The Mexican Revolution*, 120–121.
29 Jean A. Meyer, *The Cristero Rebellion: the Mexican People Between Church and State 1926–1929* (Cambridge: Cambridge University Press, 1976), 9.
30 Ibid., 33–34.
31 Joaquín Márquez Montiel, *La doctrina social de la iglesia y legislación obrera mexicana* (Mexico, 1939) cited in Quirk, *The Mexican Revolution*, 27–28.
32 Meyer, *The Cristero Rebellion*, 51.
33 Quirk, *The Mexican Revolution*, 246–247.

34 Meyer, *The Cristero Rebellion*, 198.
35 Nomland, *Teatro mexicano*, 285–289.
36 González Franco, *La perfecta alegría* (Mexico: J. I. Muñoz, 1938), 57.
37 Ibid., 31.
38 Nomland, *Teatro mexicano*, 288.
39 Rodolfo Oneto Barenque, *La realidad en las manos del hombre* (1936); Ezequiel de la Isla, *Tarsicio* (1938), *Valor cristiano* (1939), and *Una víctima de la secreta de la confesión* (1938), cited in Nomland, *Teatro mexicano*, 289.
40 See Miguel Covarrubias, "Slapstick and venom: politics, tent shows and comedians," *Theatre Arts Monthly*, 22, no. 8 (August 1938), 594–595; and Nomland *Teatro mexicano*, 145–178 on political revues and *carpas*.
41 Federico Gamboa, *La venganza del gleba* (Mexico: 1907).
42 David Poole, Introduction to *Land and Liberty: Anarchist Influences in the Mexican Revolution. Ricardo Flores Magón* (Sanday, Orkney, UK: Cienfuegos Press, 1977).
43 Ricardo Flores Magón, *Tierra y Libertad* (Mexico: Ediciones del Grupo Cultural "Ricardo Magón," 1924).
44 A strong alcoholic drink made from the fermented juice of the agave or maguey plant and popular with the lower classes.
45 Elena Alvarez, *Dos dramas revolucionarios,* (Mexico: Ediciones de la Liga de Escritores Revolucionarios, 1926), 46.
46 Mauricio Magdaleno, *Teatro revolucionario mexicano* (Madrid: Editorial Cenit, SA, 1933), 274.
47 Germán List Arzubide, *Tres obras del teatro revolucionario* (Mexico: Ediciones Integrales, 1933), 64.
48 Nomland, *Teatro mexicano*, 280–281.
49 Ibid., 264.
50 Pedro Bravo-Elizondo. *Teatro hispanoamericano de crítica social* (Madrid: Colección Nova Scholar, Playor, SA 1975), 116.
51 Esteban Rivas, *Carlos Solórzano y el teatro hispanoamericano* (Mexico: Impresos Anáhuac, 1970), 58.
52 Carlos Solórzano, *Las manos de dios*, in Solórzano (ed.) *El teatro hispanoamericano contemporáneo* (Mexico: Fondo de Cultura Económica, 1964), II, 325.
53 Bravo-Elizondo, *Teatro hispanoamericano*, 117.
54 Solórzano, *Las manos de dios*, 358.
55 Frank Dauster, "The drama of Carlos Solórzano," *Modern Drama*, 7 (May 1964), 98.
56 Ibid.
57 Emilio Carballido, "The intermediate zone" in Margaret Sayers Peden (trans.), *The Golden Thread and Other Plays*, (Austin: University of Texas Press, 1970), 141–142.
58 Eugene R. Skinner, "The theatre of Emilio Carballido: spinning a web," in Leon F. Lyday and George W. Woodyard (eds.), *Dramatists in Revolt: The New Latin American Theatre* (Austin: University of Texas Press, 1976), 21.

59 Mary Vázquez Amaral, *El teatro de Emilio Carballido* (1950–1965) (Mexico: B. Costa-Amic, 1974), 57.

60 Emilio Carballido, *La zona intermedia* (Mexico: Union Nacional de Autores, no. 26, S.F.), 52.

61 Eugenia W. Herbert, *The Artist and Social Reform: France and Belgium, 1885–1898* (New Haven, Conn.: Yale University Press, 1961), 34–35.

62 Tancredo Pinochet, *La conquista de Chile en el siglo XX* (Santiago: "La Illustración," 1909).

63 Theodore Child, *The Spanish American Republics* (New York: Harper, 1891), 177.

64 Ibid.

65 Ibid., 178.

66 Pedro Bravo-Elizondo, *Cultura y teatro obreros en Chile 1900–1930* (Madrid: Ediciones Michay, SA, 1986), 30.

67 Moisés Poblete Troncoso, *El movimiento de asociación profesional obrera en Chile* (Mexico: El Colegio de México, Jornadas – 29, 1945).

68 Bravo-Elizondo, *Cultura y teatro*, 10–12.

69 Ibid., 32.

70 Ibid., 58.

71 Brian H. Smith, *The Church and Politics in Chile: Challenges to Modern Catholicism* (Princeton, N.J.: Princeton University Press, 1982), 70–73.

72 P. Juan Vanherk Moris, *Monseñor José María Caro: Apóstol de Tarapacá* (Santiago: Editorial del Pacífico, 1963), 349–350, cited in Bravo-Elizondo, *Cultura y teatro*, 36.

73 Ibid., 121.

74 Rojo, *Los origenes de teatro hispanoamericano*, 185.

75 Egon Wolff, *Teatro* (Santiago: Ediciones Valores Literarios, 1971), 164–165.

76 Antonio Skármeta, "La burguesia invadida: Egón Wolff," in Pedro Bravo-Elizondo (ed.), *La dramaturgía de Egon Wolff* (Santiago: Editorial Nascimiento, 1985), 24, 29–30.

77 Samuel Eichelbaum, *Un guapo del 900* (Buenos Aires: Argentores, 1940), 84.

78 Enrique Giordano, *La teatralización de la obra dramática: Florencio Sánchez a Roberto Arlt* (Mexico: Premia Editora, 1982), 153.

79 See Donald L. Schmidt, "The theatre of Osvaldo Dragún," in Lyday and Woodyard (eds.), *Dramatists in Revolt*.

80 Alyce de Kuehne, "The theatre of Agustín Cuzzani," in Lyday and Woodyard (eds.), *Dramatists in Revolt*, 47.

81 My trans., *Modern International Drama*, 21, no. 2 (spring 1988), 50.

82 Ibid., 31.

83 Ibid., 58.

84 Virgilio Piñera, *Teatro completo* (Havana: Ediciones R., 1960), 134.

85 Ibid., 21–22.

86 Tamara Holzapfel, "The theatre of René Marqués: in search of identity and form," in Lyday and Woodyard (eds.), *Dramatists in Revolt*, 87.

87 Bravo-Elizondo, *Teatro hispanoamericano*, 87.
88 Holzapfel, "The theatre of René Marqués," 152.
89 René Marqués, *Teatro* (Rio Piedras: Editorial Cultural, 1970).
90 Bravo-Elizondo, *Teatro hispanoamericano*, 91.
91 Carlos Solórzano, "Miguel Angel Asturias y el teatro," *Revista Ibero-americana*, 35, no. 67. (January–April, 1969), 101.
92 Miguel Angel Asturias, *Soluna* (Buenos Aires: Ediciones Losange, 1955), 76–77.

5 LIBERATION THEOLOGY AND LIBERATION THEATRE: THE CONVERGENCE OF PARALLEL LINES

1 Gustavo Gutiérrez, *A Theology of Liberation* (Maryknoll, N.Y.: Orbis Books, 1973), ix.
2 Ibid., 6–7.
3 Alfred Hennelly, SJ, *Theology for a Liberating Church* (Washington, D.C.: Georgetown University Press, 1989), 67–68.
4 Phillip Berryman, *Liberation Theology* (New York: Pantheon Books, 1987), 65.
5 Ibid., 66.
6 Ibid., 23, 24.
7 Ibid., 43–44.
8 Gutiérrez, *A Theology of Liberation*, 35.
9 It is important to keep in mind that the Latin American understanding of "praxis" is not the North American conception of "practical" action. While we tend to take for granted the scientific attitude that "theory" is the result of an empirical, hypothesis-testing process, Latin Americans see empiricism as a pejorative term – one that deals with superficial aspects of a problem rather than its deeper roots. For them "theory" is seen as a means of cutting away the fat, the appearances of a problem, to get at its heart. Praxis derives from theory, but sends one back to theory as well. For a fuller discussion of this distinction in cultural attitudes, see Berryman, *Liberation Theology*, 80–85.
10 Gutiérrez, *A Theology of Liberation*, 37.
11 See Paulo Freire, *Pedagogía del oprimido*, trans. Jorge Mellado (Bogotá: Siglo Vientiuno Editores, n.d.), for a more in-depth discussion of Freire's process. The following eye-witness account gives a good feeling for what Freire's theory means in practice:

Freire would go into a village and enter into conversation with people. He would ask them to help him to observe the village life. He would have them help him take pictures of scenes of village activities which were familiar and common to most of the villagers. The villagers would then come together to see the pictures. Freire would ask them to describe what they saw in detail, writing words under the pictures as they reflected on what they were seeing and feeling.

Then Freire would question the villagers about the contradictions in the explanations they were giving about why things were the way they were. For example, in one village, the people described the harvest as being very poor.

Freire asked them "Why?" Some of the villager said: "Because the land is tired." Freire asked them why some of the land seemed to be very productive and other parts of the land seemed tired. They explained that the rich farmers had fertilizer and they did not. Freire then asked them how that was the case. The questions and answers continued, leading to issues related to their life situation. The topics discussed ranged from those which were primarily theological, political, or economic in nature to those which were basically philosophical in nature.

Frequently, villagers gave fatalistic answers. Freire would always come back to the contradictions that the people themselves had exposed. The people then began, as a result of this process, to think for themselves and to become aware of alternative ways of viewing and coping with what had seemed to be insurmountable problems for themselves and their communities.

In the process, people learned to read, to care, and to have a sense of worth. Freire called what happened to them *conscientizacão* (conscientization).

James A. Farmer, Jr., "Adult education for transiting," in Stanley Grabowski (ed.), *Paulo Freire: a Revolutionary Dilemma for the Adult Educator* (Syracuse, N.Y.: Syracuse University Publications in Continuing Education, 1972). The eyewitness is identified only as an expriest who had worked with Freire in South America and contributed this report in a course on adult education at UCLA. The quotation and reference were cited in Hennelly, *Theology for a Liberating Church*, 69.

12 Berryman, *Liberation Theology*, 72–73.

13 See Berryman, *Liberation Theology*, 63–79, on the Christian base communities.

14 Augusto Boal, *Theatre of the Oppressed*, trans. Charles A. McBride and Maria-Odilia Leal McBride (New York: Urizen Books, 1979), 121.

15 Boal, *Theatre of the Oppressed*, 122–123.

16 See Boal, *Theatre of the Oppressed*, Chs. 1 and 3.

17 See Felipe Navarro, "Augusto Boal: el teatro como detonador político," in Carlos Espinosa Dominquez (ed.), *Escenarios de dos mundos: inventario teatral de Iberoamérica* (Madrid: Centro de Documentación Teatral, 1988), 1, 81–84; Augusto Boal, "The cop in the head: three hypotheses," *The Drama Review*, 127 (fall 1990), 35–42; and "Boal in Brazil, France, the USA: an interview by Michael Taussig and Richard Schechner," *The Drama Review*, 127 (fall 1990), 50–65.

18 Enrique Buenaventura, *El ARTE NUEVO de hacer Comedias y el NUEVO TEATRO* (Cali, Colombia: TEC Publications, no. 5, n.d.), 1–2.

19 These methods of improvisation have been well described by Beatriz J. Rizk in her book *El nuevo teatro latinoamericano: una lectura historica* (Minneapolis: Institute for the Study of Ideologies and Literature, 1987), and in Buenaventura's writings themselves, such as *Dramaturgia del actor* (Cali, Colombia: TEC Publications, no. 7, n.d.), and *Metáfora y puesta en escena* (Cali, Colombia: TEC Publications, no. 8, n.d.).

20 Rizk, *El nuevo teatro*, 80.

21 See Adam Versényi, "Commentary from Colombia," *Theatre Three*, 5 (fall 1988), 17–26.

22 See Adam Versényi, "Brecht, Latin America and beyond; teatro del sesenta and Alan Bolt," *Theatre*, 17, no. 2 (spring 1986), 45.

23 See Claudia Kaiser-Lenoir, "Arte práctica y social: el nuevo teatro en Nicaragua," *Conjunto*, 78 (January–March 1989), 76.

24 Sergio Corrieri, "El teatro, un arma eficaz al servicio de la Revolución," in Francisco Garzón Céspedes (ed.), *Recopilación de textos sobre el teatro latinoamericano de creación colectiva* (Havana: Casa de las Américas, 1978), 421–424.

25 Laurette Séjourné, *Teatro Escambray: una experiencia*, (Havana: Editorial de Ciencias Sociales, 1977), 125–126.

26 Corrieri, "El teatro,"438.

27 Sergio González, "Las provisiones," in Rine Leal (ed.), *Teatro Escambray* (Havana: Editorial Letras Cubanas, 1978), 301.

28 Rosa Ileana Boudet, *Teatro Nuevo: una respuesta* (Havana: Editorial Letras Cubanas, 1983), 75–76.

29 See Fidel Castro, *Fidel y la religión: conversaciones con Frei Betto* (Havana: Oficina de Publicaciones de Estado, 1985).

30 See María de la Luz Hurtado, Carlos Ochsenius, and Hernán Vidal, *Teatro chileno de la crisis institucional: 1973–1980* (Santiago: CENECA, 1982), 16–49.

31 "San Pablo, Dirigente," included in Sonia Gutiérrez (ed.), *Teatro popular y cambio social en América Latina: Panorama de una experiencia* (San José: EDUCA, 1979), 424–437.

32 de la Luz Hurtado *et al.*, *Teatro chileno*, 32–38.

33 Carlos Ochsenius, Maricruz Diaz, Miguel Rubio, and Roberto Vega, *Práctica teatral y expresión popular en América Latina* (Buenos Aires: Ediciones Paulinas, 1988), 140.

34 Ibid., 147.

35 See Juan Andrés Piña's article, "Teatro chileno en la década del 80," in *Latin American Theatre Review*, 25, no. 2 (spring 1992), 79–85. This issue also contains valuable reports upon theatre throughout the region in the 1980s.

36 Julia Elena Sagaceta, "La dramaturgia de Ricardo Monti: la seducción de la escritura," in Osvaldo Pellettieri (ed.), *Teatro argentino de los '60: Polémica, continuidad y ruptura* (Buenos Aires: Ediciones Corregidor, 1989), 227.

37 For a more in-depth look at this period in Argentinian theatre see *Escenarios de dos mundos: inventario teatral de Iberoamérica*, 1; and the Special Issue on Contemporary Argentine Theatre in *Latin American Theatre Review*, 24, no. 2 (spring 1991).

38 Kees P. Epskamp, *Theatre in Search of Social Change* (The Hague: CESO, 1989), 93–104.

39 The caveat must be made here that a significant portion of younger theatre practitioners have taken up the idea of "collective creation" as just such an inviolable tenet of theatrical work. Lacking the knowledge of the international repertory that those who turned away from it to

formulate a new Latin American dramaturgy possessed, they condemn as heretical works of which they are completely ignorant. When the older groups turned away from the international repertory to try to find a new voice their experiments were based upon their knowledge of, and their experience with that repertory. The newer groups place themselves in the nearly impossible position of attempting to create a new theatrical language when they know nothing about the old theatrical language that what they are creating supposedly replaces.

40 See Sara Diamond, *Spiritual Warfare: the Politics of the Christian Right* (Boston, Mass.: South End Press, 1989).

41 This is not to say that the practice of liberation theatre or liberation theology is unproblematic. For Boal's "invisible theatre" technique in the expensive restaurant to be successful, for example, the other people in the restaurant need to join the protest willingly. There is no guarantee that they will do so. Liberation theology, as practiced in the Christian base communities, also depends upon the willingness of the participants to relate the Bible to their daily lives. Without that initial step *concientización* will not follow.

42 Gutiérrez, *A Theology of Liberation*, 205.

43 See Patricia González, "El evangelio, la evangelización y el teatro: el Nuevo Teatro Colombiano," *Conjunto*, nos. 61 and 62 (July–December, 1984), 49.

44 John Leddy Phelan, *The Millenial Kingdom of the Franciscans in the New World: a Study of the Writings of Gerónimo Mendieta (1525–1604)* (Berkeley: University of California Press, 1956), 72.

45 Miguel León-Portilla, *Aztec Thought and Culture: a Study of the Ancient Nahuatl Mind*, trans. Jack Emory Davis (Norman, Okla.: University of Oklahoma Press, 1963), 158.

46 Phelan, *The Millenial Kingdom*, 28.

47 Personal conversation with Alan Bolt, April 1986 in New Haven, Conn.

48 Gutiérrez, *A Theology of Liberation*, 146.

CONCLUSION

1 For a more extensive discussion of Sarmiento and Martí's proposals in Latin American letters and society see Anna Pizarro, "Cultura y prospectiva: el imaginario de futuro en la cultura latinoamericana," in *Diseños para el cambio* (Caracas: Editorial Nueva Sociedad, 1987), and in Latin American theatre, Marina Pianca, *El teatro de Nuestra América: un proyecto continental 1959–1989* (Minneapolis: Institute for the Study of Ideologies and Literatures, 1990).

2 See Carlos Ochsenius, Maricruz Diaz, Miguel Rubio, and Roberto Vega, *Práctica teatral y expresión popular en América Latina* (Buenos Aires: Ediciones Paulinas, 1988), 206–211.

3 See Donald H. Frischmann, *El nuevo teatro popular en México* (Mexico, INBA, 1990).

Bibliography

Alvarez, Elena, *Dos dramas revolucionarios*, Mexico: Ediciones de la Liga de Escritores Revolucionarios, 1926.

Alvarez Lleras, Antonio, *Víboras sociales: fuego extraño*, Bogotá: Editorial Minerva SA, 1936.

Amunátegui, Miguel Luis, *Camilo Henríquez*, vol. 1, Santiago de Chile: Imprenta Nacional, 1889.

Arrom, José Juan, *El teatro de hispanoamérica en la época colonial*, Havana: Anuario Bibliográfico Cubano, 1956.

Historia de la literatura dramática cubana, New Haven, Conn.: Yale University Press, 1944.

Asturias, Miguel Angel, *Soluna*, Buenos Aires: Ediciones Losange, 1955.

Azuela, Mariano, *Teatro*, Mexico: Ediciones Botas, 1938.

Barker, George C. (ed.), *The Shepherd's Play of the Prodigal Son (Coloquio de pastores del hijo pródigo*, Berkeley: University of California Press, 1953.

Barros Grez, Daniel, *Como en Santiago y otras comedias*, Santiago: Editorial Nascimento, 1975.

Becerra Celis, Concha, *Teatro y poemas infantiles*, Mexico: Ediciones Encuardernables, 1938.

Benítez, Rubén, *Ideología del folletín español: Wenceslao Ayguales de Izco*, Madrid: Ediciones José Porrúa Turanzas, SA, 1979.

Berryman, Philip, *Liberation Theology*, New York: Pantheon, 1987.

Bitterli, Urs, *Cultures in Conflict: Encounters Between European and Non-European Cultures, 1492–1800*, Oxford: Polity Press, 1989.

Black, George, *The Good Neighbor: How the United States Wrote the History of Central America and the Caribbean*, New York: Pantheon Books, 1988.

Blanco Moheno, Roberto, *Juárez ante Dios y ante los hombres*, Mexico: Editorial Diana, SA, 1967.

Boal, Augusto, "The cop in the head: three hypotheses," *The Drama Review*, 127 (fall 1990).

Theatre of the Oppressed, trans. Charles A. and Maria-Odilia Leal McBride, New York: Urizen Books, 1979.

"Boal in Brazil, France, the USA: an interview by Michael Taussig and Richard Schechner," *The Drama Review*, 127 (fall 1990).

Bonilla Picado, María and Stoyan Valdich, *El teatro latinoamericano en busca de su identidad cultural*, San José: Cultur Art, 1988.

Boudet, Rosa Ileana, *Teatro Nuevo: una respuesta*, Havana: Editorial Letras Cubanas, 1983.

Braden, Charles S., *Religious Aspects of the Conquest of Mexico*, New York: AMS Press, 1966.

Bramón, Francisco, *Auto del triunfo de la Virgen y gozo mexicano*, ed. Augustín Yáñez, Mexico: Imprenta Universitaria, 1945.

Los sirgueros de la Virgen, Mexico: Imprenta Universitaria, 1943.

Bravo-Elizondo, Pedro, *Cultura y teatro obreros en Chile 1900–1930*, Madrid: Ediciones Michay, SA, 1986.

Teatro hispanoamericano de crítica social, Madrid: Colección Nova Scholar, Playor, SA, 1975.

(ed.) *La dramaturgia de Egon Wolff*, Santiago: Editorial Nascimiento, 1985.

Brecht, Bertolt, *The Guns of Carrar*, trans. George Tabori, New York: Samuel French, 1971.

Breve historia del teatro argentino, vol. 1: *De la revolución a Caseros*, ed. Luis Ordaz, Buenos Aires: Editorial Universitaria de Buenos Aires, 1962.

Buenaventura, Enrique, *El ARTE NUEVO de hacer Comedias y el NUEVO TEATRO*, Cali, Colombia: TEC Publications, no. 5, n.d.

Dramaturgia del actor, Cali, Colombia: TEC Publications, no. 7, n.d.

Metafora y puesta en escena, Cali, Colombia: TEC Publications, no. 8, n.d.

Bustillo Oro, Juan, *Tres dramas mexicanos*, Madrid: Editorial Cenit, SA, 1933.

Canillita y otras obras: Sánchez, Trejo, Pacheco, Discépolo, Dragún, ed. Jorge Lafforgue, Buenos Aires, Centro Editor de América Latina, 1979.

Carballido, Emilio, *The Golden Thread and Other Plays*, trans. Margaret Sayers Peden, Austin: University of Texas Press, 1970.

Carpentier, Alejo, *América Latina en las confluencias de coordenadas históricas y su repercusión en la música en América Latina* in *América Latina en su música*, ed. Isabel Aretz, Mexico: UNESCO – Siglo Veintiuno Editores, 1977.

Castagnino, Raúl H., *El teatro romántico de Martín Coronado*, Buenos Aires: Ediciones Culturales Argentinas, 1962.

Castro, Fidel, *Fidel y la religión: conversaciones con Frei Betto*, Havana: Oficina de Publicaciones de Estado, 1985.

Child, Thoedore, *The Spanish American Republics*, New York: Harper, 1891.

Cid Perez, José, *Teatro indoamericano colonial*, Madrid: Aguilar, 1973.

Comedias Cubanas del Siglo XIX ed. Rine Leal, vols. 1 and 11, Havana, 1979.

Cook, John A., *Neo-classic Drama in Spain: Theory and Practice*, Dallas: Southern Methodist University Press, 1959.

Cook, Katherine M., *La casa del pueblo: un relatio de las escuelas nuevas de acción en México*, trans. Rafael Ramírez, Mexico, 1936.

Corrieri, Sergio, "El teatro, un arma eficaz al servicio de la Revolución," in Francisco Garzón Céspedes (ed.), *Recopilación de textos sobre el teatro latinoamericano de creación colectiva*, Havana: Casa de las Américas, 1978.

"Y si fuera así...," in Rine Leal (ed.) *Teatro Escambray*, Havana: Editorial Letras Cubanas, 1978.

Corti, Dora, *Noticias para la Historia del Teatro Nacional, No. 4: Abdón Arózteguy*, Buenos Aires: Instituto de Literatura Argentina, 1938.

Covarrubias, Miguel, "Slapstick and venom: politics, tent shows, and comedians," *Theatre Arts Monthly*, 22, no. 8 (August, 1938).

Cuadra, Fernando, *Teatro*, Santiago: Editorial Nascimiento, 1979.

Cultural Survival Quarterly, 4, no. 4, 8–9; 6, no. 1 (winter 1982).

Cuzzani, Augustín, *Teatro*, Buenos Aires: Centro Editor de América Latina, SA, 1971.

Dauster, Frank N., "The drama of Carlos Solórzano," *Modern Drama*, 7 (May, 1964).

Historia del teatro hispanoamericano: Siglos XIX y XX, Mexico: Ediciones de Andrea, 1966.

Davies, Nigel, *Human Sacrifice in History and Today*, New York: William Morrow, 1981.

de P. Moreno, Antonio, *Obras son amores*, Mexico: José Ignacio Durán y Cía, 1914.

Debesa, Fernando, *Mama Rosa*, Santiago de Chile: Editorial del Nuevo Extremo, 1956.

Defilippis Novoa, Francisco, *El teatro argentino, No. 8: María la tonta, He visto a Dios*, ed. Luis Ordaz, Buenos Aires: Centro Editor de América Latina SA, 1980.

de la Cruz, Sor Juana, *Obras completas*, vol. III: *Autos y loas*, ed. Alfonso Méndez Plancarte, Mexico: Fondo de Cultura Económica, 1951.

de la Luz Hurtado, María, Carlos Ochsenius, and Hernán Vidal, *Teatro chileno de la crisis institucional: 1973–1980*, Santiago: CENECA, 1982.

Diamond, Sara, *Spiritual Warfare: the Politics of the Christian Right*, Boston, Mass.: South End Press, 1989.

Discépolo, Armando., *Mateo. Stéfano. Relojero*, ed. Luis Ordaz (El teatro argentino, No. 9) Buenos Aires: Centro Editor de América Latina SA, 1980.

Obras escogidas, vols. I–III, Buenos Aires: Editorial Jorge Alvarez, SA, 1969.

Drama de la Pasión que se representa en Ixtapalapa, D.F., llamado "Los tres caídos de Jesucristo," Mexico: Imprenta Universitario, 1947.

Durán Cerda, Julio, "Civilización y Barbarie en el Desarrollo del Teatro Nacional Rioplatense," *Revista Iberoamericana*, 29, no. 55 (January–June, 1963).

"El teatro en las tareas revolucionarios de la independencia de Chile," *Anales de la Universidad de Chile*, no. 119 (1960).

Eichelbaum, Samuel, *Un guapo del 900*, Buenos Aires: Argentores, 1940.

El güegüence, Managua: Ediciones Distribuidora Cultura, SA 1977.

Epskamp, Kees P., *Theatre in Search of Social Change*, The Hague: CESO, 1989.

Escenarios de dos mundos: inventario teatral de Iberoamérica, vols. I–IV, Madrid: Centro de Documentación Teatral, 1988.

Fernández de Lizardi, José Joaquín, *Don Catrin de la Fachenda y fragmentos de otras obras*, Mexico: Editorial Cultura, 1944.

Fernández Madrid, José, *Atala y Guatimoc*, Bogotá: Ministerio de Educación Nacional, Editorial Minerva, SA, 1936.

The Itching Parrot, trans. Katherine Anne Porter, Garden City, N.Y.: Doubleday, Doran and Col, 1942.

Flores Magón, Ricardo, *Land and Liberty: Anarchist Influences in the Mexican Revolution. Ricardo Flores Magón*, compiled and Introduced by David Poole, Sanday, Orkney, UK: Cienfuegos Press, 1977.

Tierra y Libertad, Mexico: Ediciones del Grupo Cultural "Ricardo Flores Magón," 1924.

Víctimas y verdugos, Mexico: Ediciones del Grupo Cultural "Ricardo Flores Magón," 1924.

Franco, Jean, *La cultura moderna en América Latina*, Mexico: Joaquín Mortiz, 1971.

Freire, Paulo, *Pedagogía del oprimido*, trans. Jorge Mellado, Bogotá, Colombia: Siglo Vientiuno Editores, n.d.

Fuentes Cruz, Adalberto, *Drama de la pasión como se representa en Milpa Alta, D.F.*, Mexico, 1949.

Gambaro, Griselda, *Teatro: Las parades, El desatino, Los Siameses*, Buenos Aires: Editorial Argonauta, 1979.

Teatro: Nada que ver, Sucede lo que pasa, Ottawa: Girol Books, 1983.

Gamboa, Federico, *Entre hermanos*, Mexico: 1944.

La venganza de la gleba, Mexico: 1907.

Gamboa, José Joaquín, *Teatro*, Mexico: Ediciones Botas, 1938.

García, Santiago, *Teoría y práctica del teatro*, Bogotá: Ediciones CEIS, 1983.

García Icazalceta, Joaquín, *Nueva colección de documentos para la historia de México: Codice Franciscano Siglo XVI*, Mexico: Editorial Salvador Chavez Hayhoe, 1941.

García Velloso, Enrique, *Memorias de un hombre de teatro*, Buenos Aires: Editorial Guillermo Kraft, 1942.

Giordano, Enrique, *La teatralización de la obra dramática: de Florencio Sánchez a Roberto Arit*, Mexico: Premia Editora, 1982.

González, Patricia, "El evangelio, la evengelización y el teatro: el Nuevo Teatro Colombiano," *Conjunto*, nos. 61 and 62 (July–December, 1984), 45–49.

González, Sergio, "Las provisiones," in Rine Leal (ed.) *Teatro Escambray*, Havana: Editorial Letras Cubanas, 1978.

Gonzalez del Valle, Francisco, *Heredia en la Habana* (Cuadernos de Historia Habanera, No. 16), Havana: Municipio de La Habana, 1939.

González Franco, Francisco, *La perfecta alegría*, Mexico: J. I. Muñoz, 1938.

¡Maldita agrarismo! (Mexico: 1939).

Gorostiza, Manuel E. de, *Teatro Selecto*, Mexico: Editorial Porrúa, SA, 1957.

Graham, R. B. Cunninghame, *The Conquest of New Granada: Being the Life of Gonzalo Jiménez de Quesada*, London: William Heineman, 1922.

Gutiérrez, Eduardo, *Juan Moreira*, Buenos Aires: Centro Editor de América Latina, 1980.

Gutiérrez, Gustavo, *A Theology of Liberation*, Maryknoll, N.Y.: Orbis, 1973.

Gutiérrez Hermosillo, Alfonso, *Teatro*, Mexico: Imprenta Universitaria, 1945.

Hennelly, SJ., Alfred, *Theology for a Liberating Church*, Washington, D.C.: Georgetown University Press, 1989.

Herbert, Eugenia W., *The Artist and Social Reform. France and Belgium, 1885–1898*, New Haven, Conn.: Yale University Press, 1961.

Heredía, José María, *Antología Herediana*, Havana: Imprenta "El Siglo XX," 1939.

 Obras Poéticas, vol. I, New York: Imprenta I Librería de N. Ponce de Leon, 1875.

Hernández, José, *El gaucho Martín Fierro: La vuelta de Martín Fierro*, Montevideo: Editorial Síntesis, 1963.

 Martín Fierro, dramatized by José Gonzalez Castillo, vol. III, Buenos Aires: Instituto Nacional de Estudios de Teatro, Biblioteca Teatral, 1942.

Herrera, Ernesto, *El teatro uruguayo de Ernesto Herrera*, Montevideo: Editorial "Renacimiento," 1917.

Hidalgo, Bartolomé, *Obra completa*, Montevideo: Editorial Ciencias, 1979.

Historia del teatro argentino, ed. Luis Ordaz, Buenos Aires: Centro Editor de América Latina, 1982.

Horcasitas, Fernando, *El teatro náhuatl: épocas novohispana y moderna*, Mexico: UNAM, 1974.

Hughes, Lloyd H., *The Mexican Cultural Mission Programme*, Paris: UNESCO, 1950.

Huidobro, Vicente, *Obras completas de Vicente Huidobro*, vols. I and II, Santiago: Editorial Andrés Bello, 1976.

Jiménez Rueda, Julio, *Herejías y supersiticiones en la Nueva España (Los heterodoxos en México*, Mexico: UNAM, 1946.

Jones, Willis Knapp, *Behind Spanish American Footlights*, Austin: University of Texas Press, 1966.

Kaiser-Lenoir, Claudia, *El grotesco criollo: estilo teatral de una época*, Havana: Casa de Las Américas, 1977.

Karavellas, Panon D., *La dramaturgia de Samuel Eichelbaum*, Montevideo: Ediciones Germinus, 1976.

Kayser, Wolfgang, *The Grotesque in Art and Literature*, trans. Ulrich Weisstein, Bloomington: Indiana University Press, 1963.

Kubler, George, *Mexican Architecture of the Sixteenth Century*, vols. I and II, Westport, Conn.: Greenwood Press, 1972.

Las Casas, Bartolomé de, *Obras escogidas*, vols. III and IV, Madrid: Biblioteca de Autores Españoles, 1958.

Leal, Rine, *Breve historia del teatro cubano*, Havana: Editorial Letras Cubanas, 1980.

 La selva oscura, vol. I: *Historia del teatro cubano desde sus orígenes hasta 1868*, Havana: Editorial Arte y Literature, 1975.

 La selva oscura, vol. II: *De los bufos a la neocolonia (Historia del teatro cubano de 1868 a 1902*, Havana, Editorial Arte y Literatura, 1982.

Leguizamón, M., *El teatro argentino, no. 2 Calandria*, ed. Luis Ordaz, Buenos Aires: Centro Editor de América Latina, 1980.

León-Portilla, Miguel, *Aztec Thought and Culture: a Study of the Ancient Nahautl Mind*, trans. Jack Emory Davis, Norman, Okla.: University of Oklahoma Press, 1963.

Lira, Miguel N., *Vuelta a la tierra*, Mexico: Editorial Fabula, 1940.

List Arzubide, Armando, *Teatro histórico escolar*, Mexico, 1938.

List Arzubide, Germán, *Tres obras del teatro revolucionario*, Mexico: Ediciones Integrales, 1933.

Lopez Gallo, Manuel, *Economía y política en la historia de México*, Mexico: Editorial el Caballito, SA, 1972.

Luco Cruchaga, Germán, *Teatro*, Santiago: Editorial Nascimiento, 1979.

Lyday, Leon F. and George W. Woodyard (eds.), *Dramatists in Revolt: the New Latin American Theatre*, Austin: University of Texas Press, 1976.

Magaña Esquivel, Antonio, *Breve historia del teatro mexicano*, Mexico: Ediciones de Andrea, 1958.

Imagen del teatro, Mexico: Ediciones Letras de México, 1940.

Medio siglo de teatro mexicano (1900/1961), Mexico: Instituto Nacional de Bellas Artes, 1964.

Magdaleno, Mauricio, *Teatro revolucionario mexicano*, Madrid: Editorial Cenit, SA, 1933.

Magón, Ricardo Flores, *Land and Liberty: Anarchist Influences in the Mexican Revolution. Ricardo Flores Magón*, ed. David Poole, Sanday, Orkney, UK: Cienfuegos Press, 1977.

Tierra y Libertad, Mexico: Ediciones del Grupo Cultural "Ricardo Flores Magón," 1924.

Verdugos y víctimas, Mexico: Ediciones del Grupo Cultural "Ricardo Flores Magón," 1924.

María y Campos, Armando de, *La dramática mexicana durante el gobierno del presidente Lerdo de Tejada*, Mexico: Compañía de Ediciones Populares, SA, 1946.

Los payasos poetas del pueblo (El circo en México), Mexico: Ediciones Botas, 1939.

Markham, Sir Clements, *The Incas of Peru*, London: Smith, Elder, 1910.

Marqués, René, *Teatro*, Rio Piedras: Editorial Cultural, 1970.

Martí, José, *Obras completas*, vol. II, Havana: Editorial Lex, 1946.

Matas, Julio, "Vuelto a *Electra Garrigó* de Virgilio Piñera," *Latin American Theatre Review*, 22, no. 2 (spring 1989), 73–79.

Materiales para una historia del teatro en Colombia, ed. Maida Watson Espener and Carlos José Reyes, Bogotá: Instituto Colombiano de Cultura, 1978.

Medrano, Juan Espinoso (El Lunarejo), *El Hijo Prodigo*, Lima: Ediciones de la Biblioteca Universitaria, 1967.

Méndez Plancarte, Gabriel, *Humanistas del Siglo XVIII*, Mexico: Ediciones de UNAM, 1941.

Meyer, Jean A., *The Cristero Rebellion: the Mexican People Between Church and State 1926–1929*, Cambridge: Cambridge University Press, 1976.

Monterde, Francisco, *Proteo*, Mexico: Editora Intercontinental, 1944.

Monti, Ricardo, *Historia tendenciosa de la clase media argentina de los extraños sucesos en que se vieron envueltos algunos hombres públicos, su completa dilucidación y otras escandalosas revelaciones*, Buenos Aires: Talía, 1971.

Una noche con el Sr. Magnus y hijos, Buenos Aires: Talia, 1970.

Visita, Buenos Aires: Talía, 1978.

Morales, José Ricardo, *Burlilla de Don Berendo, Doña Caracolines y Su Amante*, Madrid: Tuarus Ediciones, 1969.

Teatro incial, Santiago (?): Ediciones de la Universidad de Chile, 1976.

Morante, Luis Ambrosio, *Tupac-Amarú*, vol. i, no. 9, Buenos Aires: Sección de Documentos, Instituto de Literatura Argentina, 1924.

Moriarity, James Robert, "Ritual combat: a comparison of the Aztec 'War of Flowers, and the Medieval 'Mêlée,'" *Museum of Anthropology Miscellaneous Series*, no. 9, Greeley, Colo.: Colorado State College – Greeley Museum of Anthropology, 1969.

Muñoz, Diego *et al.*, *Poética de la población marginal: teatro poblacional chileno, 1978–1985*, Minneapolis: The Prisma Institute, 1987.

NACLA Report on the Americas, 14, no. 6 (November–December, 1980); 15, no. 3 (May–June, 1981).

Navarro, Felipe, "Augusto Boal: el teatro como detonador politico," In Carlos Espinosa Dominguez (ed.), *Escenarios de dos mundos: inventario teatral de Iberoamérica*, vol. i, Madrid: Centro de Documentación Teatral, 1988, 81–84.

Navarro, Francisco, *El mundo sin deso y otros dramas*, Madrid: Espasa-Calpe, SA, 1935.

Nomland, John B., *Teatro mexicano contemporáneo (1900–1950)*, Mexico: Instituto Nacional de Bellas Artes, Departamento de Literatura, 1967.

Ochsenius Carlos, Maricruz Diaz, Miguel Rubio, and Roberto Vega, *Práctica teatral y expresión popular en América Latina*, Buenos Aires: Ediciones Paulinas, 1988.

O'Kelley, James J., *La tierra del Mambí*, Havana: Instituto del Libro, 1968.

Ordaz, Luis, *El drama rural*, Buenos Aires: Librería Hachette, SA, 1959.

Orozco Rosales, Efrén, *Liberación*, Mexico: Departamento del Distrito Federal, Dirección General de Acción Civica, 1935.

El mensajero del sol, Mexico, DF: 1941.

Pacheco, Carlos M., *Los disfrazados y otros sainetes*, Buenos Aires: Editorial Universitaria de Buenos Aires, 1964.

Pavlovsky, Eduardo, *La mueca, El señor Galíndez, Telerañas*, Madrid: Editorial Fundamentos, 1980.

Paz, Albio, "El paraíso recobrado," in Rine Leal (ed.), *Teatro Escambray*, Havana: Editorial Letras Cubanas, 1978.

Pereira Salas, Eugenio, *Historia del teatro en Chile desde sus orígenes hasta la muerte de Juan Cascabuerta, 1849*, Santiago de Chile: Ediciones de Universidad de Chile, 1974.

Perez Estrada, Francisco, *Teatro folklórico Nicaragüense*, Managua: Imprenta Nacional, 1970.

Phelan, John Leddy, *The Millenial Kingdom of the Franciscans in the New World: A Study of the Writings of Gerónimo de Mendieta (1525–1604)* (University of California Publications in History, 52), Berkeley: University of California Press, 1956.

Piñera, Virgilio, *Teatro completo*, Havana: Ediciones R, 1960.

Pinochet, Tancredo, *La conquista de Chile en el siglo XX*, Santiago: "La Illustración," 1909.

Pita, Santiago de, "El principe jardinero" Xerox in Yale Latin American Collection/Cuba/He94c/0111.

Quirk, Robert E., *The Mexican Revolution and the Catholic Church (1910–1929)*, Bloomington: Indiana University Press, 1973.

Ramírez, Susan E (ed.), *Indian–Religious Relations in Colonial Spanish America* (Foreign and Comparative Studies/Latin American Series 9), Syracuse, N.Y.: Maxwell School of Citizenship and Public Affairs, 1989.

Ramos, José A., *Almas Rebeldes*, Barcelona: Librería de Antonio López, 1906.

Teatro, Havana, Editorial Arte y Literatura, 1976.

Ravicz, Marilyn Ekdahl, *Early Colonial Religious Drama in Mexico: From Tzompantli to Golgotha*, Washington, D.C.: The Catholic University of America Press, 1970.

Rebolledo, Efrén, *Obras completas*, ed. Luis Mario Schneider, Mexico: Instituto Nacional de Bellas Artes, 1968.

Recopilación de textos sobre el teatro latinoamericano de creación colectiva, ed. Francisco Garzon Céspedes, Havana: Casa de las Américas, 1978.

Rela, Walter, *Historia del teatro uruguayo 1808–1968*, Montevideo: Ediciones de la Banda Oriental, 1969.

Teatro uruguayo 1807–1979, Montevideo: Ediciones de la Alianza, 1980.

Reyes, Alfonso, *Ifigenia cruel*, Monterrey, México: Ediciones Sierra Madre, 1974.

Reyes de la Maza, Luis, *Cien años de teatro en México (1810–1910)*, Mexico: Sep/Setentas, 1972.

Ricard, Robert, *The Spiritual Conquest of Mexico: an Essay on the Apostolate and the Evangelizing Methods of the Mendicant Orders in New Spain: 1523–1572*, trans. Lesley Byrd Simpson, Berkeley: University of California Press, 1966.

Rivas, Esteban, *Carlos Solórzano y el teatro hispanoamericano*, Mexico: Impresos Anáhuac, 1970.

Rizk, Beatriz J., *El nuevo teatro latinoamericano: una lectura histórica*, Minneapolis: Institute for the Study of Ideologies and Literature, 1987.

Robe, Stanley, L. (ed.), *Coloquios de pastores from Jalisco, Mexico*, Berkeley: University of California Press, 1954.

Rojo, Grinor, *Los origenes del teatro hispanoamericano contemporáneo: La generación de dramaturgos de 1927, dos direcciones*, Santiago de Chile: Ediciones Universitarios de Valparaíso, 1972.

Sánchez, Florencio. *Obras completas*, ed. Jorge Lafforgue, vols. I and II, Buenos Aires: Editorial Schapire SRL, 1968.

Sanchez Gardel, Julio, *Teatro*, Buenos Aires: Librería Hachette SA, 1955.

Séjourné, Laurette, *Teatro Escambray: una experiencia*, Havana: Editorial de Ciencias Sociales, 1977.

Smart, Charles Allen, *Viva Juárez!*, Philadelphia: J. B. Lippincott, 1963.

Smith, Brian H., *The Church and Politics in Chile: Challenges to Modern Catholicism*, Princeton, N.J.: Princeton University Press, 1982.

Solórzano, Carlos, "Miguel Angel Asturias y el teatro," *Revista Iberoamericano* 35, no. 67 (January–April, 1969), 101–104.

(ed.), *El teatro hispanoamericano contemporáneo*, vols. I and II, Mexico: Fondo de Cultura Económica, 1964.

Spell, Jefferson Rea, *Rousseau in the Spanish World Before 1833: a Study in Franco-Spanish Literary Relations*, Austin: University of Texas Press, 1938.

Suárez Radillo, Carlos Miguel, *El teatro barroco hispano-americano*, vols. I–III, Madrid: José Porrúa Turanzas, SA, 1981.

El teatro neoclásico y costumbrista hispano-americano, vols. I and II, Madrid: Ediciones Cultura Hispánica, Instituto de Cooperación Ibero-americano, 1984.

Teatro argentino de los '60: Polémica, continuidad y ruptura, ed. Osvaldo Pellettieri, Buenos Aires: Ediciones Corregidor, 1989.

Teatro bufo siglo XIX: Antología, ed. Rine Leal, vols. I and II, Havana: Editorial Arte y Literatura, 1975.

Teatro cubano del siglo XIX, Antología, ed. Natividad González Freire, vol. I, Havana, Editorial Arte y Literatura, 1975.

Teatro Escambray, ed. Rine Leal, Havana: Editorial Letras Cubanas, 1978.

Teatro gauchesco primitivo, Buenos Aires: Ediciones Losange, 1957.

Teatro indígena prehispánico: Rabinal Achí, ed. Francisco Monterde, Mexico: Ediciones de la UNAM, 1955.

Teatro Mambí, ed. Rine Leal, Havana, Editorial Letras Cubanas, 1978.

Teatro Quecha Colonial, ed. and trans. Teodoro L. Meneses, Lima: Ediciones Educbanco, 1983.

Teatro y Revolución, ed. Graziella Pogolotti, Rine Leal, and Rosa Ileana Boudet, Havana: Editorial letras Cubanas, 1980.

Todorov, Tzvetan. *The Conquest of America*, trans. Richard Howard. New York: Harper and Row, 1984.

Toor, Frances, *A Treasury of Mexican Folkways*, New York: Crown, 1947.

Torres, Teodoro, *El humorismo y la sátira en México*, Mexico: Editora Mexicana, SA, 1943.

Tres piezas del virreinato, ed. José Rojas Garcidueñas and José Juan Arróm, Mexico: Instituto de Investigaciones Estéticas, UNAM, 1976.

Troncoso, Moisés Poblete, *El movimiento de asociación profesional obrera en Chile*, Mexico: El Colegio de México, Jornadas – 29, 1945.

Usigli, Rodolfo, *México en el teatro*, Mexico: Imprenta Mundial, 1932.

Vargas Tejada, Luis, *Las convulsiones*, Bogotá: Instituto Colombiano de Cultura, 1971.

Las convulsiones. Doraminta, Bogotá, Ministerio de Educación Nacional, Editorial Minierva, SA, 1936.

Vasconcelos, José, *Promoteo vencedor*, Madrid: Editorial América, n.d.

Vásquez Amaral, Mary, *El teatro de Emilio Carballido (1950–1965)* Mexico: B. Costa-Amici, 1974.

Vela, Eusebio, *Tres Comedias de Eusebio Vela*, ed. Jefferson Rea Spell and Francisco Monterde (Mexico: Imprenta Universitaria, 1948).

Versényi, Adam, "Brecht, Latin America and Beyond; Teatro del Sesenta and Alan Bolt," *Theatre*, 17, no. 2 (Spring 1986).

"Commentary From Colombia," in *Theatre Three*, 5 (Fall 1988), 17–26.

Villaurrutia, Xavier, *Autos profanos* (Mexico: Ediciones Letras de Mexico, 1943).

El pobre Barba Azul (Mexico: Sociedad General de Autores de Mexico, 1947).

Invitación a la muerte. (Mexico: Ediciones Letras de Mexico, 1944).

Vodanovic, Sergio, *Teatro* (Santiago: Editorial Nascimiento, 1978).

Wolff, Egon, *Teatro* (Santiago: Ediciones Valores Literarios, LTDA, 1971).

Ximena, Pedro, *Reales Exequias por el señor don Carlos III. Rey de las Españas y Americas*, ed. Manuel Ignacio Pérez Alonso (Managua: Banco Central de Nicaragua, 1974).

Index